Teaching for Biliteracy

Teaching for Biliteracy

STRENGTHENING BRIDGES BETWEEN LANGUAGES

Karen Beeman • Cheryl Urow

Caslon Publishing
Philadelphia

Caslon, Inc.
825 N 27th St
Philadelphia, PA 19130

caslonpublishing.com

20 19 18 17 16 15 14

Library of Congress
Cataloging-in-Publication Data

Beeman, Karen, author.
    Teaching for biliteracy : strengthening bridges between languages / Karen Beeman and Cheryl Urow.
        pages   cm
    Includes bibliographical references and index.
    ISBN 978-1-934000-09-0
1. Education, Bilingual—United States. 2. English language—Study and teaching—United States—Spanish speakers. I. Urow, Cheryl, author. II. Title.

    LC3731.B44 2013
    370.117′50973—dc23   2012041745

This is a book about teaching for biliteracy—reading and writing in Spanish and English—in the United States. It is the book we wish we had had when we began as bilingual and dual-language classroom teachers and administrators over 20 years ago. It is the book we wish we had had when our school administrators handed us literacy materials in English and told us, "just translate it into Spanish." This is the book we wish we had had when, in an effort to learn how to make better use of our literacy materials, we attended workshops and seminars that offered great suggestions about strategies and curriculum but focused on the teaching of English literacy to monolingual English speakers with no mention of biliteracy. This is the book we wish we had had when we spent part of our vacations in Spanish-speaking countries in bookstores reviewing and buying Spanish-language materials for our classrooms because what we had never quite fit the needs of students developing biliteracy.

We stopped expecting the seminars on English literacy to tell us what to do in Spanish. We started observing our students' language use more closely and we identified patterns in their biliteracy development. We made notes about aspects of biliteracy that were challenging for our bilingual learners, and we developed tools, resources, and strategies that were effective in our classrooms. We reviewed current research on biliteracy in relation to our practice, and we created our own professional development workshops for practicing biliteracy teachers. We also created and taught university-level teacher-preparation courses on the teaching of Spanish literacy in an English-dominant environment. We listened to the teachers who attended these workshops and enrolled in our classes and we decided to write this book.

Major Contributions

Teaching for Biliteracy: Strengthening Bridges between Languages describes, explains, and demonstrates for practitioners how to teach for biliteracy. Although the guide focuses on teaching for biliteracy in Spanish and English in the United States, its major principles can be adapted and applied to biliteracy contexts in which languages other than Spanish and English are used. The guidebook is grounded in the latest research, and makes three powerful, practical contributions to the emerging field of teaching for biliteracy.

First, we introduce the concept of *the Bridge* as an integral component of effective biliteracy instruction. We argue that teaching for biliteracy has three parts: Spanish instruction, the Bridge (both languages side by side), and English instruction. The Bridge is the instructional moment when teachers purposefully bring the two languages together, guiding students to transfer the academic content they have learned in one language to the other language, engage in contrastive analysis of the two languages, and strengthen their knowledge of both languages. An important characteristic of the Bridge is that it is two-way: it goes from Spanish to English and from English to Spanish. Because bilinguals transfer what they have learned in one language to the other language, they do not have to learn content in both languages. For example, if students study math only in Spanish, the Bridge provides opportunities for them to attach English to that math content without relearning the math concepts and skills in English. Students also learn to use cross-linguistic strategies as they explicitly compare and contrast their two languages on the phonological, morphological, syntactic, and pragmatic levels, and they strengthen their metalinguistic awareness.

Second, we offer *three fundamental sociolinguistic premises* that educators can use to guide their decision making about teaching for biliteracy on the classroom, program, school, and district levels. These premises capture the complexity of teaching for biliteracy in Spanish and English in the United States. According to these premises, teaching for biliteracy is different than teaching for monolingual literacy for the following reasons:

1. Spanish in the United States is a minority language within a majority culture.
2. Students use all of the languages in their linguistic repertoire to develop literacy.
3. Spanish and English are governed by distinct linguistic rules and cultural norms.

The first premise highlights the stratification of languages and language users in society. The second premise reflects a multilingual perspective on bilingual learners. The third premise draws attention to the linguistic similarities and differences between the target languages and the cultural norms of those who use them in different discourse communities.

Third, we provide a *biliteracy unit framework* that teachers can use to plan, implement, monitor, and evaluate their literacy instruction for bilingual learners participating in bilingual, dual-language and Spanish-for-Spanish-speakers programs. The biliteracy unit framework shows teachers how to do the following:

- Draw on student, teacher, and community language resources, linguistic creativity, and cultural funds of knowledge as an integral part of classroom instruction
- Integrate language arts and content-area instruction
- Scaffold students' learning of content-area concepts and skills in two languages
- Provide students with opportunities to read and write grade-level texts across the curriculum
- Support students' development of academic English and Spanish across content areas
- Make cross-linguistic connections during the Bridge.

This framework is compatible with literacy frameworks and programs used in K–12 schools today, and it provides the organizing structure for the book.

Special Features

We provide practitioners with resources that enhance the teaching and learning of Spanish and English for all students fortunate enough to learn in two languages. Useful tools, strategies, and resources for teachers of Spanish and English biliteracy appear throughout the book, many of them displayed in boxes. These include tools specific to the instruction of Spanish literacy in the United States and tools for planning for the Bridge. That is, we provide classroom strategies supporting the key use of all of students' linguistic resources during that planned time where students who have completed the instructional part of a unit make cross-linguistic connections between their languages and move to extension activities in the other language. We also provide tools to assess for biliteracy, an ongoing process that provides feedback for planning further lessons. Also, each chaper ends with questions and activities for reflection, to help you evaluate your own teaching practices. To honor Spanish and to keep simultaneous translations to a minimum, we have included examples of lessons, rubrics, and other tools in Spanish. When Spanish is used for content that is crucial to understand, we have included translations in the text.

The following text and online features aid readers in using the book strategically:

- **Key Points** introduce the main ideas of each chapter.
- **Vignettes** from actual practice highlight contemporary challenges.
- **Practical tools, resources,** and **strategies** counter biliteracy instruction and assessment challenges at the classroom, program, school, and district levels
- **Profiles of prototypical bilingual learners** and **biliteracy teachers** illustrate the biliteracy tools, resources, and strategies in practice.
- **Activities for Reflection and Action** at the end of each chapter invite teachers and administrators to apply the key points of the chapter to their own practice.
- **"How Spanish Works,"** a supplemental chapter at the end of the book, highlights aspects of the internal structure of Spanish that have a direct impact on the teaching of literacy in Spanish and the development of metalinguistic awareness, a key element of biliteracy.
- **Web site resources** that supplement the text include sample biliteracy unit frameworks for 1st, 3rd, and 4th grades and high school that are described in the book; a blank biliteracy unit framework template that teachers can download, adapt, print, and use as they create their own bilingual study units; a sample survey for collecting linguistic, cultural, and academic background information on students; and recommendations for further reading. Go to casloncommunity.com/teaching-biliteracy/ to access the online resources that complement this text.

Using This Guide

In this guidebook, you are introduced to research on biliteracy, to the students and teachers engaged in developing biliteracy, and to a framework for planning, instructing, and assessing in a biliteracy context. All the ideas, suggestions, and examples can be used and adapted by a district, school, or teacher. We intentionally do not promote any one product or program. Instead, we believe in teacher professionalism and expertise, and we hope that this book supports teachers and provides them with tools and knowledge to enhance their practice.

Teaching for Biliteracy can be used as a professional development guide—in study groups, workshops, or professional learning communities— with practicing teachers and administrators who work in districts, schools, programs, and classrooms that teach for biliteracy. It can also be used as a teacher preparation and educational leadership guide for educators preparing to promote biliteracy at school to help navigate the complex task of teaching for biliteracy. We know there is no single answer for all students, teachers, and schools, and, therefore, *Teaching for Biliteracy* is offered as a guide rather than a recipe. We have written it to provide teachers with the information and direction to make the best decisions for their students, their school, and themselves.

Acknowledgments

This project began five years ago and it has led us on a journey that we could not have accomplished on our own. There are many people we wish to thank for supporting us throughout this time. Our colleagues at the Illinois Resource Center have encouraged, listened, and challenged us as we have developed our thinking. We thank John Hilliard, Jeanette Gordon, Margo Gottlieb, Tammy King, Barbara Marler, and Cristina Sánchez-López. Josie Yanguas, our director, has been unwavering in her support of our work. *¡Mil gracias, Josie!*

We could not have written this book without the suggestions and revisions provided to us by Else Hamayan. She held our hand all the way from Argentina for most of these five years, and we are indebted to her.

We have been influenced by the work of a number of researchers and experts. The work of the Literacy Squared project at the University of Colorado, Boulder, has inspired us during this journey and it has greatly influenced our thinking. We are grateful to Literacy Squared for their cutting-edge research and advocacy for emerging bilinguals. In particular, we are honored to have Kathy Escamilla write the Foreword to our book, and we thank her for her support over the years. Kim Potowski's work has also influenced us significantly; we are grateful to her for working with us and encouraging us throughout this project.

We thank the many teachers and administrators we have worked with in schools in Illinois and across the country who are developing biliteracy in bilingual-language, dual-language, and heritage-language programs. These teachers and administrators have offered practical perspectives and real life challenges that have motivated us to continue our work.

Additionally, we thank the students in our graduate level classes who have shared so much about their practice with us. We have learned the same or more from them as they have learned from us, and we are very grateful!

Caslon Publishing patiently waited for our manuscript for a long time and, once they received it, provided tremendous support. We wish to thank Charles Field for his belief in our book, Rebecca Freeman Field for teaching us so much and challenging us to reach our potential, Debby Smith for her invaluable editing "magic," and Nancy Lombardi for seeing the book through to completion.

For their patience, belief in us, and unconditional support, we thank our families. Karen would like to thank Doug and Peg Beeman and the whole Beeman clan for being her biggest cheerleaders and for their never-ending love and patience. *Paulo Gaete-Beeman ha motivado y ha apoyado a su mamá por medio de su risa, su amor y su creatividad lingüística, y este libro está dedicado a él. Las muchas conversaciones e ideas compartidas con Byron Javier están reflejadas en este libro, y su apoyo implacable y su amor palpable han sido imprescindibles para la culminación de este proyecto.* Finally, Karen wishes to thank Gabi and Rodrigo Javier for all their support and love. Cheryl would like to thank and dedicate this book to her real-life simultaneous bilinguals, Hannah and Lucía, who provided invaluable source material for the vignettes and much needed reality checks during the writing process. *También le quiere dar las gracias a su esposo, Fred Chonkan-Chan, por su amor y apoyo constante y, más que nada, por llevar a las chicas a jugar durante los sábados del libro.*

FOREWORD

There are upwards of 10 million children who enter U.S. schools speaking languages other than English; current estimates put this number at about 1 in 10 of every student in a U.S. school. The language, culture, and funds of knowledge that emergent bilingual[1] children bring to school constitute a huge and often untapped national resource. That these emerging bilingual students can benefit from educational programs that capitalize on and develop their linguistic and cultural resources is well established in the educational research (e.g., see Goldenberg, 2008[2]). Concomitantly the extant research has established that students who enter U.S. schools as monolingual English speakers also can benefit greatly from educational programs that afford them the opportunity to acquire and develop languages other than English. It is the potential for children in this double demographic that underscores the critical need for books such as *Teaching for Biliteracy: Strengthening Bridges between Languages.*

Karen Beeman and Cheryl Urow have done a masterful job of outlining *who* the children are in U.S. schools; *how* programs such as dual language can provide opportunities to become bilingual, biliterate, and bicultural; and *what* potential instructional learning units can be utilized by teachers to provide these important learning opportunities for diverse linguistic and cultural groups. They skillfully use profiles of real children and their teachers to demonstrate both the enormous heterogeneity of this population as well as how the profiles of each child can be used in the development of English and other languages.

Beginning in chapter 1, the authors take on and debunk the widely held misconception that children's non-English languages present a barrier to English acquisition and/or that they are a source of cognitive and linguistic interference. Their use of the term *Bridge* emphasizes both that first languages are resources to learning other languages, and that the language bridge is a two-way conduit, where there is crosslinguistic transfer from English to a non-English language and vice versa. This image is used artfully throughout the text to illustrate how the learning and acquisition of two languages is connected, and is an important contribution of this book.

Teaching for Biliteracy's focus on bridging as something that is informal and unplanned and also critical in the day-to-day practice of teaching emergent bilingual children is another unique contribution by this work. Too often we try to separate rather than connect children's languages, thereby limiting rather than enhancing their opportunities to utilize the totality of their linguistic repertoires as learning resources. The authors clearly explain that cross-language bridging is what separates monolingual learning from biliterate learning.

Unlike many other texts about bilingualism and biliteracy, which limit their discussion to instructional programs and practices and the children they benefit, Beeman and Urow provide a chapter that discusses the importance of teacher profiles.

---

[1] Although English language learner (ELL) is widely used, the field is moving to wider utilization of the term "emergent bilingual learner," which is a more positive synonym for ELL.

[2] Goldenberg, C. (2008). Teaching English language learners: What the research does and does not say. *American Educator, 2*(2), 8–23.

Teachers are the frontline providers of opportunities to become bilingual and biliterate, and it is their dispositions and attitudes that influence and shape the emerging biliterate identities in all of the children they teach. Understanding the developmental trajectories of bilingual teachers in the United States is critical in planning professional development activities that subsequently improve the implementation of high-quality dual-language learning opportunities for children.

Another important contribution that this book makes is the assertion that dual-language programs can coexist with the new Common Core State Standards. I would add that any educational program intent on developing biliteracy in all of its students establishes a standard and rigor that surpasses the Common Core—for biliteracy, in any form, is a higher form of literacy than monoliteracy.

Readers of this text will find it informative partly because of its firm footing in many relevant theoretical perspectives. These include the use of sociolinguistic theory to better understand teacher and student language profiles; the use of sociocultural theory as a grounding for the importance of understanding that all learning, and most importantly language learning, is social in nature and situated in particular social and political contexts; and contrastive analysis as a way of arguing effectively why the pedagogy and methodology used to teach literacy in Spanish must differ fundamentally from the pedagogy and methodology used to teach literacy in English. This grounding in theoretical perspectives makes the book comprehensive in its orientation about how to strengthen the development of biliteracy for the diverse populations of children becoming biliterate in U.S. schools.

Finally, readers of this book will benefit from the authors' broad definition of biliteracy development as including oracy and metalanguage as well as reading and writing as critical components of development of biliteracy. Quite simply, the book represents state-of-the-art thinking with regard to the building of quality educational programs designed to ensure that large and quite diverse populations of students become biliterate.

Beeman and Urow are to be congratulated for writing a book that, in concrete ways, illustrates how to build bridges to biliteracy **and** how to bridge theory to practice. Teachers and other educators will find many concrete suggestions about how to value non-English languages. Although written from a Spanish/English perspective, the book is applicable to the development of biliteracy from many different pairs or languages. It is an excellent text to read and discuss as the field builds the next generation of dual-language programs for new millennium children.

—*Kathy Escamilla*

CONTENTS

CHAPTER 4
Planning the Strategic Use of Two Languages   48

CHAPTER 5
Language Resources, Linguistic Creativity, and Cultural Funds of Knowledge   66

CHAPTER 6
Building Background Knowledge   78

CHAPTER 10
The Bridge: Strengthening Connections between Languages   133

CHAPTER 1

Foundations in Teaching for Biliteracy

KEY POINTS

- Biliteracy instruction includes the broad range of teaching and learning activities involving reading and writing that occur in Spanish and English across the curriculum.

- Effective biliteracy educators embrace a holistic, multilingual perspective on teaching, learning, and assessment that sees the two (or more) languages that each student speaks as complementary parts of that student's developing linguistic repertoire.

- Teaching for biliteracy in Spanish and English in the United States involves complex processes that are informed by fundamental sociolinguistic premises.

- The Bridge is the instructional moment in teaching for biliteracy when teachers bring the two languages together, guiding students to engage in contrastive analysis of the two languages and to transfer the academic content they have learned from one language to the other language.

- Bridging involves the use of cross-linguistic strategies and leads to the development of metalinguistic awareness.[1]

- The biliteracy unit framework is a flexible structure that teachers can use to plan and implement effective biliteracy instruction in any teaching-for-biliteracy context.

In our research, our work in the classroom, and our collaboration with other teachers and researchers, we have found that teaching for biliteracy is unlike teaching for monolingual literacy. Specifically, teaching for biliteracy in Spanish and English in the United States is unlike teaching for English literacy to monolingual English speakers in the United States and unlike teaching for Spanish literacy in Spanish-speaking countries. This understanding is the basis of this book.

Teaching for biliteracy takes place throughout the world with many different languages. Because the focus of our work is on teaching for biliteracy in Spanish and English in the United States, we draw on this case throughout this book. We recognize that many varieties of Spanish are used in the United States, and we have sought to include examples of and references to these varieties. But because our linguistic and cultural roots are in Mexico and Central America, and the students

---

[1]Throughout this book, the term "Bridge" is capitalized when used as a noun and lowercased when used as a verb; "bridging," in all contexts, is lowercased.

with whom we have worked in the United States are mainly of Mexican and Central American origin, most of our examples are taken from or refer to these cultures and languages. All of the suggestions, examples, and resources we present, however, can be adapted and used with Spanish speakers from any Spanish-speaking context.

We encourage biliteracy practitioners and researchers working with other target languages in other sociolinguistic contexts to use the case of teaching for biliteracy in Spanish and English in the United States as a springboard for their work. Our approach to teaching for biliteracy, including the sociolinguistic premises on which it is based, the concept of the Bridge and bridging, and the biliteracy unit framework that structures our work with teachers, can be readily applied to other contexts for biliteracy instruction.

What Do We Mean by Teaching for Biliteracy?

Bilingual students learn best in a classroom where teachers take a constructivist approach to literacy instruction. Constructivist teachers provide instruction in classic comprehension strategies and basic skills, such as sound-symbol correspondence within a context that is rich in meaning, builds on students' background knowledge and experiences, and requires students to apply their developing skills to authentic tasks. Most literacy programs in schools today focus on reading during the language arts period. But students need to learn to read, write, listen, and speak in all content areas throughout the day in order, for example, to read their math books, write up science experiments, talk about events in history, organize their thoughts about a favorite author, and reach high content and English-language development (ELD) standards as well as Spanish-language development (SLD) standards. A comprehensive approach to literacy instruction integrates content, literacy, and language instruction and connects reading with oral language and writing. Effective biliteracy instruction enables bilingual learners to use reading, writing, listening, and speaking for a wide range of purposes in two languages.

Educators today generally recognize an important distinction between "social language" and "academic language." Social language can be understood as the relatively informal conversational language we use among friends and family when we communicate about everyday topics orally and in writing. Academic language can be understood as the relatively formal oral and written language used in academic texts and academic settings. The term "academic language" includes many different registers,[2] such as the languages of math, science, and social studies, as well as the (English) language arts referred to in state-mandated ELD standards and in the SLD standards, Spanish language arts standards, and bilingual standards that have been developed in some states. Thus, the language of science (i.e., a scientific register) includes the vocabulary used to talk about scientific subject matter and the structures of the genres used in scientific texts within scientific discourse communities (e.g., the scientific method).[3]

---

[2] The concept of "register" involves consideration of the situation or context of use; the purpose, subject matter, and content of the message; and the relationship between participants. For example, two lawyers discussing a legal matter use the register of law; two teachers discussing student work use the register of education. Vocabulary differences—either a special vocabulary or special meanings for ordinary words—are most important in distinguishing different registers (Romaine 2000, p. 21).

[3] The term "genre" is used in sociolinguistics and stylistics to refer to a recognizable communicative event that happens with some frequency within a speech community in which oral or written language

In this book, we focus on the academic or formal language and literacy across content areas required for school success, and our work is aligned with state-mandated content and language-development standards. But we also look at the social or informal oral and written language that our students use with family and friends outside the classroom. This holistic, sociocultural view of language and literacy as communicative practice encourages teachers to build on the ways students use language and literacy at home and in their communities as a means of developing the oral and written language they need for school success.

Literacy research and practice has long been dominated by a monolingual perspective, surprisingly even in bilingual programs. Recently, however, an encouraging shift has begun to occur in language and literacy education to a multilingual perspective (de Jong, 2011; Escamilla et al., 2010). Thus, in contrast to the once widespread practice of labeling students who are developing biliteracy in dual-language programs as either "English-dominant" or "Spanish-dominant," more and more educators now refer to all students involved in developing biliteracy as "two-language learners" (Escamilla, 2000) or "bilingual learners" (de Jong, 2011), the terms we use interchangeably throughout this book. These educators see biliteracy development as a dynamic, holistic process that stands in contrast to the static notion reflected in the terms "English-dominant" and "Spanish-dominant." Furthermore, they recognize that many bilingual learners use languages in ways that challenge these traditional labels. These students come from homes and communities in which English and Spanish together or in combination with one or more other languages are used orally and in writing for a wide range of purposes.

Educators who take a multilingual perspective look at the two (or more) languages each student speaks as complementary, comparing these students with other bilingual learners and viewing their use of more than one language as an asset. They place these students in bilingual classrooms that can take advantage of their multilingual resources, and they use assessment practices that accommodate the two languages. Most important, they view these students as learners who use their knowledge and skills in both languages for learning.

In contrast, educators who take a monolingual perspective look at the two languages each student speaks as separate and compare the students to monolingual speakers in each language. These educators generally see the students' use of a second language as a deficit and label their performance in both languages as "low" (Escamilla, 2000). They place these students in a single-language literacy class in the language they determine is "dominant" and assess them only in that language.

The following incident reflects a question heard often in the field today, and it brings into focus some of the negative consequences of a monolingual perspective on bilingual learners. This incident occurred in a graduate bilingual certification course for bilingual teachers.

One of the teachers, Samuel, brought an example of student writing to class and asked his classmates for help. One of his 1st grade students, María, had written "*Voy a una party con mi broder*" as part of a language experience activity. Samuel wondered whether María has fully developed her home language and asked his classmates, "How can I teach her when she doesn't speak either of the two languages well?" Several classmates questioned

---

figures prominently. The scientific method, show-and-tell, persuasive essays, church sermons, and free-style rap are all examples of genres. The structure of the language used within a genre is relatively stable within a speech community, which makes it comprehensible to members of that community. The ways that genres are structured linguistically reflect the cultural contexts of which they are a part.

whether María was even in the right program. Some argued that since María's Spanish isn't good to begin with, perhaps she should be placed in an all-English program.

Biliteracy teachers who look at this example from a multilingual perspective do not see María's code-switching, that is, her use of both English and Spanish within the utterance, as a deficit. Rather, they see it as evidence of "translanguaging," of her taking advantage of and using all her available linguistic resources (García, 2009). These teachers value and build on the language resources and linguistic creativity evidenced in their students' use of two languages, and they make space for it.

The Bridge and Bridging

Teaching for biliteracy has three parts: Spanish (or one of the two languages) instruction, the Bridge (both languages side by side), and English (or the other language) instruction. The Bridge occurs once students have learned new concepts in one language. It is the instructional moment when teachers bring the two languages together to encourage students to explore the similarities and differences in the phonology (sound system), morphology (word formation), syntax and grammar,[4] and pragmatics (language use) between the two languages, that is, to undertake contrastive analysis and transfer what they have learned from one language to the other. The Bridge is also the instructional moment when teachers help students connect the content-area knowledge and skills they have learned in one language to the other language.

The Bridge is a simple but powerful concept: with strategic planning, the Bridge allows students who are learning in two languages to strengthen their knowledge of both languages. The Bridge is a tool for developing metalinguistic awareness, the understanding of how language works and how it changes and adapts in different circumstances. An important aspect of the Bridge is that it is two-way. It goes from Spanish to English and from English to Spanish. It recognizes that because bilinguals transfer what they have learned in one language to the other language, they do not have to learn content in both languages, even when they are tested only in English. For example, if students study math only in Spanish, the Bridge provides opportunities for them to attach English to that math content without relearning the math concepts and skills again in English.

For many years in the United States we have taught students to keep their two languages separate. One reason for this practice is to avoid devaluing Spanish, which often occurs when English comes into Spanish learning time. While the potential for devaluing Spanish and thus limiting students' ability to reach deep levels of learning in Spanish is a consideration that must be addressed, keeping the two languages separate has had the unfortunate effect of emphasizing to students that what they know in one language cannot be used in their other language. We have also assumed that students have engaged in contrastive analysis on their own. But not all students know, for example, that pairs of words like *energía*–energy are cognates. Recent research has shown that bilingual students who receive instruction in how their two languages are similar and different engage more regularly and successfully in cross-linguistic transfer, the application of a skill or concept learned in one language to another language, than do bilingual students who do not receive such

---

[4] Syntax and grammar refers to the word order within sentences (how sentences are constructed) and the rules governing this word order, as well as other rules describing a language.

instruction (Dressler, Carlo, Snow, August, and White, 2011) and that bilingual students who understand how their two languages are similar and different achieve higher levels of academic success (Jimenez, García, and Pearson, 1996). The Bridge is our response to this reality.

The Bridge is a part of a unit that has been planned and organized by the teacher. Bridging, or translanguaging, however, is more flexible and spontaneous than the Bridge and need not involve the teacher. Bridging occurs during the Bridge and whenever students and teachers make connections between the two languages. When students make these connections and tap into all their linguistic resources to learn, they are bridging. Bridging is important because it promotes cross-linguistic transfer (Koda and Zehler, 2008) and leads to the development of metalinguistic awareness. Bilingual students of Spanish and English who develop metalinguistic awareness are able to identify similarities and differences between Spanish and English. Guiding students to this awareness is critical to the effective teaching of biliteracy and sets biliteracy instruction apart from monolingual literacy instruction.

Sociolinguistic Premises about Teaching for Biliteracy

Three fundamental sociolinguistic premises capture the complexity of teaching for biliteracy in Spanish and English in the United States, and they can be adapted to any two languages used in biliteracy instruction. According to these premises, teaching for biliteracy in Spanish and English in the United States is different than teaching for monolingual literacy because of the following:

1. Spanish in the United States is a minority language within a majority culture.
2. Students use all of the languages in their linguistic repertoire to develop literacy.
3. Spanish and English are governed by distinct linguistic rules and cultural norms.

The first premise highlights the stratification of languages and language users in society. The second premise reflects a multilingual perspective on bilingual learners. The third premise draws attention to the linguistic similarities and differences between the target languages and the cultural norms of those who use the target languages in different discourse communities. These three premises shape our discussion.

THE STRATIFICATION OF LANGUAGES IN SOCIETY

Premise 1 states, teaching for biliteracy in Spanish and English in the United States is different than teaching for monolingual literacy because Spanish in the United States is a minority language within a majority culture. In this premise, the terms "minority" and "majority" refer to the status of Spanish and English in the United States today, rather than to the number of Spanish speakers relative to English speakers.

The task of learning to read and write in the majority language of a country, whether it is English in the United States or Spanish in Latin America, is supported and affirmed by a multitude of structures. In the United States, teachers and administrators receive abundant professional development in English literacy in their certification programs; researchers continue to study and publish findings that influence the way English literacy is taught; the larger school communities support literacy development by establishing networks and relationships between libraries and schools and between publishers and schools through book fairs and author days. In Latin America, Spanish literacy is supported in the same ways that English literacy is supported in the United States. Children are invited to libraries on Saturdays, for example, to see the latest puppet-show adaptations of popular books, such as *El gato en botas*. Environmental print and the use of literacy are affirmed in the majority language in both English- and Spanish-speaking countries.

The context and support that allow language-majority speakers to become literate in their own language do not exist for language-minority students. Thus, for those who are learning to read and write in Spanish in the United States, even in communities where Spanish plays a vital role in everyday life, Spanish literacy instruction can be sporadic, inconsistent, and not reflective of best practices or research (Escamilla, 2000; Freeman and Freeman, 2006; Ovando, Combs, and Collier, 2006). For example, many programs for English language learners, or ELLs (students who speak a non-English language at home and have been identified as becoming English proficient),[5] use Spanish only to "explain" what students do not understand, that is, to clarify what is occurring in English rather than as a focus for study and development in its own right. Another example of where Spanish literacy instruction falls short is in transitional bilingual programs for ELLs, which use Spanish for a limited number of years while the students learn English. Students transition from Spanish to English once it has been determined that they know enough English to get along without Spanish support, cutting short these students' literacy development in Spanish. Many transitional bilingual programs, referred to as "early exit," offer Spanish literacy instruction to ELLs only in kindergarten and 1st grade and sometimes into the middle of 2nd grade and then place the students in general-education all-English classrooms (Ovando et al., 2006). Some districts offer English-only preschools to ELLs and then move these students to bilingual programs starting in kindergarten, further jeopardizing the context for biliteracy development (Escamilla, 2000).

These approaches to the development of literacy in Spanish do not reflect current findings on bilingual education. Research has shown, for example, that for students to develop literacy, they need to go through predictable stages that require consistent, uninterrupted instruction. Furthermore, compared with monolingual students, students who acquire advanced levels of proficiency in a second language often experience cognitive and linguistic advantages (Cloud, Genesee, and Hamayan, 2000). When sequential bilingual learners (students with a base in Spanish who are new to English) learn to read and write in Spanish and English, they catch up to their native English-speaking peers in English, while those who are not taught to read and write in Spanish fall behind their peers in English (Freeman and Freeman, 2006). Simultaneous bilinguals (those who are exposed to two languages from birth) go through the same acquisition process with both languages (Ovando et al., 2006). Thus, when they are enrolled in programs that build on their two-language resources by teaching them to read and write in both languages through their elemen-

---

[5] Although "ELL" is widely used in the field, we are beginning to see a move to "emergent bilingual," which García (2009) uses as a synonym for ELL. For example, New York has recently adopted this term.

tary school years, they are more successful in school than bilingual learners who are not given the opportunity to develop biliteracy (Escamilla et al., 2010).

In the United States, the minority status of Spanish is reflected in the minimal professional development in Spanish literacy instruction that is offered. This lack of appropriate teacher preparation has important implications in the classroom (Escamilla, 1999; Guerrero, 1997). In general, teacher preparation programs do a good job of covering the foundations of second-language acquisition and methods for teaching English as a second language, but bilingual teachers are rarely taught how to teach in Spanish. Few schools provide professional development in Spanish and about Spanish instruction (Escamilla, 2000; Guerrero, 1997), and even fewer address the challenges of teaching for biliteracy as opposed to teaching for monolingual literacy. Most teachers are expected to take a mainstream, English-specific curriculum and adapt it for Spanish. But they are generally given no extra time, materials, or training to do so. As a result, English drives the instruction that takes place in Spanish, altering it significantly.

These differences between the structures and support for Spanish relative to English in the United States are explained by the fact that Spanish does not hold the same sociopolitical value as English (Cloud et al., 2000; Crawford, 1999; Cummins, 1996; Escamilla, 2000; Freeman, 2004; Ovando et al., 2006). Students, parents, and teachers understand that to be successful in the United States, one must develop English literacy. Thus, teaching literacy in English is required, whereas teaching literacy in Spanish is a choice, and it is a politically laden choice. Despite a long history of bilingual education in the United States and extensive research supporting its value, anti-immigrant sentiment and the political backlash that comes with it have made Spanish a marked language (Crawford, 1999; Cummins, 1996; Freeman, 2004), and Spanish instruction has come under attack (Freeman and Freeman, 2006). Decisions about teaching for biliteracy are often based on the sociopolitical power relationship between Spanish and English rather than on research or developmentally appropriate practices (Brisk and Harrington, 2007; Escamilla, 2000; Freeman, 2004). The result is that Spanish literacy instruction does not hold the same status as English literacy instruction.

Decision-makers therefore must analyze the infrastructure that has been created in a district to determine whether program decisions support strong literacy development and whether they are consistent with research and best practice in the field. The stratification of languages and their speakers, along with sociopolitical perceptions of the status of these languages, affects all contexts involved in teaching for biliteracy, not only Spanish and English in the United States.

In the United States, students and teachers are consistently driven to English in matters of placement, instruction, and assessment. And because parents are often led to believe that only English literacy matters, they may minimize many of the supportive activities and behaviors they could be providing and demonstrating at home in Spanish that would transfer to English, and instead they engage with their children in a learner's version of English. Even when teachers teach in programs that aim for bilingualism, and they require students to produce language and literacy in Spanish, English makes its way into the classroom. Research has shown that many dual-language programs, which strive to develop true biliteracy and bilingualism with students from both English- and Spanish-speaking homes, struggle to encourage students to value Spanish and to continue to speak, read, and write in it beyond 4th grade (Freeman, 2004; Potowski, 2007). Students tend to value English learning over Spanish learning, to choose books in English rather than Spanish

---

BOX 1.1.   Suggestions for Elevating the Status of Spanish in the School Community

- Involve teachers and parents in the design of bilingual and dual-language programs so they have a voice in determining the goals, vision, and implementation of the program.
- Offer classes in Spanish as a second language for interested teachers and parents.
- Provide teachers with professional development in how to deliver literacy instruction in Spanish.
- Hold faculty meetings in Spanish when all participants are bilingual.
- Make public announcements in Spanish and ensure that Spanish is represented in environmental print (newsletters, bulletin boards, letters, and all other print that is created in the school).
- Invite speakers to public events who highlight the benefits of biliteracy.
- Encourage teachers to speak to each other in Spanish.

---

for sustained silent reading, and to prefer English to Spanish in social situations. If literacy in Spanish is to be taught effectively in the United States, all stakeholders—students, parents, teachers, and community members—must value Spanish.

Recognizing that Spanish is a minority language, as the first premise states, is a call to action. Educators must become advocates for biliteracy, because research has shown that biliteracy instruction is the best way to educate emerging bilinguals to ensure that they reach their full potential. Research has shown also that students perform best when they feel good about themselves and about their learning (Cloud et al., 2000). If we are to maximize student potential for biliteracy development, educators need to elevate the status of Spanish in the school community. (See Box 1.1. for suggestions; these suggestions can be adapted to other minority languages.) To accomplish this change, we must have a paradigm shift in the United States to a positive view of bilingualism that sees it as a resource and a realistic goal rather than as a challenge or a problem.

A HOLISTIC, MULTILINGUAL VIEW OF BILINGUAL LEARNERS

Premise 2 states, teaching for biliteracy in Spanish and English in the United States is different than teaching for monolingual literacy because students use all of the languages in their linguistic repertoire to develop literacy. This premise, like the first one, calls for a paradigm shift. It focuses, however, on the individual and how we look at individual learning in two languages. An important consideration in teaching Spanish literacy in the United States today is the two-language background of our students. Thus, a paradigm shift from a monolingual perspective to a multilingual perspective would allow educators to see the knowledge and use of two languages as a linguistic asset rather than as an obstacle.

Many bilingual programs in place today were designed in the United States 30 to 40 years ago, when the majority of bilingual students were sequential bilingual learners, that is, students who had been exposed to one language in their home country and who were new to their second language, English (Escamilla et al., 2010). The theory behind these programs is that when children develop a solid base in content and literacy in their first, or dominant language, they will transfer these skills to English (Cummins, 1981; Ramirez, Yuen, Ramey, and Pasta, 1991; Thomas and Collier, 1997). This theory has led educators to look at bilingual education as a set of either/or issues: students are dominant in either Spanish or English; initial literacy should be taught in Spanish or English. If students are dominant in Spanish, instruction should be conducted in Spanish, with English to enter only once a solid base in Spanish has been established.

Recent demographic shifts in the Latino population, however, have resulted in an increase in the number of Latino students who are U.S. born. These students, who make up 75% of ELLs in the elementary schools, have been exposed to Spanish and English from birth (Capps et al., 2005; Swanson, 2009). They are simultaneous bilinguals to whom the principles of language acquisition created for sequential bilingual learners might not apply. Thus, we should be careful about how we characterize children's language use and consider whether it is appropriate to make pedagogical decisions based on the notion of a dominant language.

Many teachers express frustration in trying to follow the principle of identifying and then teaching in the "dominant" or "native" language when they work with students who enter school speaking Spanish and English. These teachers may use the term "semilingual" to describe students who, like the child we encountered earlier who wrote, "*Voy a una party con mi broder*," do not seem to speak either language well.[6] In what language, these teachers ask, are they to teach initial literacy?

The second premise answers this question. If students speak two languages, they should receive instruction that uses both languages strategically and in a way that makes pedagogical sense. Rather than looking for one language that is dominant, we need to view students who speak two languages as having strengths in both languages (de Jong, 2011). The term, referred to earlier, that best describes these students—because it captures their two-language background—is "two-language learners." These students should be exposed to both Spanish and English every day and be encouraged to use all they know in all their languages. They are growing up in bilingual communities where both languages are used on television, in magazines and books, in environmental print, and in everyday conversation, and their language reflects these communities.

An additional challenge for educators is to avoid the erroneous assumption that bilingual students comprise two monolinguals in one. This belief has led some educators to expect these students to speak and use Spanish as monolingual Spanish speakers and English as monolingual English speakers and to assume that we therefore need to teach them literacy in Spanish the way literacy is taught to monolingual Spanish speakers and literacy in English the way it is taught to monolingual English speakers (Grosjean, 1989). Escamilla (1999, 2000; Escamilla et al., 2010) argues that bilingual learners should not be compared with monolingual learners and that their two languages should be viewed as forming a whole. Furthermore, a student's mixing of the two languages should be seen not as a problem but as a reflection of his or her bilingual resources. For example, when a student identifies a letter sound in English (This letter says "em.") but gives an example of a word that begins with that letter in Spanish (*mesa*), rather than looking at the student as confused, or limited, in Spanish, we recognize that he or she is using both languages for learning. Inherent in the belief supported by the second premise, that students use all their linguistic resources in learning, is the recognition that students can transfer content,

---

[6] The term "semilingual" was introduced in 1975. It reflects the misguided belief that some ELLs have limited ability in both Spanish and English. Although this view has been well refuted (see, e.g., Ovando et al., 2006), the term is still in use.

language, literacy, and cultural knowledge and skills from one language to another (Crawford, 1999; Cummins, 1981; Dressler et al., 2011).

If we believe that schooling should build on what students know and can do, we should question the effectiveness of programs that teach students how to read in Spanish only and wait to transition them to English literacy once they have reached a certain level of proficiency in Spanish. Doing so makes it harder for them to develop biliteracy. If students enter with two languages, why wait to allow them to use both languages for learning? The most effective way for them to do so is through the strategic use of two languages in literacy and content instruction, and the Bridge.

CONTRASTIVE ANALYSIS BETWEEN LANGUAGES

Premise 3 states, teaching for biliteracy in Spanish and English in the United States is different than teaching for monolingual literacy because Spanish and English are governed by distinct linguistic rules and cultural norms. Some aspects of literacy development, such as the comprehension skills of predicting, inferring, summarizing, clarifying, and confirming, are universal. But each language works differently and students must understand these differences in order to maximize their learning in each language and develop metalinguistic awareness in each language and across languages.

Teachers and administrators who understand the similarities and differences between the two languages will be able to deliver a more authentic, coherent, and successful literacy experience for their students in Spanish and English. They will, for example, prefer texts written in the original language and avoid translations. Furthermore, these educators will encourage bridging and contrastive analysis in their classes. In the discussion that follows, we introduce key elements in contrastive analysis, which we develop further in subsequent chapters. In doing so, we draw on the field of linguistics to identify and explain different levels of language, including phonology, morphology, syntax, meaning relations at the word and sentence levels (semantics), and language use in context (discourse).

Spanish and English have clear phonological differences. Recognizing differences in Spanish and English phonology can help educators understand common pronunciation challenges for Spanish speakers learning English and common spelling errors by Spanish speakers who are beginning to write in English. For example, the words "very" and "berry" in English are what linguists call "minimal pairs" because only the word initial sounds are different. The difference in sound between "b" and "v" in word initial position signals the difference in meaning between the two words. In English, these two letters are phonemes, the basic units of sound in a language. In Spanish, however, "b" and "v" are not phonemic in word initial position; they are both pronounced as [b]. The lack of sound distinction between "b" and "v" in Spanish is one of many differences between English and Spanish that can help explain why two-language learners developing spelling in English need different approaches to help them, for example, distinguish between these two letters and avoid errors such as writing "beri" instead of "very."

Students can also be encouraged to contrast Spanish and English at the morphological and syntactic levels. Many words in Spanish and English emanate from the same root and have similar meanings, spellings, and pronunciations, that is, they are cognates. The languages of math, science, social studies, and language arts are full of cognates in Spanish and English, such as *geometría*–geometry; *electricidad*–electricity; *democracia*–democracy; *conservar*–conserve; *características*–characteristics. Students who are taught cognates, as well as the meaning of prefixes and suffixes, that are used in both languages engage in cross-linguistic transfer and recognize that words and the meanings of prefixes and suffixes that they know in one language can be applied in the other. For example, when studying morphology, students who have been taught that words in Spanish that end in *–ción* are written in English with the equivalent –tion (taking away the "c" and the accent and adding the "t"), are then able to write the word "multiplication" conventionally in English, using their Spanish (*multiplicación*). For students who want to write "multiplication" the way they hear it ("multiplicashun"), this lesson is very powerful. They learn that they can apply this rule to all words that follow this pattern (*comunicación*–communication; *educación*–education; *fundación*–foundation; *negociación*–negotiation), and they use this morphological pattern when reading and writing in English and in Spanish.

While there are many morphological and syntactic similarities between Spanish and English, there are also many differences. For example, students need to know about language conventions, such as the designation of gender for common nouns in Spanish but not in English, and false cognates, which are words that have similar spellings but different meanings across languages. Among these are nude–*nudo* (knot) and assistance–*asistencia* (attendance). Reflexive verbs, such as *llamarse* (to call oneself) are more common in Spanish than in English; the most common way to say, "My name is Eugenia" in Spanish is *Me llamo Eugenia* ("I call myself Eugenia"). Word order is another salient difference between the two languages; in Spanish the adjective follows the noun, as in "*el carro rojo*"; in English the adjective precedes the noun, as in "the red car." Teachers can use contrastive analysis to draw students' attention to these morphological and syntactic differences, helping them to develop metalinguistic awareness and avoid common errors.

Teachers can also encourage students to contrast their two languages at the discourse level. Discourse analysis focuses on the form–function relations of language, and contrastive analysis at this level draws students' attention to cross-cultural differences in the norms of interaction and interpretation underlying oral and written Spanish and English. Ethnographers of communication use the SPEAKING grid (Hymes, 1972) to analyze speech events in terms of the following components:

S: scene and setting

P: participants

E: ends or goals, purposes, and outcomes

A: act sequence or the form and order of speech acts (e.g., asking and responding to questions, agreeing and disagreeing)

K: key or indicators of the tone, manner, or spirit of the speech event (e.g., sarcastic, ironic)

I: instrumentalities for forms and styles of speech (e.g., oral, written, English, Spanish)

N: norms or social rules structuring the speech event

G: genre or the type of event (e.g., debate, persuasive argument, joke)

In Box 1.2 we compare similar speech events in Spanish and English, using the SPEAKING grid, to demonstrate differences in cultural norms.

In this contrastive analysis of two comparable speech events (one in Spanish and one in English), the settings, participants, ends, key, instrumentality, and genre are similar: at home, one intimate makes an oral request for help packing for a trip to visit another intimate. In both events, the request is followed by the preferred response: the other intimate provides the help that was requested. But the act

BOX 1.2. Comparing Speech Events with Differing Underlying Cultural Norms	
Event in Spanish	**Event in English**
S (scene, setting): farewell luncheon and preparation for travel	S (scene, setting): farewell luncheon and preparation for travel
P (participants): Gerardo, Sara, and Ramona	P (participants): Emily and Miriam
E (ends or goals): Ramona needs to exchange a broken suitcase	E (ends or goals): Emily would like to borrow a suitcase from Miriam

A (act sequence)
  1. Ramona describes her trip to the store.
  2. Ramona shows Gerardo and Sara the broken suitcase and describes the problem.
  3. Gerardo offers to take Ramona to the store to exchange the suitcase.
  4. Because they are siblings, Gerardo offers only once. Had they not been siblings, Gerardo would have had to offer three times so that Ramona could agree to his insistence and therefore not be a nuisance.
  5. Gerardo, Ramona, and Sara go the store and exchange the suitcase.
	A (act sequence)
	  1. Emily asks Miriam for a suitcase
	  2. Miriam says yes with conditions.
	  3. Miriam gives Emily the suitcase.

K (key): oral narrative Spanish, focused on description of event	K (key): oral narrative in English, focused on fact and need.
I (instrumentality): informal register	I (instrumentality): informal register

N (norms of interaction and interpretation):
  1. Speaker establishes cues for the listener, thereby engaging in an indirect request
  2. Listener offers help without being asked
	N (norms of interaction and interpretation):
	  1. Direct request
	
	  2. Direct response

G (genre): request of an intimate	G (genre): request of an intimate

sequences are different, and this difference reflects different cultural norms that guide request-making among intimates in Spanish and English.

In the Spanish event, Gerardo and Sara are hosting a farewell luncheon for Ramona, Gerardo's sister, who is visiting from Guatemala. Ramona is chatting with Sara and Gerardo about her packing and her return to Guatemala. After discussing her trip to the store and the purchases she has made, including a suitcase, Ramona tells Gerardo and Sara that she has just noticed that the zipper on the new suitcase is broken. She asks Sara and Gerardo whether they would like to see the suitcase, and they agree. As soon as he sees the broken zipper, Gerardo asks Ramona whether she would like to be taken back to the store to exchange the suitcase. She immediately replies she would, and the three go to the store. Gerardo later explains that if Ramona were not his sister, he typically would offer three times to take her to the store, and only after his insistence would she agree. This speech event reflects the following cultural norms:

- Ramona sets the stage by describing the situation using a variety of examples and establishing cues for Gerardo to pick up on, but she does not make a direct request for help.

- Gerardo picks up on the cues Ramona provides and offers to help solve the problem without Ramona's asking directly.

- Ramona is intentionally indirect in asking for help because to be direct would be rude.
- Ramona and Gerardo use indirectness and expect the listener to pick up on cues that the speaker presents.

In the English event, the act sequences and norms of interaction and interpretation are different. Emily is visiting her friend Miriam in Chicago. As she is packing on the day of her departure, Emily realizes that she will never be able to get all her purchases into her suitcase. She goes into Miriam's kitchen, where Miriam is preparing a farewell luncheon, and explains her quandary. She then asks Miriam whether by any chance she has a spare bag to lend Emily. Miriam goes into her closet, pulls out an old carry-on bag, and gives it to Emily, asking Emily whether she would be able to mail it back to her by the following month, because she is planning a trip. This speech event reflects the following cultural norms:

- Emily is direct and to the point in asking Miriam for a bag.
- Miriam does not take offense at the directness; in fact, she probably would not have understood if Emily had been indirect in setting the stage for Miriam to offer the bag.
- Emily would not have felt hurt if Miriam had said that she could not spare a bag.
- Both speakers used direct to-the-point language and used time efficiently.
- Miriam was just as direct in asking for the bag back by the following month.

The different cultural norms that frame language use, as illustrated in this speech event analysis, have led some researchers, comparing the two languages, to describe communication in English as more direct or linear and communication in Spanish as more circular (Brisk and Harrington, 2007; Escamilla and Coady, 2001). Because of the social expectations of the two languages, English speakers tend to be more direct, get to the point faster, and use fewer words than Spanish speakers, who use more descriptive language and take more time. Neither speech pattern is better than the other; they are simply different because they reflect the expectations of the culture and language in which they are rooted. Thus, many native English speakers are described as tending to speak and write in a linear fashion, while many native Spanish speakers are described as tending to speak and write in a circular fashion. Teachers can employ the Hymes SPEAKING grid to analyze their students' language use and draw their attention to cross-cultural differences.

Two-language learners are exposed to language that reflects both sets of cultural norms, and often both sets are used. Many teachers describe their students as speaking in Spanish using a linear discourse pattern that reflects norms of interaction from American culture or writing in English using a circular pattern that reflects oral discourse in Spanish. Students use their knowledge of English when learning in Spanish and vice versa.

Differences in cultural norms also help to explain how language varies with language user and social situation. Brisk and Harrington (2007) identify specific areas of literacy that are culturally defined, such as philosophies of and attitudes toward knowledge. The American academic context requires students to be independent learners who analyze, question, and critique knowledge contained in texts. This requirement is specific to the United States. Though many schools in Spanish-speaking countries expect students to analyze and critique text, they place less emphasis on this skill. Another distinct difference between cultures is revealed in how poetry is used in social gatherings. In many Spanish-speaking countries, the ability to *declamar* (recite) poetry from memory with appropriate intonation and emotion at gatherings where there is music and poetry, such as family celebrations or New Year's Eve parties, is highly valued. This use of poetry, which crosses socioeconomic levels and reflects the strong story-telling tradition of many Spanish-speaking countries, rarely occurs in gatherings in the United States.

In the United States, literacy skills are closely tied to the demands of the workforce and the technology that is available. Learning to write and organize original ideas and go through the "writing process" is a very common expectation in schools in the United States. Brisk and Harrington (2007) state that in the United States, the writer is expected to make the text clear to readers. In contrast, according to Escamilla and Coady (2001), Spanish narrative writing is divergent, often switching from one topic to another and then returning to the first topic.

As these few examples reveal, because of differences in context and expectations, literacy practices that work in English in the United States may not work in Spanish, and Spanish literacy practices from Spanish-speaking countries cannot necessarily be applied in the United States. Furthermore, both languages are used differently in different regions, social classes, and social groups.

Students enter school with background knowledge and experiences stored in overlapping linguistic reservoirs. The strategic use of two languages in content and literacy instruction, including the teacher-guided Bridge, is the best way to take advantage of these resources. Once bilingual students have a solid grounding in a particular content area in one language, they can transfer this knowledge to the other language by the Bridge.

Creating Bilingual Units of Instruction: A Biliteracy Unit Framework

Teaching for biliteracy requires the strategic use of Spanish and English. Literacy instruction should ensure that students acquire listening, speaking, reading, and writing skills in Spanish and English across content areas. This book is anchored in the strategic use of two languages, organized in a biliteracy unit framework. That framework has three parts: (1) learning new concepts and literacy skills in one language, (2) the Bridge where both languages are side by side, and (3) extension activities in the other language. (See the template for the biliteracy unit framework on pp. 16–17.)

In the first part, which includes planning and teaching in one language, students learn the concepts. The teacher chooses the curricular theme and accompanying big idea drawn from learning standards in the areas of math, science, language arts, and social studies. For example, for a 1st grade social studies class, the theme might be The Family with the big idea, "We all have families, but each family is unique." The teacher develops language and content targets related to the theme, language targets in Spanish for the instruction delivered in Spanish, and language targets in English for the instruction delivered in English, which she teaches and assesses throughout the unit. She initiates the unit in one language (Spanish or English) and develops new concepts using authentic tasks for reading and writing. If the policy for the school in the preceding example is to teach 1st grade social studies in Spanish, all instruction before the Bridge would be conducted in Spanish. The teacher focuses first on speaking and listening, creating a comprehensible context by building on and developing students' background knowledge and vocabulary.

She focuses next on reading comprehension and writing, often integrating the two. She then addresses and teaches the discrete skills needed to read and write, such as word study and fluency.

The second part is the Bridge, the moment when students compare the concepts in two languages. Once the students have learned and expressed the curricular language and concepts, the relevant words and phrases are written on a chart in Spanish and English, side by side. Next, students and teachers engage in contrastive analysis of the two languages.

In the third part, students engage in extension activities conducted in the other language using listening, speaking, reading, and writing. Taking the key concepts and language identified during the Bridge, they apply their learning from one language to the other language. In our example, the 1st grade students would apply the words and concepts about the family they learned in Spanish to activities in English.

During the instruction, teachers must plan their use of language carefully to ensure that they are strategic in their use of the two languages. Students, using all they know in all their languages, may switch back and forth between Spanish and English at any time. Their switching is a normal developmental process. But language use for teachers is different. Before the Bridge, teachers should choose Spanish only or English only for teaching a particular unit and ensure that they know the academic words in the language they choose. In teaching the unit, they should use language supports, such as word banks and sentence prompts, to help students develop the academic language they need in the unit.

The Bridge is student-centered. During the Bridge, the teacher visually places the two languages side by side, first guiding students to communicate what they have learned, for example, in Spanish about the family, and making a list of terms. The teacher and the students then generate the equivalent of those terms in English. The amount of teacher involvement in this first step of the Bridge depends on the students' level of knowledge in the other language. For students who are beginning to learn English, the teacher will provide the English terms; for students with an intermediate or advanced level of proficiency in English, the teacher will encourage the students to provide the English terms for many of the Spanish concepts. The second step of the Bridge is the contrastive analysis, during which students compare how their two languages work. The similarities and differences they explore and identify are captured in the Bridge anchor charts they create during the Bridge. These bilingual charts highlight the words and linguistic features studied during the Bridge, and they remain in the classroom so students can continue to refer to them. The formal, planned Bridge occurs only after students have learned the concepts and language that have been taught in a particular unit and are ready to engage in contrastive analysis. Bridging, in contrast, is informal and unplanned. It occurs every day whenever students, reading and writing in Spanish or in English, compare and contrast their two languages on their own and with the Bridge anchor charts they made in previous units.

Planning for Biliteracy at the Classroom Level from the Learner's Perspective

All biliteracy programs should have a well-articulated language and content allocation plan that tells students and teachers what is expected. The allocation plan facilitates the tasks of designing schedules and making decisions about what literacy components are used and in which language, and it helps teachers determine when and how to Bridge. In instances where there is no allocation plan, teachers may find

Biliteracy Unit Framework: Template

Content area:

Language in which this content area is taught:

Theme/Big idea:

Language allocation for this grade:

Standards:

___% Spanish; ___% English

Content targets:

Language targets
- Spanish:
- English:
- Cross-linguistic:

Summative assessment:

Building Oracy and Background Knowledge
Language of instruction: _____ (This language is maintained until the Bridge; the other language is used in the Extension Activity.)

Language resources, linguistic creativity, and cultural funds of knowledge:

Building background knowledge:

Formative assessment

Reading comprehension   Formative assessment

Writing   Formative assessment

Word study and fluency   Formative assessment

Summative assessment

The Bridge: Strengthening Bridges between Languages   Formative assessment

Language of instruction: Spanish and English

Extension Activity   Formative assessment

Language of instruction: _____ (the other language)

17

it helpful to document what is being taught in each language. If documentation reveals significant overlap, it may be good to teach the content in one language and use the Bridge after students have learned the concepts.

In addition to a language and content allocation plan, teachers should consider three other elements. First, if students are to develop literacy in two languages, they should read and write in both languages every day. In the primary grades, reading and writing in both languages may mean that students are doing the "heavy lifting of literacy" in Spanish by engaging in reading and writing activities focused on comprehension, writing, fluency, and word study and the "light lifting of literacy" (Escamilla, 2009) in English by focusing on journaling and independent and group reading.

Second, literacy should be thought of as whole. For example, if the district has established a 90-minute "literacy block," students developing biliteracy can engage in 45 minutes of literacy in Spanish in the morning and 45 minutes of literacy in English in the afternoon. Scheduling literacy components in both languages every day, however, may not be possible because of time constraints. One solution is to integrate language arts with content. Providing students with opportunities to read and write every day means that sometimes students are preparing a report on a science research project in Spanish as part of the writing process and are engaged in an author's study in English. When the school day is looked at from the students' point of view, it is easier to see how literacy activities in each language complement each other to form a whole.

Third, as noted earlier, teaching for biliteracy is different than teaching for monolingual literacy. Bilinguals are not two monolinguals in one, and therefore schedules cannot reflect two monolingual schedules in one. The schedule in a biliteracy classroom, for example, must acknowledge time for the Bridge, and because bridging allows skills to be integrated across languages, the skills and concepts need not be taught in both languages. In a biliteracy setting, literacy is integrated with content, and so the topics and themes that students read and write about in a biliteracy setting may be somewhat different than those in a monolingual setting. Skills such as predicting, inferring, understanding different genres, and applying appropriate syntax and grammar, however, are similar to those taught in a monolingual setting. Analyzing how students spend their time in school and viewing the school day from the learner's perspective allows teachers and administrators to find redundancy and other complications in students' schedules. In planning for biliteracy at the classroom level, teachers must be flexible in integrating scope and sequence in the reading and writing activities in two languages. Administrators also must be flexible in realizing that daily schedules for bilingual classrooms may need to be different than schedules in monolingual classrooms. The following questions may be used as a guide in analyzing students' time:

- Do students have the opportunity to read and write every day in both languages?
- Are students engaged in meaningful and purposeful literacy activities in both languages?
- When Spanish and English literacy instruction is looked at as a whole, are students engaged in the district's literacy curriculum?
- Are students held accountable for learning in the target language (rather than being allowed to wait to switch to the other language to learn)?
- Is it easy for teachers to see where and when Bridges will take place?

Program Considerations

Using the Bridge is most challenging in programs that do not have a clearly defined content and language allocation plan, especially in dual-language programs. The Bridge works best when it is a carefully planned activity that occurs after learning new concepts in one language. The unit framework in this book therefore places the Bridge at the end of instruction in one language, where it is followed by extension activities in the other language that guide students to use and apply the concepts learned in all their languages. This placement ensures that Spanish and English are equally valued. Rather than abandoning Spanish in preparation for standardized testing in English, students and teachers know that the Bridge will enable students to demonstrate in English what they have learned in Spanish and what they have learned in Spanish in English.

Establishing the amount of time spent in each language and the language in which each content area will be taught is essential when planning for the Bridge. In the discussion that follows, these elements are described in three types of language programs: dual-language (or two-way-immersion), bilingual (developmental and transitional), and heritage language. All teachers involved in teaching for biliteracy should understand the program structures and should know what role they play in them.

ALLOCATING LANGUAGE AND CONTENT IN DUAL-LANGUAGE PROGRAMS

Dual-language programs are designed for students who speak English at home, for students who speak Spanish at home, and for two-language students who speak both languages at home. The goal of dual-language programs is to develop cross-cultural understanding, bilingualism, and biculturalism in all students. To reach these goals, students from each group are integrated in the classroom and instructional time is divided between English and Spanish. One "non-negotiable" is that at least 50% of instructional time be delivered in Spanish. By about 3rd or 4th grade, most dual-language programs allot 50% of instructional time to Spanish and the other 50% to English. Many dual-language programs choose to spend more instructional time in Spanish than in English in the early primary grades, however, in an effort to elevate the status of Spanish and ensure that all students develop a strong foundation in Spanish by the time they reach the intermediate and upper grades of elementary and junior high school. Programs that elect to do more Spanish in these grades choose between 80/20 (80% Spanish and 20% English) and 90/10 (90% Spanish and 10% English) language allocation models in the primary grades, gradually increasing the amount of English to 50/50 by 3rd or 4th grade.

Once the language allocation plan has been decided, 50/50 or 80/20–90/10, teachers and administrators determine what content will be taught in each language. A common misunderstanding at this point is that for students to become biliterate, content must be shared across languages. While it is true that students need to be exposed to academic language in both Spanish and English, trying to teach content in both languages often results in flip-flopping, that is, teachers switch between languages randomly within a unit or teach a portion of the unit in one language and then switch to the other. When flip-flopping occurs, students typically wait for their most comfortable language (often English) and "check out" during instruction in the other language. Likewise, teachers understand that if students do not understand something in one language they can just wait until the instruction switches to the other language. This understanding often results in teachers' not using sheltered instruction and differentiation strategies that would make content comprehensible for students at different stages of English- and Spanish-language development. In the absence of a well-defined content allocation plan, teachers can, unwittingly, end up favoring instruction in English because of comfort level and anxiety over high-stakes testing.

Assigning a content area to one language is cleaner and simpler than sharing content across both languages. It is also more cost-effective: when content is shared across two languages, materials must be purchased in both languages. And, as discussed earlier, students need to learn content only once, regardless of the language in which it is taught; they do not have to learn content in both languages to demonstrate their learning. The Bridge, a fundamental element in teaching for biliteracy, explicitly teaches students that what they learned in one language can be applied in the other.

In a 50/50 dual-language program, language arts is taught in both Spanish and English. Many programs integrate parts of their language arts curriculum with content, often social studies. Math and science are taught in either language. Some programs teach science only in English K–5 (with a Bridge to Spanish) and math only in Spanish K–5 (with a Bridge to English). Other programs switch the language for these content areas by year or by several years (e.g., math is taught in Spanish K–2 with a Bridge to English and then taught in English 3–5 with a Bridge to Spanish). The simpler the content allocation plan, the easier it is to implement. In 80/20 or 90/10 programs, language arts is taught in both languages in the early primary grades, and content areas are taught in Spanish with a Bridge to English. By 3rd grade, some of the content is delivered in English (e.g., math in English and science in Spanish) with a Bridge to the other language.

Self-contained dual-language teachers can plan Bridges easily in their own classrooms. When language is divided by teacher, however, and the English teacher does not speak Spanish, who will conduct the Bridge becomes an issue. There are three options. One is to have students lead the Bridge with teacher support. This option is the most effective because students are in charge of their own learning, and it is widely used by English teachers who are not Spanish speakers but who have a good working relationship with the Spanish teacher. Another option is to have the two teachers conduct the Bridge together. The third is for teachers to collaborate in planning the Bridge so that the English teacher has enough Spanish to do the Bridge on her own.

ALLOCATING LANGUAGE AND CONTENT IN DEVELOPMENTAL AND TRANSITIONAL BILINGUAL PROGRAMS

The biggest difference between dual-language programs and developmental and transitional bilingual programs is the student population. Transitional and developmental bilingual programs serve students whose linguistic profile could be described as two-language learners or ELLs. Thus, the caution about "flip-flopping" between languages while teaching content is different; there are no English-dominant students in the classroom who will "wait" for English. But because Spanish is a minority language within a majority culture (premise 1), students and teachers often value English over Spanish and sacrifice time allocated for Spanish in the rush to get to English. Therefore, it is important to think about language and content allocation plans in transitional and developmental bilingual programs to ensure that the languages are valued equally.

Developmental bilingual programs, like dual-language programs, never halt Spanish instruction. They always plan for biliteracy by using both languages. Most developmental bilingual programs spend more time in Spanish in grades K–2 and gradually reach a 50/50 language allocation plan by 3rd or 4th grade. The 80/20 or 90/10 content allocation plan described earlier would be effective in a developmental bilingual program.

The aim of transitional bilingual programs, in contrast, is to "transition" students to English when their English-language proficiency has reached a certain level. Until that point, students are engaged in Spanish instruction in language arts and content, as well as English-language development. Bridges are done from Spanish to English, and the extension and application activities done in English after the Bridge build on the background knowledge and vocabulary developed in Spanish. Because of the research showing that when two-language learners spend more time developing both languages, they are more successful in developing literacy skills in English, many transitional programs maintain a Spanish language arts or Spanish for heritage speakers class for students in grades 3–5 to continue to support their literacy development in both languages.

PLANNING FOR BILITERACY IN HERITAGE LANGUAGE PROGRAMS

Spanish for native speakers (SNS), or heritage language programs, are typically thought of as alternatives to foreign language programs. One of the hallmarks of SNS programs is the integration of content with language instruction (Potowski, 2005). Rather than teaching discrete elements of language, as is often done in foreign-language classes, SNS classes use topics and themes that are highly relevant to the students' lives and often come from the social studies/contemporary history context. Like other biliteracy students, students in SNS programs benefit from instruction that involves the use of the Bridge from Spanish to English at the end of the instructional part of a unit. But they can also bridge from English to Spanish at the beginning of a unit. For example, background knowledge and vocabulary can be front loaded in English and then bridged to Spanish. A student-centered approach to bridging can help SNS teachers determine when bridging will be the most effective.

ACTIVITIES FOR REFLECTION AND ACTION

1 . Premise 1 for biliteracy instruction states, "Teaching for biliteracy in Spanish and English in the United States is different than teaching for monolingual literacy because Spanish in the United States is a minority language within a majority culture." Do the following on your own, with colleagues, or with your students:

- Collect evidence from your daily life that Spanish (like other minority languages) is a marked language.

- Collect evidence about how the status of Spanish affects the decisions made about literacy instruction in Spanish (e.g., policy, materials, curriculum, scheduling, program structure).

- Develop an action plan to address the preceding evidence. Make sure to plan for actions at the personal, classroom, school, and community levels.

2 . Premise 2 for biliteracy instruction states, "Teaching for biliteracy in the United States is different from teaching for monolingual literacy because students use all of the lan-

guages in their linguistic repertoire to develop literacy." Do the following on your own, with colleagues, or with your students:

- Collect evidence on how two-language learners are generally viewed in your school community.
- Classify this evidence as to whether it corresponds to a multilingual or monolingual perspective.
- Develop an action plan to move the school community to a multilingual perspective.

3. Premise 3 for biliteracy instruction states, "Teaching for biliteracy in Spanish and English in the United States is different than teaching for monolingual literacy because Spanish and English are governed by distinct linguistic rules and cultural norms." Do the following on your own, with colleagues, or with your students:

- List the similarities and differences between Spanish and English.
- Analyze the list to determine how these differences are addressed in literacy instruction in each language. Determine additional strategies to address these differences.
- Describe the current opportunities students have for bridging and contrastive analysis and plan for additional opportunities.

4. Working alone or with your colleagues, map out your current language and content allocation plan. Using instructional minutes allocated for the day or week, determine how much time you spend in Spanish and how much time you spend in English, and which content you teach in which language. Then compare these data with those of other colleagues and your program vision and plan and consider the following questions:

- How does the schedule reflect the three premises?
- When factoring in music, art, physical education, and other special subjects, are students exposed to enough minutes in Spanish in order develop biliteracy?
- What adjustments—both short term and long term—could be made to better reflect a multilingual perspective of biliteracy development?

CHAPTER 2
Students: A Multilingual Perspective

KEY POINTS

- Individual characteristics, such as linguistic, cultural, and academic background, vary widely among the students who learn to read and write in Spanish and English in the United States. These characteristics have an impact on students' learning.

- Information about these characteristics should be available to teachers.

- Instruction is most effective when it is differentiated to reflect the linguistic, cultural, and academic backgrounds of the students.

Beginning with the Learner

Pick up any book on pedagogy, and invariably you will find that teachers are advised to begin instruction with their students' experiential base. Teachers are also advised to adapt their instruction to the students' different learning styles (Tomlinson, 2001), their different language proficiency levels (Echevarria, Vogt, and Short, 2003; Fairbairn and Jones-Vo, 2010; Irujo, 2004, 2006), and their different levels of academic achievement (Tomlinson, 1999, 2001). Implicit in these recommendations is the assumption that the teacher is familiar with the linguistic, cultural, and academic background of all the students in the classroom. Gaining such familiarity can be difficult, however, because of the daily pressures of teaching and because students, like Carmen, the child in the following story, sometimes appear in the classroom with little warning.

> It's a small school, and so the principal herself walks Carmen down to Mr. Aguirre's 1st grade bilingual classroom. The principal, Dr. Weston, who does not speak any Spanish, smiles broadly and talks in calming tones as she takes Carmen by the hand. Dr. Weston pushes open the door to the classroom and waits while Mr. Aguirre finishes explaining the assignment to the class. When Mr. Aguirre turns to the principal and Carmen, Dr. Weston says, "Good morning, Mr. Aguirre. This is Carmen and she has just registered for school here this morning. Carmen doesn't speak English, but she does speak Spanish. I know she will feel very comfortable in your classroom." With that, the principal drops Carmen's hand and walks out of the classroom. Mr. Aguirre welcomes Carmen to the classroom in Spanish, and begins to introduce her to her classmates one by one.

Teachers and administrators with no easy access to background information about students may find it easier to group the students into broad categories and to attribute a common linguistic, cultural, and academic background to all the students in a single group than to try to infer their individual needs. The students who participate in biliteracy instruction in the United States are often grouped together this way and are referred to as Spanish-speaking students, Spanish-dominant students, or even English language learners. Dr. Weston made the same assumption that many do: if literacy instruction is offered in both Spanish and English, the instruction has been differentiated enough to meet the specific linguistic, cultural, and academic needs of all students who come from a Spanish-speaking background.

While literacy instruction in both Spanish and English may indeed meet one of Carmen's needs, her enrollment in a bilingual class is only the first step in matching instruction to her experiential base. The students who participate in biliteracy instruction in the United States are not a homogeneous group, and simply identifying a child as a Spanish speaker does not give sufficient information for the teacher to create effective and meaningful units of instruction. Biliteracy instruction, like literacy instruction in one language only, is more effective when it is differentiated to meet the needs of each student (Tomlinson, 2001).

Biliteracy Learner Profiles

This chapter introduces five students who are developing biliteracy in the United States. All five students are two-language learners, though their linguistic profiles vary. These students are fictitious. Their names are made up and their profiles are compiled from those of students we have known. Though these five student profiles do not include every element in the range of linguistic, cultural, and academic experiences and resources that two-language learners bring to the biliteracy classroom, they allow us to illustrate and bring to life the premises of literacy instruction in Spanish and English we present in Chapter 1. Understanding these premises will help educators use the biliteracy unit framework to create an effective learning environment for the great variety of students who are learning to read and write in Spanish and English in the United States.

These profiles also illustrate the benefits of biliteracy instruction for a wide range of students, not just children who cannot speak English. However, as the first premise states, Spanish is a minority language within a majority culture. Thus, Spanish literacy instruction in the United States has been viewed as an "add-on" to the regular curriculum and, almost universally, as merely an avenue to English literacy (August and Hakuta, 1997; Escamilla, 1994). Therefore, literacy instruction in Spanish has typically been offered only to those students who have little or no proficiency in English and only until they have developed sufficient proficiency in English to be instructed in English-only classrooms. The reality of the first premise is that students who enter schools in the United States able to speak even rudimentary English have often been encouraged to begin literacy instruction in English only. This practice is based on the rationale that there is no need for these students to "go back" to Spanish if they already have some ability in English (Cummins, 1980). It reflects a monolingual perspective on language that is challenged by the multilingual perspective the second premise supports. According to that perspective, students need a literacy curriculum that allows them to tap into all of their linguistic resources. The third premise—that both Spanish and English are governed by distinct linguistic and cultural rules—is at the center of the bilingual units of study we create to meet the needs of these five learners.

CARMEN: A NEWLY ARRIVED IMMIGRANT
FROM A SPANISH-ONLY HOME

Carmen, the child we met earlier, has just immigrated to the United States from Mexico with her parents. She attended some kindergarten in Mexico, and she has arrived in the United States in time to begin 1st grade in September. Before emigrating, she and her family lived in a small, agricultural community in Mexico. Her parents made the difficult decision to leave their home and extended family and come to the United States in a quest for economic and educational advantages. Carmen's parents were unable to continue their own schooling past 3rd grade. They are undereducated, but, according to the United Nations definition of literacy, they are not illiterate. The United Nations defines literacy as "the ability of an individual to read and write with understanding a simple short statement related to his/her everyday life" (UNESCO, 2005).

Carmen has many of the same challenges the over two million school-aged immigrants who come to the United States from Spanish-speaking countries face (U.S. Census Bureau, 2005). While the majority of these children come from Mexico (U.S. Census Bureau, 2001), Spanish-speaking students also come from other places in Latin America, including Puerto Rico, Guatemala, Argentina, and the Dominican Republic. Carmen represents the recent arrival from Latin America, a sequential bilingual with some schooling in her home language. Because she speaks only Spanish when she arrives at her U.S. school, she seems to be an obvious candidate for Spanish literacy instruction.

Literacy instruction in Spanish is most often an option for children like Carmen, new to the United States and monolingual Spanish speakers, but even students like her are sometimes denied literacy instruction in Spanish. Tests that do not allow for regional differences in language may show that these children are performing below what has been determined to be at or near grade level in Spanish literacy, and therefore schools place them directly in English-only classrooms. This monolingual approach to literacy instruction is based on the belief that if a student seems to lack a strong base in what is perceived to be his or her first language, literacy instruction should take place in English only, to avoid wasting time in getting to English. Though Carmen had some schooling in Mexico, it was minimal, since she is only six and just entering 1st grade. Her use of language reflects the cultural norms appropriate for the region and sociocultural environment in which it developed, including the use of archaic and regional expressions typical of rural Mexico, such as *ansina* for *así* and *naiden* for *nadie*, and an indirect pattern of language use. Carmen does have six years of Spanish oracy development, and because of the strong link between oracy and literacy, Carmen would benefit from a program that allows her to take advantage of her oracy resources in Spanish while developing her resources in English, that is, a program of biliteracy instruction.

PAULO: A FIRST-GENERATION U.S. STUDENT WITH ORAL
PROFICIENCY IN SPANISH AND ENGLISH

Paulo's family, like Carmen's family, came to the United States from rural Mexico in search of better academic and economic opportunities. And like Carmen, Paulo is in the early years of schooling. He is in the 2nd grade. Paulo's parents are literate in Spanish, but because of interrupted schooling, they have low levels of literacy. Unlike Carmen, however, Paulo has never lived in Mexico. He was born in the United

States and has attended school only in the United States. He reflects the current demographic trend that two-thirds of all U.S. English language learners who were born in the United States (Swanson, 2009) have parents or grandparents who are from outside the United States. Like many two-language learners born in the United States, Paulo entered the U.S. public school system with oral abilities in both Spanish and English, and language use that is reflective of both languages. He is a simultaneous bilingual who speaks Spanish at home with his parents and who learned English from television and from attending all-English full-time day care before entering school. When Paulo's language was first assessed at kindergarten registration, educators had a difficult time determining his dominant language; when Paulo spoke in Spanish, he inserted words in English. For example, when asked to talk about something that had happened to him recently, he said, using an English verb in present progressive Spanish, *"Estuve bleedi-ando"* ("I was bleeding"). And when asked to find the letter "i" in Spanish, he pointed to the "e" in English.

In educational settings that employ a monolingual perspective to literacy instruction, it might be determined that Paulo has "no language," or that he is "low in both languages" (Escamilla, 2000). It also might be determined that, because he does have some ability in English or that he sometimes uses the more direct and linear speech pattern reflective of English in his oral Spanish, literacy instruction in Spanish would be of little benefit to Paulo. Unlike Carmen, a recent immigrant who learned language in a monolingual environment, Paulo has always lived in an environment with two languages, and he draws on both linguistic resources when he speaks or writes. Paulo reflects the second premise: students use all of the languages in their linguistic repertoire to develop literacy. He would therefore benefit from a biliteracy program in Spanish and English, which would tap into and build on all his linguistic resources. Since kindergarten, Paulo has been in a bilingual classroom that supports literacy instruction in both Spanish and English and therefore takes advantage of and builds Paulo's linguistic repertoire.

ANTONIO: A NEWLY ARRIVED IMMIGRANT WITH EDUCATIONAL EXPERIENCE IN SPANISH

Antonio, like Carmen, has just arrived in the United States, and, like Carmen and the majority of Spanish-speaking immigrants in the United States, he is from Mexico. He too spent the early years of his life surrounded by Spanish and has been acculturated into the norms of his home country. But he is beginning 5th grade and is therefore older than Carmen and Paulo, and his Spanish reflects the Spanish used by an urban, upper-middle-class social group. Antonio has come to the United States because the multinational company for which his father works has transferred the family here from Mexico City. And though Antonio will initially find the culture of the United States as new and confusing as Carmen does, he enters U.S. schools with five years of education in his first language. Thus, he begins his biliteracy development as a sequential bilingual. He can read at grade level in Spanish and has the literacy skills expected of a beginning 5th grader: he can use a table of contents and a dictionary and he can write a paragraph. He enters U.S. schools with many more academic skills than Carmen. These skills are fully accessible, however, only if his education includes Spanish. If he is placed in an all-English classroom, he will not be able to demonstrate his understanding or his previous knowledge until he has developed some proficiency in English. In the meantime, he will miss the new content being taught in the 5th grade.

Antonio's parents are well prepared to navigate the new culture and the new school system. They are both college-educated professionals and come with greater academic skills than Carmen's and Paulo's parents. Antonio's father, a chemical engineer, is bilingual in Spanish and English. Antonio's mother, an accountant, has some expressive fluency in English. Antonio's parents know how to advocate for Antonio and will enroll him in extracurricular activities that will enhance his educational experience.

Although Antonio's parents can function in English, Spanish is the language of the family and of the home. They have brought many books with them from Mexico and continue to read Mexican newspapers on the Internet, watch Spanish-language television, and discuss news and current events in Spanish. To be able to demonstrate what he knows and understands about the world around him, Antonio needs to be in a classroom that allows him to access his linguistic and academic skills in his home language, Spanish, while providing him with the time and structure to add an additional language, English. Like Carmen and Paulo, he will benefit most from a biliteracy program, where he will continue to receive support in developing Spanish literacy and learn how to bridge and use the skills he already has in Spanish to the new language, English.

Because of the lower status that the Spanish language holds in this country, many parents of students like Antonio place their children in English-only classrooms because they see bilingual education as a remedial program or as a hindrance to their child's acquisition of English. Others seek dual-language, or two-way immersion, programs for their children. These programs, which are detailed later in Hannah's profile, are bilingual programs that support biliteracy, but they are often viewed as enrichment programs or programs for gifted students because they include students who come from homes where only English is spoken.

LUCÍA: A HERITAGE SPANISH SPEAKER IN A SPANISH-FOR-NATIVE-SPEAKERS PROGRAM

Lucía is in middle school in a large U.S. city. Like Paulo, she was born in the United States, but her parents immigrated to the United States from El Salvador. Lucía is the youngest of five children, all born in the United States. Lucía's parents are more comfortable conversing in Spanish, so they continue to speak Spanish at home. Lucía's older brothers and sisters, following the pattern of many immigrant children, prefer using English. By the time Lucía was born, more English was being spoken in the home than Spanish. Although Lucía's parents speak to each other and to the children mostly in Spanish, the children use English when they respond to their parents and when they speak with each other. The few times the parents use English, they use a learner's form.

Federal law requires that schools seek out children who are not fully proficient in English and mandates that these children be provided comprehensible access to the curriculum until they are proficient enough in English to participate in a public schooling setting without support (Box 2.1). States have interpreted the law in different ways. Some states require English-as-a-second-language (ESL) classes, and others require a mix of first-language instruction—also called bilingual education—and ESL instruction. Where non-English-language services are offered, they are generally viewed as temporary and only as a path to English-language proficiency. Typically, once children are determined to be English proficient, non-English-language support is withdrawn. These programs, which require students to replace

---

BOX 2.1.   Addressing English Language Learners in U.S. Schools: Federal Guidelines

Title VI of the Civil Rights Act of 1964 prohibits discrimination based on race, color, or national origin.

Lau v. Nichols (414 U.S. 563 [1974]) affirms the Department of Education memorandum of May 25, 1970, which directs school districts to take steps to help limited-English proficient (LEP) students overcome language barriers and to ensure that they can participate meaningfully in the district's educational programs.

The three-prong Castañeda standard requires programs that educate children with limited English proficiency to be

- based on a sound educational theory;
- adequately supported, with adequate and effective staff and resources, so that the program has a realistic chance of success; and
- periodically evaluated and, if necessary, revised. (*Castañeda v. Pickard*, 1981)

Office of Civil Rights, 2006.

---

their non-English language (in this instance, Spanish) with English, genrally lead to subtractive bilingualism (de Jong, 2011; García, 2009). Students like Lucía who are put into such programs learn to put aside their Spanish linguistic resources to focus on developing English only.

When Lucía entered kindergarten at her local school, tests determined that she was proficient in English because she could use English for everyday social purposes. The school authorities therefore saw no need to provide literacy support in Spanish.

In choosing English as their primary language of communication, despite the influence of Spanish in their home, Lucía and her siblings demonstrate their understanding of the predominant cultural message in this country, that the only language that counts is English (Wong-Fillmore, 1991). Little in their environment has given them any reason to value Spanish. They are heritage language speakers, children brought up in homes where Spanish is spoken and who themselves have some proficiency in the language (Wiley and Valdés, 2000).

Children like Lucía whose academic instruction builds on only one portion of their linguistic resources can function well in school in the early years, where all instruction is more hands-on and interactive, and literacy instruction focuses on letter-sound recognition and decoding (Thomas and Collier, 2002). In the later years, however, when the curriculum becomes more abstract and literacy instruction focuses on comprehension, Lucía and students like her begin to struggle. As she moves from learning to read to reading to learn, Lucía needs to be able to access all her resources, including those in Spanish. Recognizing this need in students like Lucía, more and more school districts are offering Spanish-for-native-speakers (SNS) classes (Campbell and Kreeft-Payton, 1998). These classes foster additive bilingualism and biliteracy, which gives children a reason to value their oral skills in Spanish and to develop literacy skills, thus increasing their academic and linguistic resources.

The linguistic, cultural, and academic backgrounds of older students who are developing biliteracy differ as widely as those of students who are in the early stages of biliteracy. Like Lucía, many of these SNS students enter the classroom as heritage language speakers who use social Spanish primarily with parents or other community members. And like Lucía, they may have developed literacy only in English, so while they can speak Spanish, they cannot yet read or write it. Other students involved in SNS classes in middle or high school may be newcomers from Latin America. Some of these students will enter SNS classrooms with grade-level literacy in Spanish; others will enter with low levels of literacy in Spanish, perhaps because they left school early or because migration or other forces interrupted their schooling, making it inconsistent. These students will need special consideration and support in the SNS classroom. All SNS students, however, have oral proficiency in Spanish, and oracy is a crucial part of literacy.

HANNAH: A DUAL-LANGUAGE-PROGRAM STUDENT FROM AN ENGLISH-ONLY HOME

Hannah is the only student of the five who does not use any Spanish in her home. Her parents were born in the United States and grew up here. And though neither parent speaks Spanish, they enrolled Hannah in a dual-language program. Also called two-way immersion programs, dual-language programs "integrate native English speakers and speakers of another language, providing instruction in both languages for all students." They "promote bilingualism and biliteracy, grade-level academic achievement, and positive cross-cultural attitudes and behaviors in all students" (Center for Applied Linguistics, 2010).

Hannah is in 3rd grade in a Spanish–English dual-language program. About half the children in her classroom come from Spanish-speaking or two-language homes; the rest are Spanish language learners from non-Spanish-speaking homes. Their only exposure to Spanish is what they receive in school.

Because of the rise of dual-language programs in the United States, more and more native English speakers are developing literacy in a non-English language, usually Spanish (Center for Applied Linguistics, 2011). With this trend comes the need for increased differentiation in the biliteracy classroom to accommodate the range of students represented by Carmen, Paulo, Antonio, Lucía, and Hannah, which includes students who are new to this country, students who use Spanish in their homes, and students who use no Spanish at home. Hannah exemplifies the Spanish language learner involved in learning biliteracy in the United States.

The five student profiles provide a context for talking about students of biliteracy from a multilingual perspective that looks at what students can do and what resources they bring to the classroom, rather than from a monolingual or deficit perspective that looks at what they cannot do. As you review the profiles, consider how they remind you of your students and what characteristics of your students are missing. Consider also what information is necessary and how having this kind of information about your students would help your teaching. In the sections that follow, we discuss the three most important groups of characteristics that differentiate students of biliteracy from one another—linguistic, cultural, and academic—and suggest ways that teachers can gather similar information about their students.

Key Characteristics That Distinguish Bilingual Learners

LINGUISTIC CHARACTERISTICS

Academic, or formal, language, as discussed earlier, broadly describes the language of textbooks and classrooms. Social, or informal, language in Spanish, also referred to as community Spanish, differs according to context. Language use can be determined by the following:

- Language user: a person from Puerto Rico might use *guagua* (bus); a person from Chile might use *guagua* (baby)

- Region: archaic expressions, such as *pos* rather than *pues*, have been retained in rural areas.
- Social group: community Spanish used by immigrants and their families in the United States includes *lonche* and *puchar*.

Students like Carmen and Antonio will enter the biliteracy classroom with more linguistic resources in one language and little language development in the other. If all students involved in developing biliteracy were like Carmen and Antonio, planning classroom instruction could be very straightforward: use the students' oral proficiency in Spanish to introduce and teach new concepts of reading and writing in Spanish and then bridge to English. But this plan reflects a monolingual approach and does not effectively address the needs of any of the learners we describe, including Carmen and Antonio. They may enter the biliteracy classroom with more linguistic resources in Spanish, but they live in a multilingual world. They are interacting with students like Paulo, Lucía, and Hannah and are exposed to a variety of formal and informal Spanish and English through various media and peer interactions. Their linguistic repertoires are developing and changing, and instruction that addresses literacy in a "dominant" language only does not consider the changing needs and resources of these students.

Simultaneous bilinguals like Paulo and Lucía, in contrast, enter the biliteracy classroom with linguistic resources in two languages—English and Spanish, though they are not, as Grosjean (1989) emphasizes, two monolinguals in one person. While some students may initially have the bulk of their knowledge stored in one language, simultaneous bilinguals will begin their biliteracy instruction with background knowledge stored in two or more languages.

When students like Paulo and Lucía are learning literacy in Spanish and English, they use all of their linguistic resources for classroom instruction. Classroom instruction for them, however, is less straightforward than for students who are monolingual in Spanish, like Carmen and Antonio, raising the questions, What language should be used to introduce new concepts in reading and writing? How should code-switching, the shifting between English and Spanish from sentence to sentence, or within sentences, be addressed? When does bridging occur, and what is its focus? And, how do you teach and plan bridging activities for Paulo and Lucía and also meet the linguistic needs of Carmen and Antonio as they develop their resources in two languages? We address these issues in later chapters.

Hannah represents the small but growing number of students from all-English homes. Like Carmen and Antonio, they enter the biliteracy classroom with more linguistic resources in one language. But, also like Carmen and Antonio, these students quickly develop resources in both languages and begin to look more like Paulo and Lucía.

While it is tempting to talk about these students on a continuum of language proficiency, the concept of a continuum is too restrictive and emphasizes the either/or, monolingual paradigm. Instead, we recommend looking at students and describing their abilities across languages, including their ability to identify which language is being spoken and to understand and use cognates. We provide more information on helping students to expand these metalinguistic abilities in Chapter 10.

CULTURAL CHARACTERISTICS

Although the majority of students learning literacy in Spanish in the United States are referred to as Hispanic or Latino, these children represent a wide variety of cultural backgrounds, each of which affects many elements, including how language is used. Some were born in the United States; others immigrated here. Among immigrants, their experience entering the United States profoundly affects how they view themselves and those around them. Their level of acculturation depends on how long they have been here. Newcomers like Antonio and Carmen need extra time and more explicit instruction as they adapt to U.S. cultural expectations. Children like Paulo and Lucía, born in the United States of immigrant parents, have to learn how to navigate two worlds, that of their families and that of the larger, majority culture. Children like Hannah from the majority culture go through a different form of acculturation as they interact with classmates who are adapting to the culture of the U.S. school system.

The culture of the home also affects how language is used. Lucía, for example, may prefer to use English and may feel more proficient in it, but, because she has grown up in a home where Spanish is used, her English reflects that Spanish influence. Like Gerardo and Ramona in the speech event discussed in Chapter 1, Lucía is seen by English speakers as less direct than Hannah and other native English speakers. When we compare Lucía's and Hannah's language use, we can find evidence of the social norms of the languages spoken by their parents and other community members. It should be expected that Lucía's and Paulo's written English, and how the two students comprehend oral language and written texts in English, also will be influenced by the cultural norms underlying how they use Spanish. In contrast, Hannah will use the cultural norms of English as she speaks and writes in Spanish and comprehends oral language and written texts. Texts written originally in English that reflect the linear pattern of English, though they have been translated into Spanish, may be more comprehensible to Hannah than to Lucía and Paulo because the organization of the text will be familiar to her. Antonio, Carmen, Paulo, and Lucía will find texts written originally in Spanish more comprehensible.

Linguistic differences will also be evident among students from Spanish-speaking countries throughout the world that reflect the region, social group, and social class they are from. For example, children raised in a home with parents from Costa Rica will be taught to use *usted*, the more formal form of "you," with all people, including their classmates. In contrast, children raised in homes with parents from Mexico will likely be taught to use *usted* with elders and *tú* with peers. Teachers who have a Mexican background might try to "correct" the children of Costa Rican descent, telling them to use the more formal form of "you" with their teachers and the less formal form with peers. A mismatch like this between the regional versions of Spanish spoken by the teacher and by her students can also lead to the teacher's claiming that her Spanish-speaking students do not speak "correct" Spanish. The descriptions of regional varieties of Spanish can be recorded and noted without stigmatizing the language use. The interaction between student and teacher is discussed in more detail in Chapter 3; how to take advantage of the varieties of Spanish that students bring to the classroom is discussed in Chapter 6. Socioeconomic status is as important an aspect of culture as immigration status and country of origin. Antonio's parents, for example, who are college graduates, may have more in common with college-educated, monolingual English-speaking parents in the United States than with Paulo's or Carmen's parents, though they too are from Mexico. Because of Antonio's parents' higher socioeconomic status and level of education, their cultural experiences more closely match those of the parents of middle-class students in U.S. public schools. Antonio and his parents understand how schools work, and this understanding helps them adjust to school in the United States. In contrast, because Paulo's, Carmen's, and Lucía's parents all left school at an early age, though they have rich funds of knowledge gained by life experience, they understand less about how schools work, and their children may experience more challenges when entering the public school system.

ACADEMIC CHARACTERISTICS

Students learning literacy in Spanish in the United States represent the same diversity of academic ability and achievement as all students. Some will learn to read early; others will struggle with reading. Some will demonstrate a deep understanding of mathematical concepts; others will find math more challenging. These differences, along with linguistic and cultural differences, must be addressed by teachers and administrators in planning biliteracy instruction.

Collecting Information about Students: Tools and Strategies

When teachers have adequate background knowledge about their students, they are better able to tailor instruction to the needs of each student, create meaningful and differentiated units of study, and develop lessons that build on the linguistic, cultural, and academic resources of a broad range of students (Gottlieb, 2006).

THE KIND OF INFORMATION TO COLLECT

The first step in the process of gathering background information is for teachers and administrators to identify the kind of information that is most useful and decide how best to collect it. Schools throughout the country use home-language surveys, tailored to the individual community, to identify students who speak a non-English language at home and would benefit from English-language services. To collect a full profile of each student, teachers and administrators should include in their survey questions about each student's cultural background and linguistic resources, including use of formal and informal Spanish, formal and informal English, and metalinguistic abilities. The survey should also ask about parents' linguistic, cultural, and academic background. Box 2.2 is a sample of a completed survey for Paulo, taken when he registered for kindergarten.

The responses to questions in the survey about how students use informal and formal English and Spanish tells teachers how, where, and with whom students use Spanish, whether, for example, like Lucía, they use Spanish in the home only receptively or whether, like Carmen, they converse in Spanish. The survey provides space for collecting information about the background of the parents because the parents' background affects the experiences the children bring to the classroom. Also, knowing the parents' levels of English proficiency helps teachers tailor their communication to the parents and can reveal something about the level of acculturation in the home. Parents, like Paulo's, who have little ability in English have a more difficult time navigating life in the United States than parents who have some ability, and their children are affected by the difficulties their parents have in understanding the many intricacies of life here. Such children are sometimes pressed to translate for their parents. This situation puts stress on the families and on the children, who might be asked to take on responsibility that is beyond their level of maturity.

BOX 2.2.   Sample Completed Survey for Collecting Linguistic, Cultural, and Academic Background Information on Students

Date of intake: Kindergarten registration, August 15, 20XX
Name of student: Paulo
Cultural background: Born in the United States; speaks Spanish in the home, English outside the home
Linguistic resources: Spanish
  Formal Spanish: Uses formal Spanish for some colors and for soccer terms
  Informal Spanish: Language use reflects community Spanish (e.g., *troca, lonche*)
Metalinguistic abilities: Identifies language with person (speaks English with monolingual English-speaking preschool teacher and Spanish with parents); linguistic creativity includes *bleediando* and other linguistic approximations
Linguistic resources: English
  Formal English: Uses formal English for some colors, numbers, and shapes
  Informal English: Language use reflects playground English, community and regional English
Academic background: 1 year of all-English preschool; 2 years of all-English day care
Parents' linguistic, cultural, and academic background: Parents born in rural Mexico; Spanish speakers with interrupted schooling; understand and speak some English

---

Teachers and administrators might also try to find out what literacy activities occur in each student's home and what social activities the family participates in apart from the school community, such as sports and church and club activities. It is also important to gather information about each student's health, early development, and previous educational experiences (formal and informal), such as day care and preschool, and the languages used in these environments. Another factor to consider is whether there were any lapses in each student's schooling for health or other reasons.

HOW TO COLLECT INFORMATION

The information referred to in this chapter is most effectively gathered through an intake interview and a supplemental home visit. Districts and schools should decide who will be responsible for gathering the information and how time will be allocated for carrying out this responsibility. The interviews, and any forms parents are asked to complete, should be in the language parents speak, and the person responsible for conducting the interviews should be fully bilingual. Intake interviews must be conducted with the parents or guardians responsible for the care of the students, and not with the students themselves or with school-aged siblings.

How do you find out the educational level of the parents of a new student? How do you ask a speaker of a minority, marked language what language he or she uses at home? Those responsible for conducting the intake interviews must be bilingual and must respect the sensitivity of the questions and the confidentiality of the information they receive. And parents must understand why and for what use this information is being collected. It is often necessary to collect some of the information when parents register their students and collect the more sensitive information later, after parents have had time to develop a relationship with the teacher and the school.

INSTRUCTIONAL STRATEGIES THAT INFORM WHILE TEACHING

Completing a survey like the sample one for Paulo gives teachers valuable information. But teachers also routinely learn more and more about their students during in-class interactions. Any teaching or learning strategy that allows for student choice, such as dialogue journals, allows students to write or talk about personal information. As with background information on the family, however, the teacher must be aware of situations that require discretion and confidentiality. If any information is provided that might indicate a serious problem, the teacher should consult with the proper authorities in the school.

Meeting the Needs of Different Learners

Once all this information is collected, what can teachers do with it? How would an instructor teach Carmen, Paulo, Antonio, Lucía, and Hannah in the same classroom if they happened to be at the same grade level? What materials would meet their different needs? What activities would be most appropriate to engage their background experiences? One reason for using the five sample students in this book is to demonstrate that no single activity, resource, or assignment can meet the needs of all the students. Teachers developing biliteracy in the United States, like all teachers, need to differentiate instruction. In Chapter 4, we describe the biliteracy unit framework, which reflects the three premises and allows for differentiation to meet the linguistic, cultural, and academic needs of the wide range of students learning biliteracy in the United States. In Chapters 5 through 10, we discuss the elements of biliteracy instruction and how the instruction of each element might be differentiated for the many learners every teacher will encounter.

Biliteracy Learner Profiles and the Three Premises

The three premises provide a way of understanding the needs of a diverse group of students learning biliteracy in the United States, and for communicating these needs to others. The first premise—that Spanish is a minority language within a majority culture—helps us understand why Lucía, for example, entered the classroom refusing to speak Spanish and why Paulo insists that he prefers to read in English. Spanish-speaking children in the United States quickly internalize the lower status Spanish holds in the larger society and manifest their perception by showing a preference for English. The first premise also helps us to understand why Spanish-speaking parents often insist that the school place their children in English-only classrooms. They understand that proficiency in English is necessary for success in the United States and often see little need for supporting Spanish outside of the home.

The second premise—that children use all of their linguistic resources to learn to read and write—explains why children like Paulo and Lucía, who enter school with some proficiency in English, benefit from literacy instruction in Spanish as well. Only a bilingual classroom, where literacy is taught in Spanish and English, gives two-language learners like Paulo and Lucía the opportunity to use all of their background experiences, regardless of language or cultural context.

The third premise—that Spanish and English are distinct languages that are governed by different cultural and linguistic norms—helps us understand why Lucía and Paulo, both born and educated in this country, appear to be English language learners in their academic writing, because they may be using the oracy pattern from their home language, Spanish. Although Lucía has never been formally instructed in Spanish, the Spanish she hears at home has influenced her oral language development and her written English. This premise helps us to understand that a wide range of students—represented here by Carmen, Paulo, Antonio, Lucía, and Hannah—benefit from explicit instruction in two languages, with strategies and methods that reflect each language and the needs of the different learners.

ACTIVITIES FOR REFLECTION AND ACTION

1. This chapter introduced the variety of students who benefit from literacy instruction in Spanish, and a tool for collecting information about them. Use this tool, the Sample Survey for Collecting Linguistic, Cultural, and Academic Background Information on Students (a template can be found on the Web site), to collect information about a few students in your classroom. Think about ways of collecting information that go beyond interviews, like setting up audio or video recording devices during small group work or indoor recess. Then consider the following questions:

   - In what ways does the information you collected confirm what you already knew about your students?

   - What surprised you about the information you collected?

   - How can this information help you meet the needs of your students?

2. Create your own survey for collecting linguistic, cultural, and academic information about your students. Make sure to include information that helps you plan and implement effective bilingual units of study.

   - Show this survey to other educators and solicit feedback.

   - Revise the survey based on feedback.

   - Develop a plan for collecting and using these data.

3. Based on the information you collected about your students, what kind of instructional differentiation—in addition to literacy instruction in Spanish—is needed? How can you explain and defend this need to other educational stakeholders?

CHAPTER 3

Teachers: Capitalizing on Life Experiences and Diversity

KEY POINTS

- The cultural and linguistic background of teachers affects their understanding of students and their interpretation of how to instruct in Spanish and English.

- All teachers of Spanish literacy require specific professional development on how to teach literacy in Spanish in the United States. However, few teacher preparation programs in the United States include this requirement; so many teachers who teach in Spanish require additional professional opportunities.

- Literacy learning is enhanced when teachers are reflective and aware of their own strengths and challenges.

Teacher Profiles

This chapter introduces three teachers who are teaching literacy in Spanish as part of their students' biliteracy development. Though none of these teachers is a foreign language teacher, many of the approaches and strategies recommended for them would be appropriate for foreign language teachers. Like the students profiled in Chapter 2, these teachers are fictitious. Their names are made up and their profiles are compiled from those of teachers we have worked with. Through these profiles we hope to highlight the strengths teachers in the United States bring to the Spanish literacy classroom and the challenges they face. As you read through these profiles, think of yourself and the teachers you work with, and see whether you can identify with any one profile.

ELENA: *NORMALISTA* FROM MEXICO

Elena teaches in a suburban district just outside a large U.S. city. She is originally from Mexico, where she completed the teacher preparation program, qualifying as a *normalista*, or elementary certified school teacher. Her Mexican certificate prepared her to teach monolingual Spanish speakers. Elena is taking additional coursework at the graduate level in order to be licensed to teach in the United States. She works hard at her English; while her academic English is strong, she struggles with written English. She also worries that her accent makes her sound less knowledgeable than she is. Except for details specific to Mexico, much of what we say about Elena can be applied to teachers from other Spanish-speaking countries, such as Puerto Rico, El Salvador, Colombia, and Chile.

Elena grew up in the same city in Mexico in which she taught before moving to the United States. Though diverse socioeconomically, that city is, in many respects, homogeneous, with the exception of the indigenous population, which is marginalized from mainstream Mexican society. Elena is from the middle class.

Elena taught in Mexico for three years in a private school, where she experienced a high rate of success in teaching her students to read and write in Spanish. The children she taught were also from the middle class and all used the same Spanish, which reflected their social class, geographic region, and sociocultural context. The literacy approach Elena used is best described as eclectic. Following a government education program, supplemented with materials purchased by the parents, she began by introducing a sentence, then words, then syllables, and finally vowels combined with consonants. Her students were able to decode words and sentences with a high degree of accuracy and fluency in the early primary grades.

In the United States, Elena is working with Latino and Latina students from families as culturally and linguistically diverse as the students in our profiles. Some of her students, like Carmen and Antonio, have recently moved to the United States and speak Spanish at home. Elena shares the Spanish language and the immigrant experience with these families. Somewhat challenging to Elena, however, is that the immigrant children in her class are from a rural, working-class sector of Mexican society, and they use Spanish differently than did those she taught in private school. This difference creates a tension that is most palpable when Elena's students or their parents use archaic forms of Spanish. For example, many rural Mexicans use *ansina* rather than *así* (like) or *naiden* rather than *nadie* (no one). These archaic or unconventional, forms of Spanish, used by Spanish conquerors in the 16th century (Potowski, 2005), are still used today in some rural areas of Latin America but are no longer heard in urban middle-class environments.[1] We believe it is important to note that what is now considered archaic Spanish was prestigious when it was used by the majority of Spanish speakers. Now, however, to the mainstream culture, it is a marker of people who have not participated in formal education and is therefore less prestigious. For this reason, Elena assumes that most of her immigrant students and their families have limited background knowledge and experience with school. She feels she has a lot of work to do with these students who, in her mind, do not even speak Spanish well.

The majority of the students in Elena's class are like Paulo. They are two-language learners born in the United States who have never lived outside of the country and who have developed oral language in English and Spanish simultaneously. Paulo is perhaps the most challenging student for Elena to work with because she interprets his Spanglish as a sign of confusion and deficiency. When assessing Paulo's languages, she uses a monolingual Spanish lens and a monolingual English lens rather than a multilingual lens. Thus, she assumes Paulo does not know how to speak either language (English or Spanish) well, and so she often corrects his language, waters down content for him, and expects less of him.

A few of Elena's other students, like Antonio, moved to the United States recently from urban areas in Latin America. Elena identifies more easily with Antonio's

---

[1] Potowski argues that any form of language that is used by a community is functional and therefore standard, and we agree. We therefore refer to these other ways of using Spanish as unconventional rather than nonstandard.

parents, with whom she shares a middle-class view of culture, language, and schooling. Antonio is most like the students she taught in Mexico and compares well to a monolingual Spanish learner. Elena's eclectic approach to teaching students how to read and write in Spanish initially works well for Antonio because his background knowledge and vocabulary match Elena's and also match what is expected in school.

Elena also teaches students like Hannah. Though a two-language learner like Antonio, Hannah is exposed to more English than Spanish, and she prefers English to Spanish in choosing reading materials and in oral conversation. Because Elena understands the power of English in the United States, she sees Hannah's English as an advantage. Sometimes during instructional time, if Hannah does not understand words or text in Spanish, Elena simply translates them into English, thinking she is making it easier for Hannah by focusing on her English.

Of the three teachers profiled, Elena has the most formal training and experience in teaching literacy in Spanish. Because of this background, Elena does not feel comfortable with the literacy program she is asked to use. It does not make sense to her, and she ends up changing it to make it more consistent with the way Spanish literacy instruction is conducted. The program Elena is asked to use starts with teaching the consonants and requiring students to learn the names of the letters. She adapts it by starting with the vowels and then matching the vowels to the most frequently used consonants and forming syllables. Elena knows she is deviating from the program, but she feels she must do so if she is to have success.

Elena is challenged by the requirement that she use literacy strategies she has not been trained to use: writer's workshop and reader's workshop. These student-centered strategies are meant to foster student control over their own learning. Many U.S. schools promote and teach student independence and ownership of the learning process beginning in the early grades. Elena finds the purpose of these approaches somewhat elusive, and she has trouble letting go of control in the classroom. She has particular difficulty with invented spelling in dialogue journals because she learned in her teacher training to ask students to write only words they can spell. To comply with the district expectations but stay true to her understanding of teaching Spanish literacy, Elena controls student writing with prompts and selects the books the students read.

Perhaps even more challenging to Elena than these instructional strategies that are new to her is the unconventional Spanish many of her students use. Though most often students like Paulo mix Spanish and English, Elena notices that all of her students mix the languages to some degree. For example, when describing problems on the playground, students will say, *"El me puchó"* ("He pushed me"). The verb *puchar* is an unconventional form of Spanish that uses the stem of the English verb "to push" and converts to Spanish as *"puchar."* Many two-language learners create these hybrid versions of language for verbs and, less often, for nouns, which are also blended to form mixed-language words.[2] Elena responds to these unfamiliar, unconventional Spanish words and phrases by immediately correcting students and asking them to repeat the conventional Mexican form. In doing so, she is sending a message to students that they do not speak Spanish well. We explore this issue more deeply in Chapter 5, where we discuss code-switching and the characteristics of Spanish in the United States.

Perhaps less problematic for Elena than the mixing of languages, but equally frustrating for the students, is her response to words and phrases from Spanish-

---

[2] A bilingual teacher in Zion, Illinois, reports hearing a student use the word *socketines*, a combination of socks and *calcetines* (personal communication, 2007).

speaking countries other than Mexico. When her Puerto Rican student calls a bus a *gua-gua* and her Chilean students call it a *micro*, Elena insists that they use the Mexican word *camión*. And she bans the word *coger* (grab), which she hears from her non-Mexican students. Though they use it correctly, she is uncomfortable because it has a double meaning in Mexico, with a sexual connotation. Elena has figured out that there are many versions of Spanish in the United States, but because she believes she must choose one version and stick to it, she has chosen the familiar, Mexican version, which to her is the "most correct."

MONICA: U.S.-BORN LATINA

Monica was born in the United States of parents who were immigrants from Mexico.[3] As a very young learner, Monica spoke more Spanish than English, and so she was placed in a transitional bilingual program in the urban public school she attended. Monica remembers learning to read and write initially in Spanish, though she does not remember how it was taught. Once her social English was developed, she read and wrote in English fluently. By the end of 2nd grade Monica had "transitioned" into English for all academic areas, and from that time on she used Spanish only at home and in Spanish-specific contexts. Monica and her friends communicated in English, occasionally throwing in some Spanish, and she chose all forms of entertainment in English, though as a young adult she embraced contemporary Spanish music.

Monica took a few Spanish classes in high school, but they were traditional foreign language classes, not Spanish-for-native-speakers classes, and she found them irrelevant and boring. These classes were frustrating to her because she was unable to apply the Spanish she already knew to the learning context. For example, she had learned *lentes* for eyeglasses, but the textbook used *gafas*. Though *lentes* is correct in Mexico and in Monica's life experience, the teacher considered it incorrect because it was not the term used in the book, which was based on Spanish from Spain. Monica also found the topics she read about and the dialogues she had to memorize irrelevant to her reality, and the overt attention to grammar made her feel inadequate. As a result, Monica abandoned her study of Spanish and instead took Italian in college.

Growing up in the inner city, Monica was surrounded by examples of socioeconomic inequality, and in high school she began to participate in immigrant rights organizations and to volunteer in a community organization dedicated to helping recently arrived immigrants. In these contexts she used and maintained her Spanish, and through these experiences she developed a strong sense of social justice and a desire to choose a profession that would have a direct impact on people's lives. She chose teaching and obtained her teaching certificate while an undergraduate. Though she excelled on the oral portion of the Spanish exam for her bilingual certificate, she barely passed the reading and writing portion. Reading in Spanish was always more challenging to Monica than reading in English, in part because after 2nd grade, she had read predominately in English in school and any Spanish she read involved how-to forms in very simple Spanish. Thus, Monica missed the opportunity to learn how text in Spanish, especially narrative text, is organized differently than in English. As an adult, Monica finds novels in Spanish wordy, and she has a hard time following the plots because they seem more circular than the plots in the English-language novels she prefers.

---

[3] Like many Hispanics, or Latinas, Monica prefers the term "Latina" to "Hispanic" because she wants to emphasize that her roots are in Latin America.

Monica's life experience prepared her well for becoming a bilingual teacher. She identifies with all her students, but perhaps more with students who are like Paulo. Monica understands Paulo's two-language utterances well because language mixing is so prevalent in Monica's life that it goes beyond her own use of language and permeates the entertainment in which she is immersed. For example, Monica loves the monologues by the comedian George Lopez, who might say, *"Esos 'yellow shoes' no estaban 'on sale.'"*

Though Monica has heard that it is best for teachers not to mix the two languages, she often finds herself switching to English when she does not know a word in Spanish. For example, she might say, *"A ver niños, ¿quién puede señalar el 'title page'?"* Code-switching is normal for bilingual learners and is to be expected, but the mixing of languages by the teacher in an academic setting poses problems. The teacher must plan the strategic use of the two languages to ensure comprehensibility. In this example, while Paulo may understand Monica if he knows the meaning of "title page," Carmen and Antonio will not because their vocabulary in English is still developing and they do not yet know the meaning of "title page." When working with students like Hannah, Monica may overuse English, assuming that it is appropriate to explain things in one language and do the activity in the other. When the text is in Spanish and Hannah and Paulo are struggling to understand some key words, Monica may tell them in English what the words mean rather than using instructional strategies that focus on vocabulary development and comprehension in Spanish. As a result, Hannah and Paulo are denied opportunities to develop additional academic language that will bolster their literacy skills in both languages. Simply telling a student in the other language what a text means does not ensure that the student will comprehend the meaning of the text. Students need to be engaged in instructional strategies that focus on comprehensibility so they can apply new words and strategies to future literacy tasks.

While Monica does an excellent job of addressing her students' socioaffective needs in a more comprehensive way than Elena, she is much more insecure about teaching in Spanish. The reality of the first premise, that Spanish is a minority language within a majority culture, has limited Monica's opportunities to develop Spanish academic proficiency. Monica enjoys working with children like Carmen and Antonio whose Spanish she interprets as being rich, but she is also a bit intimidated by the fact that sometimes she does not understand all the words Carmen and Antonio use. Although Monica speaks Spanish, her vocabulary in Spanish is limited, and her knowledge of instructional methodology is based on English. Furthermore, Monica's teacher preparation programs were conducted in English; the instructional materials she has for Spanish are written in English; and all of her in-service professional development opportunities are in English. She therefore applies her English knowledge to the teaching of literacy in Spanish and assumes that instructional practices that work in English should be used the same way in Spanish. Whereas Elena uses her professional knowledge to modify and adapt the Spanish literacy curriculum, Monica does not have the necessary knowledge of Spanish literacy instruction to do so. As a result, she overuses English at the expense of Spanish, making the learning of Spanish literacy more difficult and jeopardizing the development of biliteracy in her students.

SUSAN: ADULT LEARNER OF SPANISH

Susan was born in the United States and grew up here. Her ancestry is Irish and Scottish, and her family has lived in the United States for generations. Solidly middle class and suburban, Susan always found school to be comfortable, and she excelled academically at all levels. Good at languages and intrigued by other cultures, Susan chose to study Spanish after working in a restaurant in high school where many of the clientele were Spanish speakers. Susan applied herself to the formal learning of Spanish in school and practiced her social Spanish at work. During her junior year in college, she spent a semester in Spain. Susan's Spanish blossomed and she felt very comfortable living in the Spanish culture, even though she realized that she often missed cultural references at social gatherings, and that her Spanish friends assumed her Spanish-language abilities were a lot higher than they actually were.

Susan returned to the United States, finished college, and spent a year as a volunteer teacher for a national program. Her success in the program inspired her to pursue a master's degree in teaching. Determined to become a bilingual teacher because of the commitment she had felt to immigrant families since her high school work days, Susan studied for the language proficiency test in Spanish that would qualify her and passed it on the first try.

Susan has been teaching now for three years. Like most new teachers, she found her first year of teaching to be challenging and overwhelming, and she worried that having learned Spanish as a foreign language, rather than as a home language, would hamper her effectiveness in teaching in Spanish. To compensate, she has tried to keep up her social Spanish by watching television programs in Spanish and traveling to Spanish-speaking countries whenever possible. Knowing, too, that her Spanish vocabulary reflects vocabulary from Spain that does not match the Spanish of the majority of her students, she pays close attention to the vocabulary they use and often asks them for their way of saying certain things. For example, she learned from her Mexican students and their families to say, "¡Andele—que buena onda!" ("Way to go—how cool!") when she realized that the expression "¡Vale!" used in Spain to validate someone's comments was simply lost on her students.

Unlike Elena, who often corrects students when they use unconventional forms of Spanish, and Monica, who sometimes uses these forms herself and does not realize they are viewed as unconventional, Susan often is unable to distinguish between what may be an Anglicism, an archaic form of Spanish, or a regionally specific term, and so she accepts all forms of Spanish that students produce. While her acceptance of all forms is very validating to the students and their families, her inability to distinguish between these Spanish forms results in missed opportunities to highlight the nuances that abound in Spanish. Understanding these nuances in the United States is important because becoming bilingual entails developing metacognitive proficiency about unconventional forms of Spanish, regional forms of Spanish, and Anglicisms in Spanish. And this proficiency is necessary to successfully navigate the sociopolitical world of Spanish in the United States.

Like Monica, Susan feels unprepared to make independent professional decisions about Spanish literacy instruction. The district she has worked in for three years has adopted a balanced literacy approach to language arts, and while she embraces this approach philosophically, what it means to her professionally is that she is expected to implement in Spanish the scope and sequence that has been laid out by the district in English. She struggles most with the word study section of the district's plan. Because she has no comprehensive program to follow that delineates the sequence of teaching phonics to students in Spanish, she has obtained translations of some of the more salient components of the balanced literacy program and is implementing them in Spanish.

Whereas Elena has the professional knowledge to either ignore or adapt parts of these translated Spanish literacy programs, Susan relies on them too much. She has worked daily with her kindergartners to memorize the letter names in Spanish and words that match them, and she drills her students on this skill once or twice a day. A great proponent of writer's workshop and developmental writing programs, Susan has been highly conflicted about how to carry them out in Spanish. She understands that students need to be able to write spontaneously and take risks, but when she observes that some of her students, like Paulo, refer to a letter sometimes in English and other times in Spanish and that several students did not know their letters in either language at the beginning of the school year, she worries that they are becoming confused and need to build this knowledge sequentially. She therefore controls the writing students do by having them copy words she has introduced, or she uses sentence prompts that students complete with vocabulary she provides. She also designs mini-lessons and games in which students focus on letters and combine them to form syllables. She spends time researching vocabulary in Spanish to use for these activities. Students like Paulo and Hannah, however, often are not familiar with this vocabulary, and so the activities lose their effectiveness and become rote because the students focus on memorization and decoding rather than on using words they understand and that carry meaning.

Although Susan always works to strengthen her Spanish and to value her students' language, like Monica, she is challenged by the weakness of her academic Spanish vocabulary. When she does not know how to say certain things in Spanish, she tries circumlocution, describing the word or the concept without being able to produce the word. Often Antonio is the only student who can provide her with the appropriate vocabulary, and when students like Paulo and Hannah do not understand the Spanish word, she uses the English equivalent. She also sometimes switches to English during Spanish time. Because all the teaching materials, professional development opportunities, and faculty meetings are in English, Susan finds it difficult to continue to develop her academic Spanish. And though she enjoys speaking Spanish with her bilingual colleagues, they usually gravitate to English either because it is the lingua franca of the school or because they wish to accommodate Susan, who is more proficient in English.

Where Susan excels with her students is in the area of advocacy. As a U.S.-born American who has felt enriched by being exposed to other cultures and becoming bilingual, Susan is a strong voice at the school in favor of immigrant families and the rights of immigrant students. Whenever possible, she emphasizes to her students that being bilingual is a gift and that the students are lucky to speak both languages. By also sharing these thoughts with her students' parents, she has developed a good rapport with them and improved communication about their children. The confidence she feels when dealing with sociopolitical issues, however, does not carry over to the Spanish literacy classroom, and, like Monica, Susan feels unsure about whether she is teaching her students the way she should be.

Teacher Collaboration and Reflection

The reality of the three sociolinguistic premises about teaching for biliteracy is that bilingual teachers like Elena, Monica, and Susan often feel that they do not have support from colleagues, administrators, and community members in their efforts to make good decisions about teaching in Spanish. Bilingual teachers also receive mixed messages from the academic and political communities who support bilingualism and extol its cognitive benefits but, contradicting research conclusions, legislate to reduce the amount of time students can participate in the program. As the teacher profiles suggest, bilingual teachers often have to create their own materials, translate the existing texts from English to Spanish, or sift through published material created by publishers who tend to cater to the requirements of administrators by providing Spanish materials that are translated from English rather than developing appropriate materials in Spanish that reflect how Spanish works.

We encourage teachers facing these challenges to focus on the aspects of teaching they do control, to engage in ongoing professional development, and to collaborate with other teachers. Though Elena, Monica, and Susan complement each other in the strengths and areas of expertise they bring to their teaching, for true collaboration to take place among them, as among any group of teachers, three key ingredients must be present: trust, flexibility, and a shared philosophy (Wagner, 2001). If these three teachers met regularly to discuss and develop a shared philosophy, each bringing her particular strengths, they could complement each other and strengthen their collaboration. Elena's academic Spanish is strong, she has professional knowledge about Spanish literacy, and she is working on understanding two-language learners and the U.S.-specific context of bilingualism and the literacy expectations of U.S. schools. She could help Monica and Susan by identifying and explaining the methods she learned about teaching Spanish literacy in Spanish-speaking countries. Monica is most similar to her students in her sociocultural background, she understands the U.S. bilingual context firsthand, and she is working to develop the academic Spanish she needs to develop academic proficiency in her students. She could help Elena and Susan better understand their students by discussing her own experiences being bilingual and a two-language learner. Susan may be the most outspoken advocate for her immigrant bilingual students, and she understands the literacy expectations of the U.S. education system. Like Elena, she is developing an understanding of the U.S.-specific context of bilingualism, and like Monica, she is focusing on her academic Spanish proficiency so that she can develop it in her students. She could help Elena and Monica understand the universal literacy strategies that are highly valued in the United States and develop ways to merge those strategies with Spanish literacy instruction. It is easy to see the possibilities of collaboration among these three teachers.

To prepare for collaboration, teachers must reflect on their own experiences and professional development. They must assess their professional strengths and needs, examine their own assumptions in relation to the three sociolinguistic premises about teaching for biliteracy, and find creative ways to develop a shared philosophy. Our experience with practicing teachers has shown that what is most often missing in discussions and planning for biliteracy is attention to and acknowledgment of the three premises. Teachers instead often work with unspoken assumptions about teaching for biliteracy that make development of a shared philosophy difficult. For example, many teachers, like Elena, believe that Spanish literacy instruction is appropriate only for students like Carmen and Antonio, who are monolingual Spanish speakers. The assumption is that students like Paulo, Hannah, and Lucía, who use English and unconventional forms of Spanish, do not have the foundation in Spanish to participate in Spanish literacy and therefore should not participate in such a program. Rather than working to create a program of instruction that matches the students, these teachers assume that the students should match the program of instruction. Other teachers assume that the solution to the problems plaguing Spanish literacy instruction is to adopt a curriculum from Peru or some other Spanish-speaking country, overlooking the differences between these countries and the United States that would make such adoption inappropriate, including the minority status of Spanish in the United States, the variety of Spanish-speaking regions from which Spanish-speaking families have come to the United States, and the influence of English on Spanish in the United States. By acknowledging and understanding the three sociolinguistic premises, teachers can avoid misguided assumptions that can impede effective planning and instruction of Spanish literacy in the United States. By reflecting on some of the principles presented so far in this book, teachers can identify their own strengths, needs, and possibilities for collaboration. This exercise will equip them to engage in a discussion with their peers that can lead to the development of a shared philosophy. Once that philosophy has been negotiated, the other two key factors in successful teacher collaboration, flexibility and trust, tend to emerge naturally.

ENGAGING IN SELF-REFLECTION

The more teachers reflect on their practice, the better they teach. A major challenge in teaching is finding time to think about what we do and why and then make changes in our practice based on our reflection. Keeping a journal is one effective way for individual teachers to keep a consistent focus on their practice. Teachers can record two or three times a week or, better, daily, what is going well and what is not in their teaching for biliteracy practice. Gradually, the writing itself becomes the reflection, and the reflection becomes a planning tool.

Journaling can begin with questions such as the following:

- What went well? Why?
- What surprised me? Why?
- What do I want to improve? Why?

Teachers can meet regularly in professional learning communities to set goals based on a common vision, plan instruction, discuss professional reading, and observe each other's classrooms in person or by video and then exchange feedback. This structured setting offers supportive and shared leadership and promotes collective creativity and shared values and vision (Hord and Rutherford, 1998). Also, two teachers in partnership can observe each other's classrooms, about every two weeks throughout the school year, and offer feedback through a formal peer-support program that has established a shared vision and supports teachers with materials and training. The teacher who is observing can focus on one student or look for evidence that supports the teacher's goals.

Teachers also can use a self-reflection survey, such as the one in Box 3.1, which looks at professional development background, linguistic and cultural background, and awareness of students' background. This survey can also be used as a part of a professional learning community's focus on the development of biliteracy or as the backdrop of a formal peer-collaboration system.

ADDRESSING THE STRENGTHS AND CHALLENGES OF EACH TEACHER

If Elena, Monica, and Susan were to engage in self-reflection and participate together in a professional reflection structure, they would find that each of them has something to share that could improve the instruction of Spanish and English literacy for all three teachers and help them build a common vision that would guide their work with their students.

Let us imagine Elena, Monica, and Susan participating in a professional learning community sponsored by a teacher resource center in their district. All three

BOX 3.1. Sample Teacher Self-Reflection Survey

	Strongly agree			Strongly disagree

PROFESSIONAL DEVELOPMENT BACKGROUND

	4	3	2	1
1. I know and understand the research that supports initial literacy instruction in Spanish for Spanish speakers in the United States.	4	3	2	1
2. I know and understand the factors that affect literacy development.	4	3	2	1
3. I have studied (been trained in) best practices for teaching literacy in Spanish.	4	3	2	1
4. I have studied (been trained in) best practices for teaching literacy in English.	4	3	2	1
5. I feel comfortable teaching literacy in Spanish.	4	3	2	1
6. I have the materials I need to teach literacy in Spanish.	4	3	2	1
7. I understand how differences in student cultural, linguistic, and socioeconomic backgrounds affect literacy development.	4	3	2	1
8. I understand how to differentiate literacy instruction to meet individual student needs.	4	3	2	1
9. I understand how oral language development influences literacy development.	4	3	2	1
10. I understand how children develop biliteracy and how the two languages intersect.	4	3	2	1
11. I know how to use formative and summative assessments to inform my teaching and for communication to other stakeholders.	4	3	2	1

LINGUISTIC AND CULTURAL BACKGROUND

	4	3	2	1
1. I am orally fluent and literate in Spanish.	4	3	2	1
2. I have a college-level command of oral and written academic Spanish.	4	3	2	1
3. I have the Spanish academic language required to teach the grades or subject matter for which I am currently responsible.	4	3	2	1
4. I have access to the resources necessary to develop the academic language required to teach the grades or subject matter for which I am currently responsible.	4	3	2	1
5. I feel most comfortable speaking and writing Spanish in academic situations.	4	3	2	1

AWARENESS OF STUDENT BACKGROUND

	4	3	2	1
1. I know the country of origin of each of my students or of his or her parents.	4	3	2	1
2. I have assessed the linguistic abilities of all my students in both in English and Spanish.	4	3	2	1
3. I have assessed the academic achievement of all of my students in both English and Spanish.	4	3	2	1
4. I understand and respect my students' oral language use, even when they may differ from my own or from "conventional" Spanish.	4	3	2	1
5. I understand two-language learners.	4	3	2	1

teachers agree that they want to create a program that meets all their student needs, and after reading our student profiles and completing the survey in Box 3.1, they realize they have misunderstood students who are like Paulo and Hannah and that they must make a special effort to understand each of their students and avoid making assumptions. They agree that they want to create a program that accommodates their students rather than requiring the students to assimilate into the program. The facilitator of the group (in this instance, the district's curriculum director) asks each teacher to describe her students, using the student profiles as a template. Monica describes the benefits and challenges she has faced as a two-language learner. With the help of the facilitator and drawing on their discussion and readings, all three teachers begin to change their paradigm. Rather than labeling some two-language learners as confused and deficient, they will now look for the strengths of all two-language learners, regardless of their social class or educational background.

The three teachers discuss their struggle to accept their students' Anglicisms and unconventional forms of Spanish and avoid correcting this language and expelling it from the class. After reading this book and other resources, guided by their facilitator, they decide to call their students' social expressions *el español informal* (informal Spanish) and the academic language found in books that students need to learn in school as *el español formal* (formal Spanish). By using these terms, the teachers feel they are acknowledging and integrating what their students know and can do, and they are moving them from oral expression to the technical academic language found in school.

In a discussion of methods for teaching Spanish literacy, Elena describes those used in Mexico and other Spanish-speaking countries. Monica and Susan ask questions and begin to understand the differences between initial literacy in Spanish and initial literacy in English. As a team, the teachers agree that they do not need to use spelling tests or focus on the names of letters as part of their Spanish literacy instruction, and after several meetings, they build a consensus about the methods they will use in their Spanish literacy instruction.

During the discussion about how to reconcile the curriculum and methods of Spanish-speaking countries with the reality of teaching Spanish literacy in the United States, Susan explains the reasons for writer's workshop, reader's workshop, and other practices that are widespread in U.S. schools. Her knowledge and the three teachers' growing understanding of the impact that the bilingual context of the United States has on the instruction of Spanish literacy results in a shared understanding of how to implement teaching strategies that work toward the goals of literacy instruction in the United States.

As part of the professional learning community they have created, Elena, Monica, and Susan continue to meet weekly to discuss this book, other resources, and their practice. They put their shared vision into writing, and they use this vision of teaching for biliteracy to guide them as they adopt new materials and determine how to implement new district initiatives that are meant for monolingual English instruction and how to respond to other challenges they encounter.

Teacher Profiles and the Three Premises

Because Spanish, as the first premise states, is a minority language in the United States, Monica was quickly transitioned to English in her early school years and was never able to develop her Spanish as a student. Now teaching biliteracy, she is challenged by the weakness of her academic Spanish. Elena has learned about the minority status of Spanish through difficult personal experiences, such as the parents of her students who complain about her accent in English and who value English learning activities over Spanish. To compensate for this reality, Elena speaks English to her colleagues, even those who are Spanish-speaking, and she reduces the time she spends in Spanish in order to teach more English. In the bilingual programs all three teachers work in, exiting students from the program is a sign of success.

Elena struggles most with the reality of the second premise, that students will use their two languages to learn, because she interprets the use of both languages for learning as a sign of confusion and a "bastardization" of Spanish. When it was suggested to her that teachers should accept their students' use of language as a launching point for learning, she maintained that accepting approximations of Spanish is wrong and that her students do not know how to speak Spanish well. Monica and Susan also need to better understand the second premise. Until then, they will worry that their students are "low in both languages."

Elena understands the third premise, that Spanish and English are governed by distinct linguistic rules and cultural norms, and that therefore the two languages are taught differently. Her challenge is to figure out how to apply what she learned about teaching Spanish to the reality of the United States, where her students live and learn in a bilingual context. Monica and Susan, who understand the instructional context and expectations of literacy instruction in the United States, are unaware of how some literacy strategies used in English do not make sense in Spanish. When asked to teach in a balanced literacy program where the teacher selects the materials, methods, and assessment, Monica and Susan went with what they knew, English literacy instruction.

We recommend that teachers reflect on their perspectives and experiences and continually review the three premises and how they affect practice. The more teachers think about how these premises affect practice, the more actively they will address them in their teaching.

ACTIVITIES FOR REFLECTION AND ACTION

1. In this chapter, you were introduced to three different teachers responsible for teaching for biliteracy. Complete the survey in Box 3.1 and reflect on your responses. Of the three teachers, which teacher do you identify with the most? Why? In what ways are you different from the teachers in the book?

2. As part of a professional learning team (or in another type of professional collaborative setting) share your survey responses and reactions to the teacher profiles with colleagues, and develop a professional development plan that takes advantage of strengths and addresses the needs of the members of the group.

3. Reflect on the insights you have gained about your own teaching and learning as a part of these activities. Think about how your own teaching is influenced by your own linguistic, cultural, and academic background.

4. This chapter described the three elements needed for effective collaboration among teachers: trust, flexibility, and a shared philosophy. Think about the teachers with whom you work and brainstorm ways you can establish these three key elements.

CHAPTER 4

Planning the Strategic Use of Two Languages

KEY POINTS

An effective unit framework for developing biliteracy in the United States does the following:

- Tackles the issue of allocation of time and resources

- Provides a structure for planning for the strategic use of Spanish and English

- Includes activities and strategies that reflect the distinct linguistic and cultural rules of Spanish and English

- Includes strategies for transferring skills and understanding between languages

- Integrates instruction in literacy skills with meaningful content

This chapter and those that follow take a close look at the biliteracy unit framework introduced in Chapter 1 and how it can help teachers create units of study that meet the needs of the range of students learning biliteracy in the United States. The biliteracy unit framework provides a structure for planning for the strategic use of Spanish and English in the classroom. It also provides the structure for the balance of this book. Developing an effective bilingual unit of study begins with information gathering. Teachers gather information about their students' linguistic, cultural, and academic background information through surveys, parent-teacher interviews, and in-class activities (such as those discussed in Chapter 2). Teachers also reflect on their own backgrounds and experiences, as discussed in Chapter 3. An important element of self-reflection that influences the development and implementation of an effective bilingual unit of study is choice of language: the language for instruction, the language or languages the teacher uses, and the language or languages students use.

Planning for the Teacher's Use of Language

The language used for instruction of a particular unit is determined by the program's language allocation plan. That plan identifies how much instructional time is spent in Spanish and how much instructional time is spent in English. The content allocation plan identifies in which language each subject area is taught in each grade. With these two pieces in place, teachers are ready to plan units. The instructional elements that come before the Bridge—developing oracy and background knowledge, reading comprehension, writing, word study, and summative assessment—are planned and conducted in one program language, the language of heavy lifting. During the Bridge, when students and teacher engage in contrastive analysis of their languages, the two languages come together. After the Bridge, extension activities are conducted in the other program language. The sample units of study in this book identify Spanish as the language of instruction before the Bridge and English as the language of instruction after the Bridge. In dual-language and developmental bilingual programs, several content areas are taught in English. For units in these areas, English is the language of heavy lifting and Spanish is the language of extension activities after the Bridge.

Students will use both their languages throughout the day when they are learning either English or Spanish literacy. It is expected, however, that the teacher who is delivering Spanish literacy instruction will deliver an entire lesson in Spanish. To ensure that they do so, teachers must first reflect on and then plan their own language use. This point seems obvious. But experience has shown that teachers in bilingual classrooms often unconsciously switch to English or informal Spanish. Code-switching during social interactions is natural and acceptable. Language mixing by the teacher in the bilingual classroom, however, is inappropriate. Monica, whose story is told with that of Elena and Susan in Chapter 3, provides an example. Often she begins a lesson in Spanish, but when she comes to an unfamiliar term, she simply inserts the word in English. Another example is the teacher who, in presenting a lesson on how to use the cover and text illustrations to help predict the content of a book, says, "*Niños, aquí se ve el* cover *del libro. Fíjense en el dibujo en el* cover. *¿Qué es lo que ven? ¿Pueden decirme de lo que trata el libro? ¿Pueden* predict *de lo que trata el libro?*" This teacher is teaching an important prereading strategy to aid comprehension. What she failed to do, however, was to fully reflect on and plan her own language use. While we know that it may be acceptable for Paulo and Lucía, both of whom were born and grew up in the United States, to enter the Spanish literacy classroom speaking this way to each other, it is essential that the teacher model the use of formal Spanish during the time reserved for Spanish instruction. Moreover, students like Antonio and Carmen, who have recently arrived in this country, will find it very difficult to follow and understand content delivered in such a haphazard mix of Spanish and English.

The teacher must plan to use and model formal language that will expand the language of her students beyond the informal language they might currently use. By planning her own language use, the teacher becomes a model for the formal language used in the classroom. In her planning for the unit on predicting as a prereading strategy, for example, the teacher would think about all the terms she will need in order to conduct the lesson in Spanish. High on the list of important vocabulary would be *portada* (book cover) and *predecir* (predict). Also, she would plan to use language that goes beyond the informal language her students use. Thus, instead of, "*Fíjense en el dibujo en la portada del libro,*" she would plan to say, "*Observen la ilustración en la portada del libro.*"

Even teachers like Elena who have a deep background in formal Spanish need to think about their language use. They make more of a connection with their students when they are aware of the regional terms their students might use and when they prepare for responding to informal and regional language with comprehension and respect. When student language includes regional terms such as *queque* (the word for cake in Costa Rica), community Spanish terms such as *lonche* for lunch and *troca* for truck, or words in English, it is expected that the Spanish literacy teacher will maintain her use of comprehensible academic Spanish at all times during instruction without switching to English and without belittling student language use.

Rather than scolding a child for speaking "incorrect" Spanish, teachers can view student use of words such as *lonche* or *troca* as opportunities to discuss the difference between language used at home or on the playground and language used in more formal interactions. Discussions like this that focus on language use promote metalinguistic awareness, which contributes to literacy development (Cloud, Genesee, and Hamayan, 2009).

Planning Students' Cross-Linguistic Development: The Bridge

Because students enter the classroom with background knowledge and experiences stored in overlapping linguistic reservoirs, the biliteracy unit framework allows for the explicit and consistent connection and transfer of knowledge and skills between Spanish and English. This connection and transfer is made during the Bridge, the time when students are taught to examine the similarities and differences between English and Spanish using contrastive analysis. This exercise might include a study of cognates and an examination of false cognates and conventions and constructions specific to each language. The Bridge is used also to help students distinguish between informal language and formal language.

The unit theme and big idea determine the focus of the Bridge. A unit on photosynthesis, for example, would provide an opportunity to highlight cognates between Spanish and English such as *la fotosíntesis, el gas, el aire, la clorofila, el proceso, convertir, el oxígeno, el dióxido de carbono, la planta,* and *la energía*. A unit on community helpers would allow the teacher to demonstrate that Spanish nouns have gender (*el doctor/la doctora, la maestra/el maestro*), whereas English nouns do not.

The Bridge always involves the students in some active way and always begins in the language of heavy lifting used to learn the new content before the Bridge. For example, once students have studied community helpers in Spanish and have completed a summative assessment activity in Spanish, the teacher would move into the Bridge part of the unit. She might display pictures of the community helpers they have studied and ask the students to work with a partner to come up with the English labels for the same people. As two-language learners, many of the students in the classroom will know the English equivalents for the community helpers. The teacher will provide those they do not know. By explicitly teaching, talking about, and naming elements of language within a comprehensible context, the teacher is fostering metalinguistic awareness. A consistent focus on fostering metalinguistic awareness will encourage students to transfer information between their two languages so they learn to use all of their linguistic resources independently.

In addition to focusing on linguistic elements and involving the students in an active way, the Bridge is an opportunity for students to summarize their understanding of newly learned content and to learn how to express this new understanding in the other language. For example, during the Bridge portion of a unit about photosynthesis in which Spanish was used before the Bridge, the teacher might ask students to summarize their learning on the subject by choosing the 5 to 10 words most important for explaining the process by which plants change energy to food. The teacher can use these lists to assess her students' understanding. A student who has chosen the words *la flor* and *el tallo* (flower and stem), for example, probably does not understand as much about the concept of photosynthesis as a student who has chosen *el sol* and *la clorofila* (sun and chlorophyll). This exercise would tell the teacher what content she needs to clarify before beginning to focus on the English portion of the unit. Too often, students are asked to communicate in English about concepts they have not fully understood in Spanish.

To review, the Bridge is a strategy in a biliteracy unit for connecting content learned in one language to the other language. It is interactive and involves the student as a full participant. It prepares the student to use and express knowledge gained in one language in the other language and to compare the two languages in terms of phonology, morphology, syntax and grammar, and pragmatics. It allows the students to summarize content and review important academic vocabulary, and it provides an opportunity for the teacher to address specific student language errors. When students learn content in Spanish and then bridge to English, they generate a list of words or phrases in Spanish and compare them with the English equivalent, which they or the teacher provide. They do not take a list of words or phrases provided by the teacher and look them up in a bilingual dictionary, nor do they simply read the same or a related story in English. How the Bridge fits into the unit as a whole is discussed in more detail as we go through the unit cycle.

Unit Planning for the Strategic Use of Two Languages

A biliteracy unit framework that reflects a planned and strategic use of two languages follows the school's language allocation and content allocation plans. It specifies which language will be used before the Bridge (Spanish in all examples in this book) and which language will be used after the Bridge (English); both languages will be used during the Bridge. And it includes instruction in the four language domains: listening, speaking, reading, and writing. The biliteracy unit framework includes a time for explicitly teaching metalinguistic transfer, where the instruction moves from Spanish to English in a planned, strategic way.

The following story reveals that in one classroom the teacher does not use the biliteracy unit framework and does not plan for the Bridge.

> It's early Monday morning and the teachers are hurrying into the building. One by one they put their weekly lesson plans in the principal's mailbox. As the veteran bilingual teacher, Mr. Santiago, pulls his lesson plans out of his briefcase, his fellow bilingual teacher, Mrs. Gálvez, asks, "How do you designate when you use English and when you teach in Spanish?"
>
> Mr. Santiago responds, "Oh, *tú sabes*, I use English most of the day, but, *por si a caso*, I can use Spanish if they don't understand. Oh, *antes de que se me olvide, puedo usar tu* projector after lunch? Mine is broken."

The rather haphazard way that instruction in Mr. Santiago's classroom moves from Spanish to English could leave the students confused and does not support biliteracy development.

INTEGRATING LANGUAGE ARTS AND CONTENT-AREA INSTRUCTION

The biliteracy unit framework described in this book is based on the idea that the most effective way to teach for biliteracy is by integrating language arts and content-area instruction. Instruction begins with a theme and a big idea (or essential understanding) related to the grade-level content areas that will be the focus of study, rather than with a discrete skill. The big idea may come from science or social studies learning standards and the Common Core State Standards for English Language Arts and Literacy in History/Social Studies, Science, and Technical Subjects. The content-area standards guide the development of content targets for each unit of study. Because the biliteracy units of study in this book integrate language arts and content-area instruction, they are able to teach to both content-area and language arts standards, and to support the move toward the integration and study of more informational text throughout the grades. In addition, because these are units of study that focus on language and content, Spanish language development standards and English language development standards, such as those by the WIDA (World-Class Instructional Design and Assessment) Consortium, can guide the development of language targets for the unit. The WIDA CAN DO descriptors can be used also for formative assessment and for planning for differentiated instruction. WIDA is developing academic Spanish-language development standards, one of which will capture student "bridging," the understanding students have about how their two languages intersect. Also known as translanguaging or dynamic bilingualism (García, 2009), this standard will document and validate students' multilingual abilities.

A major goal of these units is to have students read and write about the content areas while developing specific language arts and language skills. Integrating language arts and content-area instruction allows students to learn and practice literacy skills within a highly comprehensible context and allows for more effective bridging between Spanish and English. Cross-linguistic targets, the focus of the Bridge, are also stated. The explicit teaching of skills, such as word study and fluency, is integrated within a larger and richer context of study. And, because it is most effective to begin a unit of study with the end in mind, the summative assessment is stated in the beginning of the unit, right after the theme, big idea, standards, and content and language targets. This summative assessment is not implemented, however, until later in the unit of study. Note how the summative assessment is directly reflective of the big idea stated for each unit of study.

In the following sections of this chapter, and through the next four chapters of the book, we will take you through the process of putting together units for the instruction of biliteracy in the United States. A template of the full biliteracy unit framework appears in Chapter 1. The 3rd grade unit on animal adaptations, which is used as an example, is at the end of this chapter.

As its big idea, "Authors use a wide variety of literary elements in fictional narratives," makes clear, this 3rd grade unit has a clear focus on teaching language arts concepts and skills within the framework of a highly comprehensible science theme. The sample unit focuses on animals and the adaptations that help them survive in their habitats. The teacher has taken advantage of this highly motivating area of study to also teach literacy skills.

BEGINNING WITH A CONCRETE ACTIVITY

The unit begins in one language, Spanish, which is maintained until the Bridge. A highly comprehensible, concrete activity designed to help develop academic oracy and provide an experiential base of background knowledge launches the unit. Too often, teachers begin units by talking to students about the new content and then asking them to read a text. Talking and reading are very abstract activities. Not until the end of the unit do the students participate in activities that illustrate the concept. By reversing the order and beginning with the concrete, teachers can provide the background knowledge and teach the oral academic language that make the text comprehensible. This first phase of the unit may take several days. In the 3rd grade sample, the teacher has planned to take at least two full class periods to build the oral academic language and background knowledge associated with the big idea. By dedicating this much time to oracy development, the teacher allows students to use the informal language they bring to the classroom and then acquire and practice the academic language they need to be able to engage in literacy activities about the topic. The oracy development is interactive, with students involved in listening and speaking activities. Because language use is language learning, strategies used at this point in the unit are more effective if students, rather than the teacher, are doing most of the talking, and thus practicing the academic language that is key to success in school. This first part of the unit is dedicated to learning academic language and building background knowledge.

Speaking in Spanish only, the teacher begins with a highly engaging strategy called concept attainment, a constructivist strategy designed to help students understand a new concept through a series of examples. This approach contrasts with the more teacher-centered transmission approach, in which the teacher tells the students what concept they will study and describes it. In the 3rd grade unit, the teacher tells the students they must guess from the examples what animal they will study. To provide ample opportunity for the students to interact orally, the teacher has the students ask her yes/no questions until they guess the secret animal. The teacher could have simply provided clues, but by requiring students to ask questions, she is inviting them to begin with their own language, whether formal or informal. She will then lead them to using the more formal language. In this way, the teacher increases opportunities for student talk and decreases teacher talk. Students will begin to internalize the academic language if they are involved in activities that require them to use the language.

The teacher tells the students that she will bring in a live animal for them to study the next day but that they must guess what animal it is. She guides them to the correct formation of yes/no questions in Spanish by providing sentence prompts: *¿Tiene* ———*?* (Does it have ———?); *¿Puede* ——— *?* (Can it ———?); *¿Vive* ———*?* (Does it live ———?); *¿Es* ———*?* (Is it ———?) Before taking questions from individual students, the teacher tells the class, "*Habla con tu pareja*" ("Talk to your partner") to come up with a bank of *sí/no* (yes/no) questions in Spanish. This strategy gives students time to explore the subject in pairs or small groups before they begin asking the teacher questions in front of the whole class. It is important to remember that this unit is being conducted entirely in Spanish. By providing the sentence prompts and the opportunity to collaborate with peers, the teacher is addressing the needs of students like Paulo, Lucía, and Hannah, who might not have the vocabulary in Spanish to form the questions they want to ask. The sentence prompts help guide the students to use Spanish, and the *habla con tu pareja* strategy gives them time to talk with peers and get help with Spanish vocabulary. For example, Paulo might ask, "*¿Tiene* scales?" ("Does it have scales?"). Paulo's code-switching is typical and expected of a two-language learner. The sentence prompts help Paulo to focus on Spanish (*¿Tiene* ———*?*) Without it, he may simply have asked, "Does it have scales?" The planned time to talk with his strategically organized small group or partnership gives him the opportunity to see whether his peers can come up the word in Spanish. Even if his peers do not understand the word "scales" in English, or do not know the word in Spanish, the discussion time allows Paulo to draw or explain what scales are, and either elicit the Spanish word or learn how to describe the concept in Spanish.

The second premise tells us that students learning biliteracy in the United States will use all their languages in an endeavor like this. It is inevitable, therefore, that in preparing questions with their peers, the 3rd grade students will use all their linguistic resources to communicate and to construct meaning. Using sentence prompts and the *habla con tu pareja* strategy gives support while allowing time for students to explore their linguistic resources and refine their questions using formal Spanish. Consistent use of paired or small-group activities throughout a unit is an important part of teaching literacy in Spanish and English. Providing opportunities for students to interact with other students in a low-stress situation encourages their participation. Because of the importance of these interactions, teachers must be thoughtful and strategic about putting partnerships and small groups together. For example, it would make sense to put students like Paulo and Lucía, who have extensive background information about life in the United States, with students like Antonio and Carmen, who have greater linguistic resources in Spanish. While the students work together to formulate questions during concept attainment, they may speak a mixture of informal Spanish, Anglicisms, English, and formal Spanish, and that is acceptable.

After giving students time to collaborate, the teacher then calls the class back to focus on the T-chart, a graphic organizer on which she will record their *sí/no* questions in two parallel columns. It is important that the T-chart be written on chart paper rather than on the board, because the completed chart will be posted in the classroom to serve as a vocabulary list and word wall for the duration of the unit.

Because the teacher has provided support for all students by giving them sentence prompts and collaboration time, she can hold them all accountable for participating, leaving her free to call on any student. Some teachers choose to call on students randomly by name; others pick student names out of a can. Whatever strategy is used, it is important to remember not to choose only students who raise their hands. We know that often the same students raise their hands and that other students quickly learn that they do not need to pay attention if they do not raise their hands. When the teacher calls on a student who does not have a ready response, the student understands that he or she can look to his or her partner or small group for help. The practice of calling on students randomly increases their accountability. It is not meant to trick or to punish the students. The more students understand that they can work together to formulate their responses, the more language and interaction—and therefore the more content and language learning—will occur in the classroom.

During initial interactive activities, such as eliciting *sí/no* questions to post on a T-chart, teachers engage in a dialogue with the students that allows them to simultaneously do the following:

- Maintain their own use of formal Spanish
- Respect and take advantage of all student linguistic resources
- Introduce new, formal vocabulary in a highly contextualized and comprehensible way

In this 3rd grade example, if a student asks, "*¿Vive en el agua?*" ("Does it live in water?"), the teacher has the opportunity to introduce the academic term *agua dulce* (fresh water) first by responding to the question and acknowledging that the animal does indeed live in water, "*Sí, vive en el agua,*" and then by elaborating, "*Pero no vive en agua del mar, o agua con sal. Sólo vive en agua dulce, agua de los ríos o lagos.*" ("Yes, it does live in water. But not in salt water, like in the ocean. It lives in fresh water, like the water in rivers or lakes.") In this way, the teacher introduces academic language by building on student language. She then writes the phrase *vive en agua dulce* (lives in fresh water) on the *sí* side of the T-chart.

This teacher knows the vocabulary she wants to introduce to her students and has a list prepared. She could have simply given the students this list and either provided a definition or explanation of each word or asked them to look the words up in a dictionary, but a guessing game about a secret animal is much more motivating to students than a list of vocabulary words. In addition, by using concept attainment, the teacher is able to listen to and assess the level of academic language her students currently have about animals. She can provide the academic language where needed, but she begins with what the students know, in either language.

The teacher accepts English words but puts them on a different chart and highlights them as different by using a different color. The teacher also illustrates potentially new words with actions, such as moving her hands like claws, or with pictures, such as drawing a fish with scales. In addition, she uses formal Spanish expressions, such as *a pesar de que* (although) as she converses with the students. Notice, in the exchange that follows, how the teacher's actions show that she understands the first two premises. For example, she does not switch to English but maintains her use of Spanish when Paulo responds in English, and she encourages all students to do the same, because she knows, as stated in the first premise, that Spanish is a minority language that is often marginalized in the United States. Also, she knows that students use all their languages when developing biliteracy in the United States, and she prepares for their use of English by setting up a separate chart for utterances in English. It is also evident that she has prepared her own language use by looking up some of the many labels her students might use, such as *tenazas*, and *pinzas* (claws.) (The following exchange is not a transcript, though it is based on real classroom interactions. It is offered for illustrative purposes only.)

Original Spanish

> **Antonio**: *¿Tiene pinzas?*
>
> **Maestra**: *Sí, tiene pinzas. ¿Alguien sabe otra manera de decir pinzas? (La maestra abre y cierra sus manos como pinzas para ilustrar el significado de la palabra.)*
>
> **Paulo**: Claws?
>
> **Maestra**: *Sí, así es en inglés. (Escribe "claws" en otra hoja y con un marcador de diferente color.) ¿Alguien sabe otra palabra en español?*
>
> **Lucía**: *¿Tenazas?*
>
> **Maestra**: *Sí, tenazas. (Escribe las pinzas y las tenazas en la columna titulada "sí.")*

English Translation

> **Antonio**: Does it have pincers?
>
> **Teacher**: Yes, it has pincers. Does anyone know another way of saying pincers? (Teacher opens and closes her hands like pincers to illustrate the word.)
>
> **Paulo**: Claws? (He says it in English.)
>
> **Teacher**: Yes, that is how you say it in English. (She writes "claws" on another piece of paper, in a different color marker.) Does anybody know another word in Spanish?
>
> **Lucía**: *Tenazas*? (Another way of saying claws in Spanish.)
>
> **Teacher**: Yes, *tenazas*. (She writes *las pinzas* and *las tenazas* on the board under *sí*.)

The students would continue asking questions until they had enough clues to determine the correct answer. As the students ask their questions, the teacher adds information to the *sí* and *no* sides of the T-chart, taking every opportunity to introduce academic vocabulary in Spanish. Once students have gathered enough *sí* responses, they will begin guessing animals by name. If a student asks whether the animal is a crab, the teacher can introduce the word crustacean: "*No, el animal secreto no es un cangrejo. Pero, como un cangrejo, es un crustáceo.*" ("No, the secret animal is not a crab. But, like a crab, it is a crustacean.") Although few of the 3rd graders may know what a crustacean is, they can get enough background information from the clues on the board (lives in fresh water, has claws, has a shell, has ten legs) to have an understanding of the word. The teacher is giving the students the opportunity to listen to, understand, and interact with the academic vocabulary before they will be called on to read or write the words.

When the students, using the many clues gathered, are able to figure out that the secret animal is a crayfish, the concept attainment activity is over. Now it is time for them to see and, if they are brave enough, to handle live crayfish. This next step is highly motivating for students. It also gives them an opportunity to practice the language they have just learned. When the teacher brings in live crayfish on the second day, which is also dedicated to oracy development, she first reviews the list of words under the *sí* column on the T-chart and then provides sentence prompts so the students can use this new vocabulary as they observe and interact with the live crayfish: *Veo* ———. (I see ———.); *Observo* ———. (I observe ———.); *Este es*———. (This is ———.); *Estos son* ———. (These are ———.). By reviewing in Spanish, the teacher is sending a clear message that Spanish is important and that the students are expected to use Spanish for academic interactions. Also, in keeping with her understanding of the first premise, she is setting aside time for explicitly teaching in Spanish.

As the teacher circulates and observes students' interactions with the animals, she encourages them to use the T-chart as a resource and introduces new vocabulary when necessary. For example, when one student picks up a crayfish and notices it has a hole on its underbelly, the teacher explains to the small group of students: "*Sólo las hembras tienen un orificio en el abdomen. Las hembras ponen huevos. Los huevos salen del orificio en el abdomen. Los machos no tienen el orificio.*" ("Only females have an orifice in the abdomen. The females lay eggs. The eggs come out of this orifice in their abdomen. The males do not have an orifice.") She then adds *la hembra* (female), *el macho* (male), and *el abdomen* (abdomen) to the T-chart. When other students ask her what the words mean, she directs them to consult with the group of students with whom she had been talking. These students, in turn, use the crayfish to explain the meaning of the new words. By using live animals and allowing the introduction of new vocabulary words to be directed by the students themselves, the teacher has created more opportunities for student-to-student interactions.

After students have experienced the live animals, the teacher asks them to report their observations. Once again, she gives them time to collaborate with their peers before calling on any one student. The T-chart of vocabulary words is clearly posted, along with the sentence prompts. As the students speak, the teacher records their observations on another chart, continuing until most students have spoken. This chart, like the T-chart created during the concept attainment, will serve as an anchor chart and will provide vocabulary and language support for students as they move through this unit of study.

MOVING FROM THE CONCRETE TO THE ABSTRACT

The lessons and activities in the 3rd grade classroom to this point suggest that the class is working on a science unit rather than a language arts unit. Now, however, the unit moves to a more traditional language arts focus that includes writing original stories and reading a variety of texts with similar literary elements. This shift reflects the big idea of this unit, which is solidly focused on a language arts concept: the author's choice of literary elements.

The more traditional way of studying these concepts would be to begin with a discussion of literary elements, such as first person, point of view, and personification, or perhaps with the reading of texts that illustrate these elements. But a unit that begins like this, with the students reading a new and unfamiliar text or listening to the teacher talk, is beginning with the more difficult and abstract activities. A new text, even one written in Spanish for students who speak Spanish, will not be comprehensible to all the students who are learning literacy in Spanish. Paulo will understand some of the words of the text, but, as a two-language learner, he will not have all the vocabulary in Spanish. Some of it he will have in English. Antonio will have the words in Spanish, but if the text was not written by someone from Mexico, he may not be familiar with all the vocabulary. Or he may not have the background knowledge and previous experience to understand the text, especially if the topics reflect the culture of the United States. A story written in Spanish about cooking and eating crayfish, for example, will be difficult for any student to understand who has never seen an animal like a crayfish before and has had little or no experience eating such creatures. Lucía and Hannah may not have the Spanish academic vocabulary in the text, regardless of the topic. Lucía may not have it because she has never, until now, been formally instructed in Spanish. All her formal instruction up to this point has been in English. Hannah may not have the vocabulary because, as a native English speaker, she is still learning Spanish. To make a text comprehensible to all the students involved in learning literacy in Spanish, a highly comprehensible, interactive activity must precede the reading of any new text.

The concepts of first person, point of view, and personification can be taught through a variety of texts and writing activities. In this instance, however, the teacher decided to tie the study of these literary elements to her science curriculum. She is responsible for teaching about animal adaptations in science, and so she takes advantage of this highly concrete and highly engaging subject to teach about literary elements as well. Too often teachers feel tied to a reading series, a basal reader, or the book the other classes in the same grade level are reading to teach literacy skills and concepts. Because this teacher understands the three premises of Spanish literacy instruction in the United States, she understands that her literacy instruction will look different than that of teachers of English literacy teaching to monolingual English speakers. She knows that because of the great variety of linguistic, cultural, and academic backgrounds that her students bring to class, she must start with a highly comprehensible, concrete activity in order to create a comprehensible context for reading and writing.

READING AND WRITING COMPREHENSIBLE TEXT

In a traditional unit, the teacher begins by talking with the students about the theme—a highly decontextualized and abstract act—and then moves to reading. Writing follows reading and is the activity just before the hands-on activity or the field trip, which is usually saved for last. Writing is viewed as a form of assessment or as a product of learning rather than as part of the learning process.

In this sample unit, however, the teacher puts writing before reading and uses the language experience approach (LEA) to introduce her students to the writing activity. The LEA takes advantage of a highly comprehensible activity students have participated in together and models how oral language is connected to written language. Here, the shared activity is the students' first interaction with the crayfish. All the students observed and, if they wished, picked up the crayfish. The next day, the teacher tells the students they are to describe what it was like meeting the crayfish for the first time. She asks them to think of a good opening sentence for their narrative and tells them, "*Cada uno hable con su pareja para pensar en una buena oración introductoria para nuestro relato de nuestro primer encuentro con los langostinos.*" When all students have had time to talk to their partners, she asks for a volunteer for a first sentence. Notice how she accepts children's responses while at the same time looking for an appropriate opening sentence. Also note how the teacher reinforces conventional Spanish verb conjugations, introduces the idea of indenting, and reviews the use of capital letters.

Original Spanish

Maestra: *Niños, los alumnos de cuarto grado están muy interesados en nuestros langostinos, y quieren saber cómo nos fue ayer cuando los conocimos por primera vez. Aquí (la maestra señala la cartulina que ha preparado) les vamos a escribir acerca de lo que nos pasó ayer. Quiero que me cuenten lo que sucedió, y yo lo escribiré aquí. Cada uno hable con su pareja para pensar en una buena oración introductoria para nuestro relato de nuestro primer encuentro con los langostinos. (La maestra les da tiempo a los estudiantes a que hablen con sus parejas.) Ahora, ¿quién me puede decir lo que sucedió ayer?*

Lucía: *El langostino pinchó a Estefania.*

Maestra: *Es cierto, Lucía. El langostino sí le pinchó a Estefania. Pero no creo que esa sea una oración introductoria. ¿Quién me tiene una oración introductoria?*

Hannah: *Ayer nosotros vemos langostinos.*

Maestra: *Si, ayer nosotros vimos a los langostinos. (La maestra repite la oración haciendo correcciones gramaticales mínimas.) No voy a empezar a escribir aquí (señala la parte extrema izquierda de la hoja). Voy a dejar un espacio—la sangría—porque estoy empezando el párrafo. ¿Con qué tipo de letra empieza una oración?*

Alumnos: *¡Mayúscula!*

English Translation

Teacher: Children, the students in 4th grade are very interested in our crayfish, and they want to know how it went yesterday when we met them. Here (the teacher points to the chart paper she has on an easel) is where we are going to write about what happened yesterday. I would like you to tell me what happened, and I will write it here. Talk to your partner and think of a good introductory sentence for our story about what happened to us yesterday. (The teacher gives the students time to talk to their partners.) So, who can you tell me about what happened yesterday?

Lucía: The crayfish pricked Estefania.

Teacher: It is true, Lucía. The crayfish pricked Estefania. But I don't think that is an introductory sentence. Who has an introductory sentence?

Hannah: Yesterday we seed crayfish.

Teacher: Yes, yesterday we saw crayfish. (The teacher repeats the sentence making slight grammatical corrections.) I am not going to start writing here (signals the far left of the page). I will leave a space—indentation—because I am beginning a paragraph. With what kind of letter do I begin a sentence?

Students: Capital letter!

The teacher uses the LEA as a source of teachable moments. In addition to modeling some of the writing conventions her students are still learning, she encourages the students to comment on the content of the text, emphasizing elaboration by adding more details or explaining things more fully. The LEA works well in the biliteracy unit framework. It enables the students to use their own words to create a text that is comprehensible to them because it is directly related to their experiences.

After writing a few paragraphs with the students, the teacher introduces point of view. She explains to the students that they have been recounting their first interactions with the crayfish from their own point of view. She now asks them to think about the crayfish's point of view. Might a crayfish have experienced this first interaction differently? She asks the students to take a crayfish's point of view and to say something about yesterday. Again, she gives them a chance to talk with their partners before volunteering to speak to the class. As students describe their reactions from the point of view of a crayfish, she helps them decide whether this version of the story will be in the first person or the third person. The teacher can use the sentences on the chart to show examples of first and third person. Once the students have decided, as a group, whether the new writing piece will be in first or third person, the teacher continues to elicit ideas. As she records their ideas, she also points out examples of personification—instances where students have given the crayfish humanlike thoughts, emotions, or abilities. The teacher notes these student comments on another sheet of chart paper.

After the students offer several statements from the point of view of the crayfish, the teacher gives them a writing assignment: they are each to write a narrative in first person or third person from the point of view of the crayfish, making sure to include elements of personification. By now the students have the background knowledge and vocabulary to write about crayfish, and they have the background knowledge and vocabulary to understand what narrative, first person, third person, point of view, and personification mean. Too often, students are asked to write a first-person narrative but are not given a subject. The 3rd grade teacher dedicated two days to developing background knowledge and vocabulary for the combined science and language arts unit. By integrating the content areas and language arts, she made good use of class time.

The students will spend several days using a writer's workshop approach that will take them through the steps of writing a first draft of the story, participating in several peer reviews, revising the story, and conferencing with the teacher before completing a final draft.

During this time, the teacher will provide mini-lessons on such topics as the elements of personification and the consistent use of the past tense in a story that narrates a past event. She will use dictado to address word study and fluency, drawing examples from the sentences the students created during the LEA part of the unit for mini-lessons in spelling, grammar, and punctuation. For this unit, the teacher will focus on the use of accents in the simple past tense in Spanish. The dictado is explained in more detail in Chapter 9.

After completing a final draft of the crayfish story, students will read several books that include personification. All the books will be in Spanish and from a variety of reading levels. While the students are reading, the teacher will work with small groups using guided reading to study and practice the literary elements and reading skills. After reading several books, students will complete a table with examples of personification, point of view, and other literary elements from their own story and from the books they have read. The table serves as the summative assessment for this unit, and, like all instruction up to this point, will be in Spanish. Along with the crayfish narrative, it will tell the teacher to what extent each student understands the concepts of personification, point of view, first and third person, and other literary elements studied.

MAKING CROSS-LINGUISTIC CONNECTIONS THROUGH THE BRIDGE

After completing the first part of the unit in Spanish—beginning with a concrete activity, then moving to writing and reading activities, then to word work and fluency practice, and finally to the summative assessment—the class moves on to the Bridge, the time for explicit instruction on how Spanish and English interact. Throughout their lives in the United States, students learning biliteracy are confronted with the interaction of Spanish and English. While the ability to make connections between their two languages has demonstrated benefits for bilingual students (Jimenez, García, and Pearson, 1996), few students are explicitly taught to make these connections and fewer still will make the connections without explicit instruction (Dressler, Carlo, Snow, August, and White, 2011).

The teacher uses the big idea to guide her planning for the Bridge. Thus, she focuses the Bridge not on crayfish vocabulary or the vocabulary of the books the students were reading but on the vocabulary of literary elements, as stated in the big idea. She begins by asking students, in Spanish, to summarize the literary elements they have studied and what they know about them. As always, she gives them the opportunity to discuss their answers in small groups before they volunteer information to the class as a whole. As the students name the literary elements to the class and what they know about them, the teacher lists the elements on a chart and records the students' responses. This exercise offers an additional opportunity for summative assessment. It is important to mention, however, that this before-the-Bridge assessment happens in Spanish, the language in which students have studied the concepts. It would make little sense, and would be unfair, to assess students in English on the content they learned in Spanish. Once the responses have been posted, the teacher asks the students to work collaboratively to come up with a movement for each key word, that is, to create their own total physical response (TPR).

Because the focus of the Bridge is on the relationship between the students' two languages, the teacher now moves to English. Using the movements the students have created, she elicits from them (or provides for them) the terms in English. When she asks the students whether they can name the literary elements in English, Paulo, Lucía, Hannah, and other students who have linguistic resources in English have the opportunity to show what they know. At this time, the teacher consults the lists of English words she has maintained throughout the unit to see whether there are any that would support this activity.

The teacher posts the Spanish and English words side by side and works with the students to compare and contrast their two languages, focusing, for this unit, on cognates, such as *la personificación*–personification and *la narrativa*–narrative. As part of the contrastive analysis portion of the Bridge, the teacher can guide students in identifying patterns, pointing out, for example, that -*ción* in Spanish usually becomes -tion in English.

The Bridge is part of all bilingual units. In this school, one teacher is responsible for both the Spanish and the English literacy instruction of these students. In bilingual programs or schools that divide this responsibility between two teachers, the Spanish literacy teacher and the English teacher work together to help the students make these metalinguistic connections.

It should be noted that throughout the part of the unit that preceded the Bridge, the teacher maintained her use of Spanish. She respected and acknowledged the students' use of English, but she herself did not code-switch. She had preplanned her own language use so she could continually model the use of formal Spanish. In addition, she made sure to match her materials to the language of instruction, following the practice in effective bilingual or dual-language programs of ensuring that when the medium of instruction is Spanish, the materials are in Spanish. During the Bridge, when the focus is on the relationship between the students' two languages, she uses both languages to talk about a word in Spanish and its equivalent in English.

After the Bridge, the teacher assigns an extension activity in English in which students can use the language modeled during the Bridge. This activity becomes the English literacy lesson. For Carmen, Paulo, and Antonio, it is an ESL lesson, but for Lucía and Hannah it is simply an English literacy lesson. The teacher continues the study of point of view, personification, and first- and third-person narrative using the differentiation strategies she used during the Spanish portion of this unit—flexible groupings, sentence prompts, concrete activities, texts at a variety of reading levels—for the English portion, including those appropriate to ESL instruction but with different texts. The biliteracy unit framework offered in this book guides teachers to base English instruction on concepts and themes studied in Spanish—rather than following a separate book or curriculum for ESL—in order to integrate units of study and promote metalinguistic transfer.

The Biliteracy Unit Framework and the Three Premises

This biliteracy unit framework respects and reflects the three premises in the following ways:

- Begins in Spanish and sets aside time specifically for Spanish
- Includes a planned time for teaching about the connection between the two languages—the Bridge
- Supports the teaching of elements unique to each language

Beginning in Spanish and setting aside time for Spanish respects the first premise by raising the status of Spanish. Using the Bridge reflects the second premise, that students use both their languages when learning Spanish literacy in the United States. Supporting the teaching of elements unique to each language respects the third premise, that Spanish and English are governed by distinct linguistic rules and cultural norms. Studying accents in the past tense in the word study part of the unit, for example, is crucial in developing literacy in Spanish but is not part of any English literacy scope and sequence.

The biliteracy unit framework described in this chapter shows teachers how to put together the elements of instruction that are unique and basic to the teaching of biliteracy in the United States. If teachers and administrators keep in mind the key elements—beginning with the concrete and moving to the abstract, moving from oracy to literacy, integrating content and language instruction, explicitly articulating the language of instruction, and creating time for providing a Bridge between the two languages—they will be able to create effective and meaningful units for Carmen, Paulo, Antonio, Lucía, Hannah, and their peers in biliteracy programs.

ACTIVITIES FOR REFLECTION AND ACTION

1. This chapter describes a biliteracy unit framework. Review the elements of the framework and the order in which they are taught, then compare them with your teaching. Consider the following:
   - What elements do you teach or not teach?
   - How is the order in which you teach these elements similar and different to that in the biliteracy unit framework?

2. Consider the implications for adopting this framework for instruction on these elements:
   - Scheduling (literacy time in two languages; integration of reading, writing, and content instruction)
   - Materials (resources in Spanish, informational text)
   - Professional development (strategies, standards, writing big ideas)
   - Collaboration (time, goals, roles and responsibilities)

3. Look at the sample 3rd grade unit shown and described in this chapter. What additional elements of literacy could be taught during the reading comprehension phase of the unit? During writing? During word work? During fluency? During the extension activity in English?

4. Collect audio or video of yourself teaching and analyze your own language use. How do you code-switch? When and why? How do you use informal Spanish? How do you use formal Spanish?

Biliteracy Unit Framework: Sample for 3rd Grade

Content area: Language arts integrated with science | **Language in which this content area is taught:** Spanish

Theme/Big idea: Animal adaptations/Authors use a wide variety of literary elements in fictional narratives. | **Language allocation for this grade:**
__70__ % **Spanish;** __30__ % **English**

Standards
- Applicable Common Core English language arts standards[1]
- Spanish language arts standards (e.g., WIDA standards)[2]
- Science standards
- Spanish-language development standards
- English-language development standards (apply after the Bridge)

Content targets: Students will identify literary elements within stories. Students will write a narrative using point of view, first-person narrative, and personification.

Language targets
- **Spanish:** Students will ask yes/no questions orally. Students will justify their hypothesis about the secret animal. Students will describe and define literary elements. Students will use past tense in writing.
- **English:** Students will describe and define literary elements.
- **Cross-linguistic:** Students will identify, describe, and provide examples of cognates. Students will describe and provide examples of the *-ción/-tion* pattern in Spanish/English.

Summative assessment
- Students will write a fictional narrative that includes a variety of literary elements.
- Students will identify and describe literary elements (point of view, first-person narrative, and personification) in their own writing, in the writing of other students, and in stories read in class.

Building Oracy and Background Knowledge

Language of instruction: Spanish (This language is maintained until the Bridge; the other language is used in the Extension Activity.)

Language resources, linguistic creativity, and cultural funds of knowledge
- Students use multiple varieties of Spanish and refer to animals in different ways. For example, some students say "*chancho*" while others use "*puerco*" or "*cochino.*"
- Students use descriptive language to tell stories about their interactions with animals. Students often use regional terms, or English words in their stories, especially when the stories take place in the United States (e.g., *Le compramos un "leash" a mi perro ayer*).

---

1. The Common Core State Standards for English Language Arts and Literacy in History/Social Studies, Science, and Technical Subjects ("the Standards") are available at www.corestandards.org/
2. The WIDA (World Class Instructional Design and Assessment) Consortium standards are available at www.wida.us/standards

continued

Biliteracy Unit Framework: Sample for 3rd Grade *continued*

- Students write and talk about these animals in a way that personifies them, and the teacher wants to take advantage of this natural affinity with animals to teach point of view and narrative.
- Students use the past tense appropriately, in both regular and irregular verbs, in their speaking and in their writing. (Note: The writing of narratives provides the opportunity to expand student skills and teach the use of accents with past tense.)

Building background knowledge

- Concept attainment: Teacher requires students to ask a series of yes/no questions in order to obtain the concept of "crayfish."
- Hands-on activity with realia: Students observe and interact with live crayfish. Teacher posts T-chart and provides sentence starters (*Veo . . .; Observo . . .; Este es . . .; Estas son . . .*) to promote Spanish use during hands-on activity.
- Students' shared observations: As students share observations, teacher records observations on an anchor chart that will provide additional vocabulary and language support.

Formative assessment

- Checklist and anecdotal records on student use of sentence prompts during the concept attainment activity and during the small group work
- Checklist and anecdotal records that capture formal and informal Spanish use, English use, and types of questions offered

Reading comprehension

- Guided reading in small groups: Students read a variety of books that include personification. The focus of the guided reading groups is to look at the author's choice of literary elements: point of view, first-person narrative, and personification.
- Table: Students complete a table on literary elements in the books they have read.

Formative assessment

- Anecdotal records on comments and connections students make during guided reading
- Rubric to evaluate completed table

Writing

NOTE: In this sample unit, writing precedes reading.

- Language experience approach (LEA): Students narrate their first interaction with live crayfish. Then, later . . .
- Writing process: Students write original first-person narratives from the point of view of the crayfish, using personification. Teacher models prewriting, drafting, peer revising, editing, and publishing.
- The teacher provides writing mini-lessons on the following:
  - Elements of personification
  - Consistent use of past tense in a narrative
  - Using a variety of words, rather than the same words again and again
  - Creating complete sentences with capitals and periods
  - Paragraphing

Formative assessment

Writing rubric that respects and reflects the integration and use of two linguistic resources at both the word and the discourse level

Word study and fluency

- Using a dictado created from the text of the LEA, the teacher provides mini-lessons on the following:
  - Use of accents in the simple past tense in Spanish, with special focus on those words whose meaning changes with the use of the accent (e.g., *hablo/habló; pico/picó*)
  - The b/v pair of *letras tramposas* (e.g., iba, not iva; caminaba, not caminava).
- Students practice reading their own stories to help build fluency, with a special emphasis on prosody.
- Students do some read aloud during guided reading to further practice skills learned in reading their own stories.

Formative assessment
Checklist that records student performance on word study and fluency activities

Summative assessment

- Students will write a fictional narrative that includes a variety of literacy elements.
- Students will identify and describe literary elements (point of view, first-person narrative, and personification) in their own writing, in the writing of other students, and in stories read in class.

The Bridge: Strengthening Bridges between Languages
Language of instruction: Spanish and English

- Students collaboratively choose key words from unit of study, in Spanish.
- TPR: Students collaboratively create movements to associate with each key word.
- Students and teacher move into English, and associate each movement with the word in English. Students provide the English equivalents that they know, and teacher provides those terms students do not know in English.

Formative assessment
Checklist that records student participation in English and student metalinguistic skills

Metalinguistic focus

- Cognates
- The *-ción/-tion* pattern

Extension Activity
Language of instruction: ___English___ ___(the other language)___

Students study the same literary elements but within English books, although NOT the same books or stories as read in Spanish.

Formative assessment
Checklist and rubric that respect the resources of the two-language learner

CHAPTER 5

Language Resources, Linguistic Creativity, and Cultural Funds of Knowledge

KEY POINTS

- Bilingual learners develop and use oral language differently than monolingual learners. Teachers must understand these differences so that they develop appropriate expectations for their students.

- One of the major characteristics of Spanish in the United States is its relationship with English.

- Bilingual learners use variations of Spanish that come from different Spanish-speaking countries.

- Background knowledge is crucial for learning and plays a key role in literacy development. Teachers are most successful when they build on what students already know and can do.

The Importance of Oral Language

Human beings develop oral language to communicate with each other, and from oral language launch into learning how to read and write (Gough and Tumner, 1986). Thus, oral language development is the crucial first step in developing literacy skills. The development of oral language leads to expanding vocabulary, language skills, background knowledge, and phonological awareness. Young children learn that print is simply a representation of what they can say, that writing represents the spoken language (Burns, Griffen, and Snow, 1999). To ensure success and avoid inappropriate assumptions about how bilingual students use their languages for learning, programs for teaching reading and writing must acknowledge the fundamental link between oral language and literacy.

Also to ensure success, teachers should learn as much as they can about their students' language development, their use of languages, and their experiences. They can then construct lessons and activities that build on how their students use language and on what they have learned in their families and communities. This chapter offers strategies teachers can use to obtain this information.

Oral Language Development of Bilingual Learners

Like monolingual learners, bilingual learners develop vocabulary, language skills, and phonological awareness, but they do so in two languages. To understand the development of bilingual learners, we must respond to these key questions:

- How do children become bilingual?
- What does it mean to be bilingual?
- What does bilingual oral language look like?
- How is bilingual oral language different from the oral language developed by monolingual learners?
- What expectations are appropriate for bilingual learners?
- How do we build on bilingual learners' oral language to develop biliteracy?

People become bilingual and exhibit bilingualism in different ways. Bloomfield (1933) narrowly defines a bilingual as an individual who has full fluency in two languages. Grosjean (1982) states that bilinguals are people who can function in each language according to given needs. We prefer Grosjean's definition of bilingualism because it is flexible enough to include the many variations of bilingualism we have encountered in our students. We consider all of our students to be bilingual because they are developing skills in all four language domains—listening, speaking, reading, and writing—and they are doing so in two languages.

All five of the students profiled in Chapter 2, Carmen, Paulo, Antonio, Hannah, and Lucía, are bilingual learners and, as such, have oral language resources in English and Spanish. But they are developing these bilingual resources in different ways. Understanding how each student develops oral language in two languages helps us establish appropriate expectations that translate into optimal pedagogy. We must be aware of the different ways children develop their two languages orally so that we do not mistake normal use of language for a sign of confusion or other problems. Though there are some parallels between the oral language development of monolinguals and bilinguals, the differences are striking, and it is imperative that we understand them so that we do not mistakenly compare the oral language use of bilinguals to that of monolinguals.

SIMULTANEOUS BILINGUAL DEVELOPMENT

Paulo and Lucía are simultaneous bilinguals, and Antonio, Carmen, and Hannah are sequential bilinguals. A simultaneous bilingual may have one parent or family member who interacts with the child in one language and another parent or family member who interacts with the child in the other language. In some families, as in Paulo's and Lucía's, the parents speak Spanish to each other and to their children, but the children, who are exposed to English outside of the home, speak English among themselves. Bilingual learners like Paulo and Lucía incorporate all the languages they are exposed to into their oral language.

Simultaneous bilinguals go through the same stages of development as monolinguals (Genesee, 2010). An important difference, however, is that from their earliest development, simultaneous bilinguals share their vocabulary knowledge between their two languages. At age 1, most children say their first words; at age 2, most children speak in two-word phrases; and by age 3, most children speak in full sentences.

One of the differences between the monolingual and the bilingual is in vocabulary. Whereas the monolingual learner will use only English words, the simultaneous bilingual learner, from the beginning, will use both languages, often mixing them in one phrase or sentence. A 2-year-old, for example, might say, "*mi pelota*" ("my ball") or "my *abuela*" ("my grandmother"); a 3-year-old might say, "*No quiero ir al* supermarket" ("I do not want to go to the supermarket"). Educators who do not understand how simultaneous bilingual learners develop language will misunderstand the mixing of languages and, comparing a student like Paulo, who might say, "*Me gustan los* video games" ("I like video games") to a monolingual speaker, conclude that he does not speak either of his two languages well (Paradis and Genesee, 1996).

Context plays an important role in shaping vocabulary development. Simultaneous bilinguals like Paulo may, for example, have a more extensive vocabulary in Spanish about such topics as religion, family, and soccer, and a more extensive vocabulary in English about television programs and playing games with siblings. They may eventually acquire more proficiency in one language than the other, and the dominance of one language over the other may change with increased exposure to one language (Espinosa, 2007; Genesee, 2008, 2010). Despite such changes, however, Paulo will continue to have linguistic resources in both his languages and access them in the classroom. We misread Paulo when we look for a dominant language and ignore the other language in instruction and assessment.

SEQUENTIAL BILINGUAL DEVELOPMENT

Carmen, who was born in Mexico and went to school through kindergarten in Mexico, is a typical sequential learner. As the research on children like her shows, when she entered 1st grade in the United States she knew and understood the structure of one language, Spanish, and needed to learn the specific features, grammar, vocabulary, and syntax of a new language, English (Espinosa, 2007). Most sequential bilinguals add the second language after age 3 and before age 7 (Tabors, 1997). Sequential bilinguals who acquire their second language after about age 7 but before adulthood are identified as "late bilinguals" (Baker and Prys Jones, 2006). When sequential bilinguals learn a second language, they go through four predicable stages, whether, like Hannah, they are English speakers acquiring Spanish or, like Antonio, they are Spanish speakers acquiring English. The length of each stage varies by child. In the first stage, sequential bilinguals will use their home language even when others do not understand or when the context requires the use of the second language (Espinosa, 2007). Then, realizing that their home language does not work, they move into the next stage, a nonverbal period during which they speak rarely or use nonverbal means to communicate. They are developing receptive language, and they demonstrate their understanding through actions and other means that do not require language. Language assessments at this stage may result in misleading information that underestimates their true language capacity. Carmen, for example, might seem to have no ability in English, though she is developing her receptive language in English and has not yet had a chance to develop her expressive language.

In the third stage, students begin using telegraphic and formulaic speech, characterized by the use of simple words or phrases to express whole thoughts. Someone like Carmen in an English context might say, "Me go bathroom." During this stage young children use phrases they have heard from others, sometimes not completely understanding the whole meaning of the words they use. During the fourth and final stage, productive language emerges. Students experiment with the new language as they learn its rules and structure. They create their own phrases and thoughts, which at first are basic grammatical patterns but which gradually become more controlled and reflective of the second language (Espinosa, 2007).

Sequential bilingual learners may know some words in one language and not the other, especially if they speak one language at home and the other at school. But the number of words young sequential learners, like young simultaneous learners, know in their two languages combined is comparable to the number and range of words young monolingual learners know (Espinosa, 2007). Teachers, therefore, must consider all languages when assessing and working with students like Carmen to understand the full range of their strengths and abilities.

Sample sentences by our five learners reveal the different ways they have been exposed to two languages and the different ways they have developed oral language. Carmen and Antonio, using Spanish syntax with English vocabulary, might say, "I have five years." Hannah, using English syntax with Spanish vocabulary, might say, "*Voy a mi tío Mario's casa.*" Paulo might say, "*Voy a una* party *con mi* broder." He may have mixed the two languages because he is surrounded by people who mix them in conversation or because he does not know the Spanish equivalent of "party" or 'brother," since these terms are always said in English in his home. Lucía, who understands Spanish but uses it sparingly, might say, "I left my shoes in the *sala*" because the living room she is familiar with is in her home, where it is consistently referred to in Spanish.

Though the paths by which students developed their oral language proficiency become indistinguishable once they are biliterate, teachers who instruct students must be aware of the multiple pathways for becoming bilingual so that their expectations are appropriate. Appropriate expectations also depend on teachers knowing the different ways that students use their languages.

Recognizing and Building on Students' Oral Language and Background Knowledge

Recent demographic shifts in the United States have led to an increase in the number of bilingual students who were born in the United States and are now in elementary school. This means that more and more students entering school have been exposed to Spanish and English since infancy. These simultaneous bilinguals are very creative in how they use their two languages orally.

LINGUISTIC CREATIVITY OF BILINGUAL LEARNERS: USING SPANISH AND ENGLISH TOGETHER

One of the major characteristics of Spanish in the United States is its relationship with English. Spanish and English are contact languages that develop side by side and intersect. Thus, Spanish is influenced by English, and English by Spanish (Potowski, 2010; Valdés, 2011), and students learning Spanish in the United States will develop their language differently than students in Spanish-speaking countries. Our students live in bilingual contexts where they continually witness their languages interacting, and this interaction has a major impact on their oral language development.

A common form of using Spanish and English together is code-switching. Contrary to popular belief, code-switching follows grammar and phonological rules and is not the haphazard use of languages. Bilinguals, whether developing as sequential or simultaneous bilingual learners, always have access to languages that may be used separately or together in countless forms. When teachers recognize that their students' code-switching follows predictable patterns, they avoid falling into the trap of viewing them through the deficit paradigm that arises from comparing their oral language to that of monolingual English or Spanish learners.

Poplack (1980) identifies three types of code-switching: tag-switching, inter-sentential switching, and intra-sentential switching. Tag-switching is the insertion of a tag phrase or a word from one language into an utterance that is entirely in the other language, for example, "She missed the bus again, ¿verdad?" Inter-sentential switching occurs at a clause or sentence boundary. In the example, "¡No me gustó, come here and do it again, pero esta vez lo haces bien!" the English phrase falls between two complete Spanish phrases. Intra-sentential switching occurs within a clause or sentence boundary, as in, "She went to buy the salsa verde for the enchiladas" (Goodman, 2007).

Code-switching has always been common among bilinguals, and it has been considered a marker of bilingualism since the 1970s (Grosjean, 1982). Nonetheless, many educators still view code-switching as a problem rather than viewing the use of two languages together as a sophisticated communicative approach that is governed by rules.

Potowski's (2005) research on heritage language speakers helps to explain how and why many bilingual students combine their languages when speaking. She identifies four categories—code-switching, linguistic borrowing, semantic extensions, and calques—that reflect the ways Spanish and English intersect in the United States, and they illustrate the reasons our students use Spanish and English together.

Potowski points out that there are many reasons for the code-switching. When students say, for example, "Tengo el eight," they may know the Spanish word for eight, ocho, but intentionally use the label that is socially acceptable in that context, or they may not know ocho because they learned their numbers in English but not in Spanish. Another example, "Vamos a ir camping," suggests that the speaker does not know the Spanish word for "camping" or assumes his listeners do not. A major use of code-switching is for emphasis, and in some cultural groups code-switching is the norm.

Linguistic borrowing, especially common among younger students, involves creating new words by borrowing between languages, as in "Estoy bleediando" ("I am bleeding"). In this example, the student is speaking Spanish and using the present progressive tense, but because she does not know the Spanish word sangrando, she uses the verb she knows from English, "bleeding," and conjugates it appropriately. As with code-switching, words created through linguistic borrowing reflect the bilingual environment in which students live. Nouns like la troca (the truck) and verbs like puchar (to push), tochar (to touch), and wáchale (watch out), borrow the English word and make it Spanish-like by making the nouns feminine or masculine or by adding the appropriate verb endings and conjugations.

Semantic extension is the use of words in one language that come from the other language but have taken on a new meaning. One example is Vamos a comprar las groserías, which translates as, "We are going to buy the vulgar [or obscene] words." Though groserías sounds like the English word "groceries," it has a very different meaning in Spanish. Students often use words from one language in a sentence that is in the other language. Sometimes the meanings are the same, as in cognates, such as posición–position; sometimes the meanings are very different, though the two words sound like cognates, as in groserías/groceries, sopa (soup)/soap, and, the classic example, embarazada (pregnant)/embarrassed. In some communities, Spanish has been so influenced by English that Spanish words like *groserías* have taken on a second meaning from English.

Potowski's final category, calques (from the French word *calquer*, "to copy"), are linguistic elements copied from one language and used in the other, for example: "*El está corriendo para alcalde*" ("He is running for mayor"); "*Quiero aplicar para éste trabajo*" ("I want to apply for this job"); and "*Siéntense en la carpeta*" ("Sit on the carpet"). In these three examples, the words *corriendo*, *aplicar*, and *carpeta* have taken on the meaning from English as opposed to the monolingual Spanish meaning *corriendo* (running [literally, moving quickly]), *aplicar* (to apply oneself), and *carpeta* (binder).

Examples of how students use their languages together are endless. The linguistic creativity that reflects the oral language used in their communities can be seen also in commercial signs in the community that combine the two languages. In class students often use the language of signs they see in the community, such as, "*Haga sus* taxes *aquí*" ("File your taxes here") and "*Pague sus* bills *aquí*" ("Pay your bills here"), two examples of code-switching through the use of both languages within one statement. The currency exchange sign "*Pague sus* bills *aquí*" uses the English word "bills" because most Spanish-speaking people in the United States, when they are speaking Spanish, use the English word rather than either Spanish word for bills, *facturas* or *cuentas*, because it is the term used in this country. Accepting and bringing attention to the linguistic creativity of bilingual students in the classroom is an important element in teaching for biliteracy, and it should be done with respect and as part of a strategic plan to move students from using informal language to using the formal, academic language needed in school.

To answer the final question posed at the beginning of the chapter, How do we build on bilingual learners' oral language to develop biliteracy? we must first answer a question many teachers ask, What Spanish are we supposed to teach, and how do we deal with the "incorrect" forms of Spanish that our students speak?

VARIETIES OF SPANISH

To Juanito, *guagua* means baby, but to Sheila, it means bus. Juanito's family is from Chile, and Sheila's family is from Puerto Rico. In Guatemala and Spain, *chucho* means dog; in Peru it is a very offensive word; in Mexico City, it is the nickname for Jesús. A turkey is a *guajolote* in México, a *chompipe* in Central America, and a *pavo* in Spain. A young man in Guatemala might refer to himself as a *patojo*, in Chile as a *cabro*, in Mexico as a *muchacho*, and in Spain as a *chico*. Like nouns, grammar can vary dramatically from country to country. In Argentina, where the familiar form of "you," *vos*, is used in a command, a common expression meaning "come look" is "*vení a ver*"; the same expression takes the form *ven a ver* in Puerto Rico. These are just a few examples of how varied and interesting the Spanish language is, and all these words are accepted in the *Real Academia Española*, where their meaning and cultural context are explained.[1] And these are the socially acceptable words—there is a large body of words with meanings that vary greatly from region to region and that can unintentionally offend other Spanish speakers.

Teaching for biliteracy in the United States requires extensive knowledge about how language works and how language reflects roles, regions, and functions. Archaic forms of Spanish remain from the days of the Spanish conquest and include

---

[1] The *Real Academia Española* is the official agency that documents the Spanish used all over the world. Entries are frequently updated and often include new words, reflecting the fact that Spanish continually evolves.

terms such as *ansina*, *pos*, *naiden*, and *truje*, which have evolved into the contemporary Spanish words *así* (like that), *pues* (therefore), *nadie* (nobody), and *traje*" (brought). These archaic forms of Spanish are still used in small villages in Spain and in rural parts of Puerto Rico, Mexico, and other parts of Latin America and still serve a function. Nonetheless, signs still appear in classrooms that say, "*Estas palabras no existen*" ("These words do not exist") heading lists of archaic forms of Spanish; and at times, when students use these words, they are reprimanded and told that they are "incorrect." Similar signs might be found in urban Mexico, where the *palabras del rancho* (words from the rural area) are looked down on because they are seen as reflecting a less formal use of the language. Reprimanding students for their language makes the teacher's job harder, and it demeans the students whose families teach them the language they use. Deciding that some words are acceptable and that others are unacceptable is a no-win strategy. It does not lead to consensus and does not build on what students know and can do.

The positive approach is to incorporate into teaching and programs what students bring with them to school and to address what they need to be academically successful. Acknowledging and accepting students' social language and using it as a stepping-stone to academic language is a more effective strategy. Chapter 6 explains how to implement this strategy.

A teacher of Spanish literacy in the United States can expect to have students who are linguistically creative in their use of Spanish and English, students who speak different varieties of Spanish from different geographical regions, and students who use archaic forms of Spanish. It would be unreasonable to expect this teacher to know all the different forms of Spanish and to have an understanding of sociolinguistics that covers all contexts. But if she accepts that all language that is functional and understood by its speakers is valid language, if she is willing to learn about different varieties of Spanish, and if she draws her students' attention to the similarities and differences between how Spanish and English are used, she will have the tools to build a successful Spanish literacy class.

Some educators have emphasized the use of "standard" versus "nonstandard" Spanish in their classrooms (Potowski, 2005; Valdés, 2011). But the variations in words and grammar and the linguistic creativity found among bilingual students reveal that there is no standard Spanish that must be sought or taught. The inappropriateness of insisting on a standard form of Spanish is clear to anyone who has traveled to many countries where Spanish is spoken or who have conversed with Spanish speakers from different areas. We prefer Potowski's terminology of "formal" and "informal." Our students enter our classrooms with informal language and it is our job to add to that repertoire the formal language required for success in school.

STUDENT BACKGROUND KNOWLEDGE

When there is a match between the students' background knowledge and experiences and the school's curriculum and materials, that is, when students have had exposure at home to the topics and themes studied at school and the language used at home and at school are similar, students are better able to connect their experiences between the two places and achieve academic success. For example, think of a girl who loves animals, whose parents read books to her about animals, and whose grandmother takes her bird watching and talks to her extensively about animals. This child will enter school already knowing some of the academic language she will encounter in the school's curriculum and materials, and she will have developed a strong foundation of knowledge about animals. When she encounters lessons on this topic, she will use all her background knowledge and language as a foundation for new learning.

Getting to know the students is important to teachers in every classroom, monolingual or bilingual, so they can build on what the students know. Diversity exists even within the same cultural and socioeconomic groups. But teachers may encounter even more diversity among bilingual learners than is found among our five student profiles, and many bilingual learners do not experience a match between home and school. It is therefore the teacher's responsibility to build connections between what students already know and what they are learning in school. Mismatches occur either when the teacher assumes background knowledge that her students do not have or when she misses opportunities to tap into their background knowledge. It is always harder to learn something you know nothing about, and it is always easier to learn something you know a little bit about. When students' experiences and language are not incorporated into the learning at school, it is harder for them to learn. Often teachers do not share the same cultural, socioeconomic, or linguistic background as their students. The difference in backgrounds and experiences makes it all the more important for teachers to learn about their students.

STUDENT FUNDS OF KNOWLEDGE

González and Moll (2002) worked with teachers to develop a pedagogical approach that builds on the cultural resources of local communities. They refer to the cultural resources that the teachers learn about in the homes and communities of their students through interviews and study group discussions as "funds of knowledge." This is the knowledge that governs the productive activities of a household.

In interviews with families to identify funds of knowledge, teachers often learn that students and their families are extremely knowledgeable in distinct realms, such as gardening, repairing cars, caring for crops, and making and selling tortillas. Teachers can connect this information to curricular standards. For example, a family that runs a *tortillería* (a business that makes and sells tortillas) out of their home has extensive knowledge about marketing, distribution, mathematics, and decision-making. A teacher who learns about this family business might, for example, start her math lesson using concrete examples from the home-run *tortillería*. Similar examples abound in all of our schools and are available to any teacher who understands that part of teaching includes exploring what students and their families know.

Teachers must be sensitive to the customs and traditions they learn about in family interviews to ensure that they match learning activities with student background knowledge appropriately and avoid a mismatch. A successful match might involve a unit with the big idea, "saving is a practice that involves putting money aside consistently." An extension of that idea might be that community members can provide services to each other that would not be achieved individually. The teacher knows that some of her students' families participate in *La Tanda*, a form of savings that is a tradition among many immigrant groups. Every month all members contribute a set amount of money and about every six months they divide the total among them. The teacher uses *La Tanda* as an example of a savings plan and community collaboration. She invites the parent of one of her students to explain to the class how *La Tanda* works and visually demonstrates the properties of multiplication. Once the concrete example is introduced and the students understand the concept, the teacher connects the example to the math and language arts standards she is teaching, which include the concept of savings in financial institutions.

A mismatch could occur when teaching the curricular understanding "becoming independent and learning how to interact with other families contributes to the social-emotional growth of children" as the big idea for a unit. She might assume that one way children learn about other families and gain independence is by staying overnight at their friends' homes. Before reading a story, she asks her students to talk about the last time they packed a suitcase and spent the night at a friend's house. When few students raise their hands, the teacher wonders why these students do not know anything about overnights. Because she is unaware that the practice of visiting overnight does not match the life experience of the students, she may incorrectly conclude they do not understand or have not experienced opportunities to become independent and establish friendships. An example that focuses on how children develop independence by caring for younger siblings and helping around the home would provide a match between the learning activity and the students' funds of knowledge.

González and Moll (2002) created a process through which high school students and teachers learn about the funds of knowledge of certain school communities using questionnaires and interviews during home visits.[2] Their project is called Puente, and the information the researchers seek covers three topics teachers will find especially useful to learn about. The first topic is family and labor history and often leads to discussion of networks of support and patterns of immigration. Work history provides many clues about the type of skills and knowledge families possess. The second topic is basic household activities, such as hobbies, family businesses, and home improvement projects. The third topic is issues regarding parenting, school experiences in the parents' home country, and language use in the home (how both languages are used). One benefit of the program is that, with several visits, the researchers, who gather the information in a respectful manner, develop a rapport with each family. This kind of information-gathering project is a logical extension of the home language and literacy survey discussed in Chapter 2.

The Puente Project is an example of a funds-of-knowledge approach. This approach is effective because of the assumptions behind it:

1. All people have knowledge that comes from their life experiences.
2. Teachers need to learn about their students' knowledge by observing, by asking questions (not assuming they have the answers), and by building relationships with students and their families.
3. The role of the teacher is to adapt the curriculum and materials to incorporate student experiences and knowledge.

This approach is effective also because students and their families play a significant role in the learning process. Teachers who adapt their materials to their students' funds of knowledge are less likely to create mismatches.

Teachers as Learners: Strategies for Learning about Students

Teachers can learn about their students by making home visits, asking families to complete questionnaires, and observing their students inside and outside the classroom. They can attend community events and celebrations, accept invitations from

---

[2] For a more extensive explanation of funds of knowledge and teachers as practitioners, see the full text of González and Moll, 2002.

students and their families, and network with colleagues who are an integral part of the community. Assigning dialogue journals in which students choose the topics they write about and asking students open questions and listening carefully to their answers about what they do with their families can also be greatly informative.

The two exercises discussed in the next section can help teachers learn more about students' oral language and background knowledge.

ANALYSIS OF STUDENT LINGUISTIC CREATIVITY

The purpose of the first exercise is for teachers to increase their understanding of their students' use of language by observing and analyzing their language inside and outside the classroom. The first step is to gather examples of students' oral language use in a natural setting, for example, by placing a tape recorder in a strategic part of the classroom while students are working collaboratively. The machine can also be set up to record whole-class discussions, though the data will probably yield more information if it captures small group discussions.

The second step is to choose some sample sentences from these recordings or from speech overheard inside or outside the classroom, write them in a chart like the one in Table 5.1, and select the appropriate category to describe how each sample mixes Spanish and English. While it is helpful to choose the appropriate category, it is more important to understand how students use both their languages. For example, if the student sample is "*El me dijo gordo y no me gustó, estaba* hurting my feelings" ("He called me fat, and I didn't like it; he was hurting my feelings"),

---

TABLE 5.1.

Analyzing Oral Language

Complete the chart with sample sentences from taped or overheard speech.

Student name: _____

Sample Sentences	Code-Switching	Linguistic Borrowing	Semantic Extension	Calque

the appropriate category is code-switching. One explanation for why students mix languages as in this example is that many classrooms in the United States have character education programs in English that help students talk about feelings. Thus, while one also might say, "He was hurting my feelings" in Spanish ("*Lastimando mis sentimientos*"), it may be more spontaneous and natural for students to express this idea in English because they are more likely to have learned the terminology in English.

Completing the chart for all students would probably not be feasible because of time constraints. It may be helpful, however, for teachers to select samples periodically from three to five students whose language is sometimes surprising or perplexing. When these three to five charts have been completed, the following questions can be used to analyze their language and assess the teacher's use of language:

1. Why did the student use language this way?
2. What social or linguistic rules is the student following?
3. How should I respond to this type of student language use in the classroom?

And when all samples have been analyzed, these questions can be asked:

1. Have I used linguistic creativity, such as code-switching, in the classroom with my students?
2. What context was I responding to?

Teachers should also consider what impact this analysis and reflection on language use might have on the language they use while teaching bilingual learners and on their practice in general.

TAPPING INTO STUDENT LANGUAGE AND CULTURAL RESOURCES

The purpose of the second, easy, authentic, and informative exercise is to learn about the specific varieties of Spanish students use. The exercise is to send home photographs or other illustrations of upcoming themes and ask students to label them with their families. The labels are likely to yield many different varieties of Spanish. For example, if the upcoming science unit is on light and sound and the activities include using several instruments and tools to demonstrate how sound travels and how it produces energy, include photos of these objects in the assignment. If a kite is included, the captions may come back identifying it as a "*papalote*," a "*cometa*," or a "*barrilete*." All of these words can be added to the *Regionalismos* (Spanish regionalisms) wall, enhancing students' knowledge of and understanding of Spanish across different regions.

Oral Language, Background Knowledge, and the Three Premises

Because, according to the first premise, Spanish in the United States is a minority language within a majority culture, when we teach for biliteracy, we tend to analyze, interpret, and evaluate the performance and growth of our students through a monolingual English lens. Students also respond to the reality of this premise. Those who know Spanish are often reluctant to use it in school, where English predominates. When Spanish literacy teachers strive to incorporate oral language activities in the classroom, students who feel more fluent or are more proficient in Spanish often choose to speak in English. Even very young children recognize that English is the language of power in this country and therefore prefer to speak in English. A student's choice of language is not necessarily a reflection of language development in that area. In multilingual settings, it is therefore imperative that teachers value and build on both Spanish and English. Pointing out to students the benefits of being bilingual and using what they know in both of their languages will help to address the reality of this first premise.

As educators, we must continue to develop our professional understanding of how bilinguals use language and the varieties of Spanish that they use, and we must build on this knowledge in the classroom. Instructional programs or lessons designed for English that have been translated into Spanish do not reflect the linguistic richness students bring to the classroom. We also need to understand how background knowledge and experiences form our bilingual learners so that we can match our curriculum to their linguistic and cultural knowledge.

ACTIVITIES FOR REFLECTION AND ACTION

1. This chapter describes the different ways two-language learners in the United States use Spanish and English together. Collect examples of the linguistic creativity of your students and then do the following:
   - Categorize them (code-switching, linguistic borrowings, semantic extensions, calques, archaic expressions, regionalisms)
   - Give the context and an explanation from a multilingual perspective for all these utterances.

2. Share with other stakeholders in your school community how these utterances reflect bilingualism and reflect the characteristics of Spanish in the United States. Discuss how the students' linguistic creativity reflects your school community's sociopolitical context.

3. Through home visits and informal exchanges with parents, collect examples of the funds of knowledge your students have. Then list their funds of knowledge and match them to content-area instruction.

4. Consider the units of study you are currently teaching. Plan ways you can build on your students' funds of knowledge in your instruction.

CHAPTER 6

Building Background Knowledge

KEY POINTS

- Effective biliteracy instruction begins with the establishment of a comprehensible context.

- Strategies that build on student language and experiences also develop background knowledge and academic oral language.

- While the development of background knowledge and academic oral language is the focus of the first part of literacy development in the biliteracy unit framework, academic oral language must be supported throughout the unit.

Student Funds of Knowledge and Linguistic Creativity in the Classroom

The following exchange demonstrates why teachers of biliteracy need to set aside time to develop background knowledge and academic vocabulary before initiating literacy activities in a new unit.[1]

Original Spanish

> **Maestra**: *Niños, ¿recuerdan el libro que leímos ayer? En el libro, Manuel se enojó mucho con Carlos. ¿Qué le hizo Carlos a Manuel para que se enojara tanto?*
>
> **Lucía:** *Maestra, ¡yo sé!*
>
> **Maestra:** *¿Sí, Lucía?*
>
> **Lucía:** *Manuel se enojó con Carlos porque pensó que Carlos lo puchó muy duro, pero actualmente se le cayó encima por accidente.*

English Translation

> **Teacher**: Children, remember the book we read yesterday? In the book, Manuel becomes angry with Carlos. Why does Manuel become angry with Carlos?
>
> **Lucía:** Teacher, I know!
>
> **Teacher**: Yes, Lucía?
>
> **Lucía:** Manuel became angry with Carlos because he thought Carlos pushed him (*puchó*—an English verb conjugated as a Spanish verb) but actually (*actualmente*) he fell on him accidentally.

---

[1]This exchange is not a transcript, though it is based on real classroom interactions. It is offered for illustrative purposes only.

As discussed in Chapter 5, students bring their background knowledge and the language of their homes and communities into the classroom. They use this social, informal, and regional language along with their previous experiences in effective ways to make sense of what they are studying in the classroom and the world around them. In the dialogue, Lucía uses her background knowledge and experiences to understand the actions and motivations of the characters in a book her 6th grade class read. Her answer is correct. In the book, Carlos did fall on Manuel, and Manuel did interpret the fall as a push. Lucía clearly understands that an accidental fall can be interpreted as an intentional push. She comprehends what she read, and she communicates her understanding effectively by using a complete sentence with the verbs conjugated correctly for the simple past in the third-person singular. But she uses informal language to engage in oral discourse about an academic subject, demonstrating her comprehension and her understanding of Spanish grammar and syntax in the language of her community—the language in which she is most comfortable.

Despite all that Lucía does well, however, she demonstrates that she needs instruction in formal Spanish. *Puchar* is not recognized by the *Real Academia Española*. Lucía's use of the word is an example of linguistic creativity, specifically, linguistic borrowing. Also, the word is a stigmatized language form. That is, it tends to be viewed among some Spanish speakers as reflective of a lack of formal education or a lack of proficiency in Spanish. In addition, Lucía, like many other two-language learners, has used "*actualmente*" to mean "actually." Lucía is using a semantic extension that reflects how her community uses Spanish. As teachers of biliteracy in the United States, part of our responsibility is to teach students about the language they are using. While *puchar* and *actualmente* serve the purpose of language—to communicate information—these words and the way Lucía uses them have sociopolitical connotations that students of Spanish literacy in the United States need to understand. *Puchar* may be appropriate within Lucía's local community, but another word, *empujar*, is the term used in more formal situations. Lucía and her peers may use *actualmente* in the way she used it in the dialogue, but she will not find it used like this in Spanish textbooks or novels. When she finds this word in a Spanish text, it will mean "currently."

Teachers need to have strategies for responding to the kind of informal language Lucía uses, and they need to plan and implement prereading and prewriting activities that focus on developing background knowledge and formal, academic language.

Implementing the Biliteracy Unit Framework

This chapter and the four that follow explain how the components of the biliteracy unit framework fit together to support effective biliteracy instruction. Each chapter, like the parts of the biliteracy unit framework, builds on the one before it. The complete, multiphase biliteracy unit framework is explained in Chapter 4. The sample units that appear in Chapter 4 (3rd grade) and on the Web site (1st grade, 4th grade, and high school) are based on the following themes, which illustrate the integration of language, literacy, and content: 1st grade: The family; 3rd grade: Animal adaptations; 4th grade: Regions of the United States; High school: Folk tales.

This chapter focuses on the development of background knowledge and formal language. Here we present strategies to build the background knowledge and academic oral language necessary for reading, writing, and developing other literacy-related skills in Spanish. Oral language is the first element in the biliteracy unit framework because it is the foundation for literacy.

Teachers and administrators are often surprised to discover that students of literacy in Spanish in the United States do not know key words or concepts in Spanish and that they need prereading and prewriting activities in Spanish to understand and produce the formal language expected. These educators believe that if a student speaks Spanish, he or she behaves like a monolingual Spanish speaker living, for example, in Honduras or Spain. They understand how to teach students like Carmen and Antonio but find teaching students like Paulo and Lucía challenging and assume that, because they may not produce formal Spanish, they will not benefit from literacy instruction in Spanish. As our student profiles demonstrate, however, students of Spanish literacy in the United States enter the classroom with a wide range of academic and linguistic resources in Spanish and English and bilingual learners are qualitatively different from monolingual learners in Honduras or Spain. We teach units that introduce academic oral language precisely because students of Spanish literacy like Paulo and Lucía, and even Hannah, do not know key words in Spanish. It is the job of Spanish and English literacy teachers in the United States to teach the range of language registers and genres, including formal language.

Strategies That Support the Development of Background Knowledge and Formal Language

Where possible, teachers should adapt the curriculum to build on the background knowledge and experiences the students bring with them to the classroom. For example, if students are required to study immigration, it is more effective to begin the unit by focusing on the challenges immigrants face today because these challenges are likely to be part of students' personal experiences or those of their parents. The unit can then move on to the less familiar topic of the challenges faced by immigrants in the early twentieth century. The literacy skills of listening, speaking, reading, and writing are learned and practiced within this comprehensible context.

However, simply beginning with a concept within the students' background experiences is not enough. It is also important to begin any unit with a concrete introduction to the topic, because no single concept or focus of study ever matches the background knowledge and experiences of every student and because the concrete, interactive activity provides the context for moving students from social language to more formal language.

Many teachers' guides recommend beginning a lesson or a unit with an informal class discussion. But in the absence of a concrete experience and the key vocabulary to discuss the concepts of the unit, some students are effectively excluded from this discussion. Beginning a unit with an informal discussion, a highly abstract, decontextualized activity, usually involves a great deal of teacher talk and much less student talk. Only those students who have the appropriate background experience and vocabulary can contribute. The same holds true for beginning the unit with any kind of brainstorming activity that asks children to contribute what they know about a concept. To ensure that all students can participate in all parts of the unit, teachers should begin the unit with an activity that provides all students with the background experiences and academic oral language and vocabulary they need to discuss, read, and write about the key concepts. Once a concrete, interactive activity is conducted, the teacher can move to a more traditional brainstorming activity.

Many of the strategies described in the following sections will be familiar to those who have a background in teaching ESL. These ESL strategies, which focus on teaching academic content and language in highly comprehensible ways, call for the same kinds of supports we recommend for teaching biliteracy in the United States. While each strategy is unique and may lend itself more to one topic or content area than another, all of the strategies can be adapted for use in grades pre-kindergarten through high school, and even with adult learners. It is up to the teacher to decide which strategy best matches the content she wants to teach and best meets the needs of her students.

TOTAL PHYSICAL RESPONSE AND ADAPTED READERS' THEATER

Total physical response (TPR) was developed by James J. Asher (2000) for ESL and foreign language instruction. We describe a slightly modified form of the strategy here and add to it the use of pictures, sentence prompts, and realia (real, concrete objects). TPR is a favorite strategy among ESL teachers because it can be used to introduce many academic concepts concretely and comprehensibly, and it requires little in the way of productive language (speaking or writing) by the students. In our modified version of TPR, the teacher models academic oral language accompanied by a visual or concrete support. Each key vocabulary word or concept is represented by a gesture or pantomime, allowing students to associate new information with a picture or real object and an action.

In the sample unit for 4th grade on regions of the United States, for example, the teacher begins the unit of study with TPR, associating actions with pictures to introduce key vocabulary drawn from the big idea for this unit. As she presents each picture, she says the word and mimes an action. After the first few words, she asks the students to join in by doing the actions with her but not yet repeating the words. Slowly she increases the activity by adding more actions and more words until actions have been associated with all the words and images. Students then move from the teacher-led activity to a collaborative small-group activity in which they continue to practice the words and accompanying actions. In these small groups, one student may volunteer or be chosen by the teacher to lead the TPR activity as modeled by the teacher. Students take turns being the leader in these small groups.

Adapted readers' theater (ART) is similar to TPR but minimizes the emphasis TPR places on associating a specific vocabulary word or phrase with a specific movement. In traditional readers' theater, the students read a text and act it out; in ART, the teacher summarizes or paraphrases a text as she and the students act it out. Through the teacher's narration and the interaction and movement of the students, the concepts and vocabulary are previewed.

TPR and ART are versatile strategies that can be used to introduce topics ranging from the different properties of solids and liquids to the procedure for simplifying fractions.

CONCEPT ATTAINMENT

In concept attainment, based on the work of Bruner, Goodnow, and Austin (1956), students are provided with a series of appropriate and inappropriate examples of a concept. By analyzing these appropriate and inappropriate examples, students are able to formulate a definition or a description of the concept, even if they are unable to name it using specific formal language. The teacher then provides the formal language. For younger students or for certain concepts, the teacher may choose to provide only appropriate examples. Concept attainment prepares students in the sample 3rd grade unit of study on animal adaptations to read and write about crayfish. As the discussion of the unit in Chapter 4 illustrates, students may not know the word *langostino* or ever have heard of a crayfish, but they are able to describe an animal that has a hard shell, that lives in water but has lungs, and that has a tail and claws. They learn the characteristics of a crayfish along with the key vocabulary to describe that animal and develop an understanding of the animal they are about to study.

FISHBOWL

The fishbowl strategy involves selecting a group of students to model an activity in the center of the class while the other students gather around and observe their actions, as if they were fish in a bowl. The teacher then orally directs the "fish" through the activity so that they model the formal language she wants the students to use when they work in pairs or small groups. The "fish," along with the teacher, walk around the room to help students with the activity.

One benefit of the fishbowl is that it teaches the students how to carry out a cooperative learning or center activity in an explicit way with a minimum of explanation from the teacher. It also allows the teacher to take advantage of the attention-seeking behaviors of some students by channeling their need for attention in a positive way (letting them become the teacher's helpers). Teachers will want to be strategic in choosing the students to be the "fish," recognizing that students who dislike being the center of attention and shy away from speaking in front of a large group of their peers will do much better in the low-stress setting provided by TPR.

The sample units for 1st grade, 4th grade, and high school further describe how the fishbowl might be used.

FIELD TRIP, EXPERIMENT, AND MOVIE

Three interactive and concrete activities, field trips, experiments, and movies, which are always fun, are usually left for the end of a unit, though they can be especially effective and create a highly comprehensible context when they are used to introduce a unit. As an introductory activity, for example, a field trip gives the teacher the opportunity to point out important elements of the concepts or central theme and introduce formal vocabulary while students see and interact with the realia. Similarly, participating in an experiment from a science unit first rather than last gives all students background experience and the appropriate formal vocabulary in a real-life situation.

Showing a movie or video also provides background experience at the beginning of a unit. Some teachers balk at the idea of showing a movie first, especially if it is a movie adaptation of a novel that the students are about to read, because they feel that watching the movie will interfere with teaching and assessing reading comprehension. Our suggestion is initially to show only part of a movie, with the sound off, if it is an adaptation of a novel the students will read. This approach is especially useful for teaching Spanish literacy in the United States because teachers often do not have access to videos in Spanish. An added benefit to showing the movie with the sound off is that the teacher can focus on specific concepts and academic vocabulary words without overwhelming the students with the entire audio portion of the movie.

WORD SORT AND SENTENCE PROMPTS

The word sort is a strategy in which pairs of students are asked to categorize words, pictures, or realia into predetermined categories (a closed word sort) or into categories of their own choosing (an open word sort), or they are directed to create a narrative using keys words and phrases. The word sort, though a hands-on activity, is abstract and therefore more appropriate as an introductory activity for older students who have some established literacy skills. With younger students, the word sort can be adapted by using pictures or realia rather than words.

As a prereading activity, the word sort allows the teacher to introduce and assess students' understanding of key academic vocabulary and background knowledge through a low-stress and enjoyable exercise. Working in pairs, students are asked to categorize a set of words. Because this is a prereading activity, the teacher has no expectation that the students will categorize all the words "correctly" or in a way that reflects the content to be taught. If the students are involved in an open word sort, they can categorize the words any way they would like, as long as they can explain their categorizations. In a closed word sort, the categories the teacher provides must be comprehensible to the students.

In the 4th grade unit on regions of the United States, student partnerships sort the key vocabulary terms, which are introduced previously through TPR, into four categories: *la topografía* (topography), *el clima* (climate), *los recursos naturales* (natural resources), and *los habitantes* (inhabitants). This is a closed word sort. The teacher provides and models some sentence prompts, and she may decide to use the fishbowl strategy to emphasize the language and behavior expected during the word sort activity. For example,

- *Creo que . . . pertenece al grupo . . . porque. . . .* (I believe that . . . belongs to the . . . group because. . . .)
- *¿Qué opinas tú?* (What do you think?)
- *Estoy de acuerdo.* (I agree.)
- *No estoy de acuerdo porque. . . .* (I disagree because. . . .)

When students have sorted the words into categories, the teacher asks partnerships to explain the reasons for their choices and to clarify any misunderstandings about the meanings of the category headings. For example, if it becomes clear that students do not understand the word *topografía* because they placed a random assortment of words in this category, the teacher reviews the movements and illustrations used to introduce that term during the TPR and guides the students through a revision of their categories.

In the high school unit on folk tales, students are asked to sort words in order to create a narrative. This use of a word sort can be adapted to other grade levels as well.

OTHER STRATEGIES FOR DEVELOPING BACKGROUND KNOWLEDGE AND ACADEMIC ORAL LANGUAGE

The strategies described in the preceding sections are only a sampling of strategies that can be used to develop background knowledge and academic oral language in the first part of the biliteracy unit framework. Strategies that are appropriate for the first part of the biliteracy unit framework are highly comprehensible and concrete; they also do the following:

- Promote student-student interaction
- Encourage active participation of students
- Structure the oral interaction between and among students
- Provide students with a structure in which to experience new concepts and practice new academic vocabulary in Spanish
- Prepare students for literacy activities
- Allow all students (Carmen, Paulo, Antonio, Lucía, Hannah, and others) to participate
- Respect the language the students bring into the classroom
- Model and teach formal vocabulary
- Reduce teacher talk and increase student talk and student movement

Strategies for the Continued Support of Academic Language in the Classroom

Even when teachers implement strategies such as TPR and fishbowl, students will often continue to use social or informal language in the classroom rather than practicing the formal vocabulary previewed in the concrete activity. Moreover, the teacher might not be able to address all the formal language students need before they participate in the literacy activities, or a student may want to discuss a concept the teacher did not preview. For these and other reasons, teachers will need to have strategies that support the use of formal vocabulary throughout the unit, not just in the first part. The following three groups of strategies support the use of formal or academic Spanish throughout the unit:

1. Model and redirect
2. Anchor charts comparing formal and informal language
3. Contrastive analysis of language

These strategies are important in the teaching of biliteracy in the United States because students of biliteracy will use all their linguistic resources in English and Spanish when they are learning literacy and concepts. To repeat a point made in Chapter 1, students who recognize the relationship between their languages reach higher levels of language proficiency in their languages and have the potential for higher academic achievement than those students who see their languages as separate and unrelated. Whether students of biliteracy see this connection, however, is often left to chance. Instead, a focus on metalinguistic awareness should be explicitly incorporated into classroom instruction. While the purpose of the Bridge is to teach about the connections between English and Spanish, throughout units designed for teaching for biliteracy in the United States, the teacher should continually be looking for ways to help students develop metalinguistic awareness through contrastive analysis.

The following three sections give brief examples of the support strategies. In each, the teacher responds to the need to address formal language use, but she also returns to the focus of the unit. Teachers charged with teaching biliteracy in the United States continually integrate and balance the teaching of language and content.

MODEL AND REDIRECT

- The teacher accepts all forms of language use, including social, regional, and informal forms of Spanish.
- The teacher models the target formal language and redirects the student to use it.
- Redirection is carried out most effectively with a support such as a sentence prompt, word bank, or graphic image (for very young students who are still learning to read).

Benefit

Modeling and redirecting can be done quickly, with little interruption to the flow of the lesson or unit.

Challenges

- Students may repeat the key language but not understand why they are being asked to use it.
- Other students may hesitate to participate in discussions or oral activities if they fear being asked to repeat new or unfamiliar language.

Example

Lucía: *Manuel se enojó con Carlos porque pensó que Carlos lo puchó muy duro, pero actualmente se le cayó encima por accidente.*

Maestra: *Sí, es cierto, Manuel malinterpretó las acciones de Carlos. Lucía, di por favor: Manuel se enojó con Carlos porque pensó que Carlos lo empujó muy duro, pero en realidad se le cayó encima por accidente.*

FORMAL AND INFORMAL LANGUAGE ANCHOR CHARTS

- The charts are initiated by the teacher and are added to and maintained by the students.
- The charts illustrate how words can be categorized according to their most appropriate use: in formal or informal situations.

Benefits

- Increases student understanding of how and why certain words or terms are used in specific situations
- Provides a permanent record of formal and informal examples to build on and use with future units

Challenge

Creating anchor charts can take a long time, thus interrupting the flow of the lesson or unit.

Example

Lucía: *Manuel se enojó con Carlos porque pensó que Carlos lo puchó muy duro, pero actualmente se le cayó encima por accidente.*

Maestra: *Sí, es cierto, Manuel malinterpretó las acciones de Carlos. ¿Lucía, me puedes hablar de las palabras informales que acabas de usar?*

Lucía: *Oh, dije "puchó" en vez de "empujó."*

Maestra: *Sí. Por favor Lucía, pon "puchó" en la tabla de palabras informales, y después escribe la palabra formal en la otra tabla.*

CONTRASTIVE ANALYSIS OF LANGUAGE

The teacher leads students through an explicit analysis of language use, including the following:

- Regional uses of language
- Archaic forms of Spanish
- Cognates
- Syntax
- Cross-linguistic influences
- Different linguistic registers

Benefits

- Provides students with a deeper understanding of how their languages are connected
- Promotes active use of all linguistic resources by students
- Provides students with the language and strategies to talk about and understand their own language use

Challenges

- Can take a long time, thus interrupting the flow of the lesson or unit
- Can be cognitively challenging for very young learners

Example

Lucía: *Manuel se enojó con Carlos porque pensó que Carlos lo puchó muy duro, pero actualmente se le cayó encima por accidente.*

Maestra: *Cuando se usa de manera formal, la palabra "actualmente" quiere decir "ahora mismo." Tenemos otro ejemplo en nuestra tabla de un cognado que, cuando se usa de manera formal, no es un cognado. ¿Cuál es?*

Antonio: *Librería como "library." En México, se dice "biblioteca."*

Maestra: *Muy bien. Y en los libros, casi siempre cuando leemos librería, el autor se refiere a una tienda donde se compra libros o papelería. ¿Por qué aquí se usa "librería" para decir "library" mientras en México se usa "biblioteca"?*

Building Background Knowledge and Academic Oral Language and the Three Premises

The use of highly concrete, comprehensible activities in Spanish to initiate a unit reflects the three premises. Beginning the unit in Spanish helps to raise the status of Spanish. Employing strategies to move to more formal or academic expression of the relevant concepts and vocabulary encourages students to draw on all their academic and linguistic resources and in doing so respects their background knowledge. These strategies also reflect the distinct linguistic and cultural rules of the Spanish language.

ACTIVITIES FOR REFLECTION AND ACTION

1. This chapter began with a vignette that typifies the linguistic creativity two-language learners bring to the classroom and went on to outline how to build on and expand this linguistic repertoire. How did you react to Lucía's response to the teacher when you first read the vignette? How, if at all, did your opinion change as you read through the chapter? Strategize answers to a response like Lucía's in your own classroom that respect and build upon the languages in the students' linguistic repertoire.

2. Think of a unit you are about to teach. Choose one of the interactive, concrete strategies described in this chapter and use it to introduce the formal language and to build background knowledge for the unit of instruction. Using the following questions, reflect on your use of the strategy:
   - What went well? Why?
   - What surprised you about your own teaching?
   - What surprised you about student learning?
   - What improvements or changes would you make in the future?

3. Take the examples of student linguistic creativity you collected for the activity in Chapter 5 (or collect new examples). Use these examples to create anchor charts, such as the informal and formal anchor chart described in the chapter, and to explicitly teach metalinguistic skills.
   - Document how students respond when their informal language is posted and studied alongside more formal language.
   - Plan for future mini-lessons focused on teaching additional metalinguistic skills and for contrastive analysis.

CHAPTER 7
Reading Comprehension

KEY POINTS

- Comprehension is the focus and goal of all literacy instruction.

- Skills taught separately from comprehension send the message that comprehension is not an integral part of reading and writing.

- Comprehension is a complex task that requires specific strategies for teaching, learning, and assessing.

The Importance of Comprehension in Literacy Instruction

The goal of all literacy instruction is to instill in students the ability to read and write comprehensibly. This goal seems obvious, but it is worth emphasizing because in many classrooms students are taught to decode text without learning to comprehend. Teaching students to read means teaching students how to comprehend text, and literacy instruction includes reading and writing. But sometimes teachers put so much emphasis on the elements of reading—the discrete word-level skills—that those skills become the goal. Daily lessons on word-level tasks can send the message that the comprehension of text is secondary and optional.

When comprehension becomes secondary, scenes like the following can occur.

The students in Mrs. Martinez's 2nd grade class are working in small groups. The students in one group raise their hands to signal that they have finished reading the assigned text. Mrs. Martinez sits down at the table with them and begins asking the students about the text. She also asks some general comprehension questions. The students have difficulty with the task. Mrs. Martinez says, "*¿Leyeron la historia de verdad? Les dije que no me llamaran hasta que terminaran de leer la historia.*" ("Did you really read the story? I told you not to call me until you finished reading the story.") The students explain that they each took turns reading a paragraph aloud. Then, after a pause, one student speaks up, "*Sí, maestra, todos leemos muy bien. Pero no entendemos nada.*" ("Yes, teacher, we all read very well. But we didn't understand anything.")

THE INSEPARABILITY OF READING COMPREHENSION AND READING SKILLS

Because Spanish is a phonetic language and students can learn quickly to decode, it is easy to focus on the success students are having in decoding without really looking at whether they are comprehending. Students who appear to be proficient at decoding may not really understand what they are reading. Later, when their inability to comprehend what they are reading is revealed, they may be blamed for their deficiency. But the fault is with the literacy instruction that did not consistently emphasize comprehension. Too often, early Spanish literacy instruction, focused on decoding, assumes that students understand what they are reading simply because the students have some language proficiency in Spanish and because the words they are decoding are in Spanish.

The biliteracy unit framework provides a corrective by placing activities that focus on these small pieces of language after reading comprehension and writing activities. While it is imperative that students of Spanish literacy know how to identify vowels and how to use syllables to decode Spanish, with the biliteracy unit framework they develop these skills only after a comprehensible context has been created—through the kind of concrete activities described in Chapter 6—and students have read it, comprehended it, and written about it. These word-level skills are studied in the part of the unit called "Word study and fluency" and are explained in more detail in Chapter 9.

The assumption that all students of Spanish literacy understand what they are reading, as long as it is in Spanish, is unfounded. Carmen and Antonio, for example, enter the Spanish literacy classroom as monolingual Spanish speakers, but the Spanish they speak does not necessarily match the variety of Spanish from which the words they are learning to decode are drawn. The assignment described in the following paragraph provides an example of the separation of decoding and comprehension.

First grade students who have been introduced to the syllables *la*, *le*, *li*, *lo*, and *lu* are given a worksheet that asks them to identify the objects among those pictured that begin with one of the syllables they just learned. The objects pictured on the worksheet are a parrot, a piece of a paper, a hand, a pair of glasses, a magnifying glass, and a wolf (Figure 7.1). At first glance, this may look like a highly comprehensible assignment because the emergent readers are not asked to read new words. They are required only to use their background knowledge and oral vocabulary in Spanish and match it to newly learned print symbols—the syllables. But Carmen may use the word *gafas* or *anteojos* rather than *lentes* for glasses, or she may never have seen a magnifying glass before and therefore not know the word *lupa*. Antonio may use the word *cotorro* or *papagayo* rather than *loro* for parrot. Suddenly, an assignment that seemed straightforward becomes less so when we consider the varieties of Spanish that students bring to the classroom.

The assignment is also ineffective for students like Paulo, Lucía, and Hannah who have grown up in the United States and have linguistic resources in Spanish and English. Paulo, for example, may not know the word *lupa*, but he may know the term "magnifying glass." If students do not have all the Spanish vocabulary or background knowledge to correctly match the syllable with the picture, the assignment becomes one of rote decoding rather than one where students are going from known oral language to literacy. While it is possible to prepare students for this type of assignment by previewing the vocabulary, the objects pictured have no real relationship to one another, and even less of a relationship to the students. They are not the key words needed to study the family, the regions of the United States, or Latin American legends, for example. The only thing the words have in common is that they begin with one of the key syllables. An assignment that becomes no more than a matter of learning random vocabulary words does not make effective use of the teacher's or the students' time.

To avoid having students learn to fragment reading so that it becomes simply saying the words fluently without necessarily comprehending them, teachers must present literacy activities—reading and writing—in the context of comprehensible

Figure 7.1.   Early Spanish literacy assignment: *la, le, li, lo, lu*

text. Unless Carmen, Antonio, Lucía, Hannah, and Paulo have been prepared explicitly for the text through an initial activity that respects the language they bring into the classroom and builds additional vocabulary and background knowledge, they may not be able to understand what they are reading in Spanish. Therefore, they may not be learning that reading means comprehending. Though an initial concrete and highly comprehensible prereading activity prepares students to understand the text, it is not enough. Further strategies that focus on the importance of comprehension during reading and writing are needed.

In this chapter, we outline how to ensure that literacy instruction occurs within the context of comprehensible text and how, therefore, to avoid separating reading skills from comprehension.

THE INTERACTING ELEMENTS OF COMPREHENSION: READER, TEXT, AND CONTEXT

Comprehension is a complex process that involves the successful interaction of three elements: the reader, the text, and the context in which the reading occurs (Duke, 2007; Duke and Pearson, 2002; Pardo, 2004; RAND, 2002). It is imperative that teachers of biliteracy plan for the successful interaction of these three elements in a Spanish literacy unit.

Beginning with the Reader

In planning for comprehension, the teacher begins by understanding the reader and the experiences, background knowledge, and oral language and vocabulary knowledge that he or she brings to the text. The students involved in developing biliteracy in the United States make up a diverse group of learners with a wide range of linguistic abilities across their languages and with a great variety of background experiences. Knowing the students and creating a biliteracy unit that takes advantage of the knowledge they bring to the classroom while introducing them to new ideas and vocabulary is the first step in creating a unit focused on comprehension.

The Text

With an understanding of the reader, the teacher can look for texts that are culturally relevant and interesting. Though some teachers have little control over the texts they use, the strategies described in Chapter 6 that focus on building background knowledge and academic language can prepare students to read books that may not match their funds of knowledge. Students who are prepared for reading through interactive strategies such as TPR, ART, and word sorts can comprehend new and unfamiliar text and therefore read the text more fluently. Still, though students can be prepared for unfamiliar themes or topics through concrete activities in the first part of the unit and then read these texts fluently, it is difficult to prepare students for texts that are inherently uninteresting or that defy comprehension.

This phenomenon is easily illustrated. Highly controlled texts, such as "*El pato pone la piña en el plato del papá*" ("The duck puts the pineapple on his father's plate"), are often used to give students practice with syllables (both simple and complex) beginning with a particular letter, in this instance, "p." A student who is able to read this sentence with fluency clearly demonstrates an ability to decode syllables beginning with "p," but what about comprehension? The text, while grammatically correct, does not make sense. In effect, it defies comprehension. The student is asked to ignore the need to make sense of the text (why would a duck be putting pineapple on his father's plate? do ducks eat pineapple? do they use plates?) simply to perform the discrete task of decoding. In addition, use of this text creates the same challenges as the *la, le, li, lo, lu* worksheet described earlier. Are we even sure our students know all these words? How much experience do children growing up in the Midwest, for example, have with pineapples? Or, how much experience do city dwellers have with ducks? It is clear that a significant amount of background knowledge and (random) vocabulary is required to make any kind of sense of this text. What is even more concerning is that this text was not written to convey a message, to entertain, or to persuade—which reflect the kinds of authors' purposes we ask students to identify—but to provide practice with decoding syllables beginning with "p." When children are asked to read text simply to practice decoding or to increase fluency, we are teaching them that comprehension is optional and we are asking them to practice reading skills on a type of text they will never encounter again.

The goal is that students comprehend text; therefore, they should not be taught that comprehension is optional. We must provide them with text that is rich and interesting enough to be comprehended, and we must prepare them to comprehend the text through concrete, comprehensible activities.

The Context

The sociopolitical or cultural environment in which students live affects their reading comprehension. We increase the ability of students to comprehend text in Spanish when we create learning environments that attach great importance to the act of reading in that language. Because Spanish is a minority language in the United States, literacy instruction in Spanish is sometimes reduced to a focus on letter and word-level skills with little attention given to comprehension, as if it were not warranted by the status of that language. The focus on text comprehension, with the subsequent integration of other literacy skills, elevates the thinking level in the classroom and, in turn, elevates the status of the minority language. To create a context that supports comprehension, we need to create a context in which the status of Spanish is elevated within the school community.

Creating a Classroom That Is Focused on Comprehension

Teachers can create a comprehension-focused classroom by regularly implementing strategies that actively involve students in taking meaning from text and that emphasize comprehension as an intregal part of reading. These strategies, which can be referred to as active reading strategies, help move students and teachers away from an emphasis on word-level tasks to a greater emphasis on text-level activities. These strategies make explicit the active interaction between text, reader, and context. In active reading strategies, students are taught and then given the opportunity to practice strategies that help them actively engage with the text. Active reading strategies can be implemented at any grade level from kindergarten through college and can be used in any content area.

ASSESSING COMPREHENSION

An added benefit of the inclusion of comprehension-focused strategies at this place in the biliteracy unit framework is that they provide ample opportunities for teachers to gather information about their students' comprehension abilities through formative assessment and to use that information to adapt their instruction as necessary. At this phase of the unit, summative assessments and the kinds of assessments that appear at the end of lessons or readings and that serve as final exams are inappropriate.

In the sections that follow, we describe the comprehension-focused strategies that appear in the sample units.

PICTURE WALK, READ ALOUD, TALK TO YOUR PARTNER, AND SENTENCE PROMPTS

Picture walk and read aloud are often used in the early grades, especially with texts that may be too difficult for students to read independently. The addition of talk to your partner and sentence prompts make them active reading strategies focused on comprehension. These four strategies are used in the sample unit for 1st grade.

In the sample unit for 1st grade, the teacher begins this part of the unit with a picture walk. She involves students in practicing the active reading strategy she will use as she reads the book. She tells the students to look at the picture on each page and tell their partner what they see in the picture. In addition, she asks the students to suggest similarities or differences between the family in the book and their own families.

She tells students that she will call on them to tell the class what they observed and that they should make sure to practice with their partner what they are going to say. The teacher gives the students the following sentence prompts: *Noto_____.* (I note _____.); *Veo _____.* (I see _____.); *Observo _____.* (I observe _____.);

Tenemos _____ en común. (We have _____ in common.); *Los dos tenemos_____.* (We both have _____.); *Somos diferentes porque _____.* (We are different because _____.) She then reads the title of the book and models how to use the prompts with the cover picture.

Noto que hay una niña y cuatro adultos. Observo unas flores en un florero. Veo a un señor con anteojos. Tanto la niña como yo tenemos familias grandes. Las dos también tenemos abuelos. Pero, somos diferentes porque mientras que la niña tiene abuelos, yo solo tengo abuelas.

I see a little girl and four adults. I notice some flowers in a vase. I see a man with glasses. Both the girl and I have large families. We both also have grandparents. But, we are different in that while the girl has grandfathers, I only have grandmothers.

Then, using a big book or a document reader, the teacher shows the students the first page of the book. As students raise their hands or begin to shout out what they see, she directs them to use the sentence prompts and to tell their partners, not the class. Here, the teacher's use of sentence prompts rather than questions is deliberate. The sentence prompts in Spanish support the students in the following ways:

- They help the students focus on the specific academic task at hand.
- They emphasize the importance of Spanish, and in that way raise the status of Spanish in the classroom.
- They provide a framework for students to speak, and subsequently write, in complete sentences.
- They provide students an opportunity to use and practice new academic language in a natural, comprehensible context.

The teacher encourages the students to use the sentence prompts and talk with their partners until she has observed that all students have participated. As students interact, the teacher observes and records their oral use of the key vocabulary introduced in the first part of the unit. At this point in the unit, it is important for the teacher to know how much of the Spanish vocabulary, including the sentence prompts, the students are using in their interactions and to note the use of social or regional Spanish and when and where students use English. A clear understanding of student oral language use is crucial for effective Spanish literacy instruction because it allows the teacher to plan units that respect, build on, and expand student linguistic resources.

The teacher continues with this picture walk routine for the whole book. She shows each picture to the class, directing students to talk with their partners using the sentence prompts and then to share their comments with the entire group. During these interactions, students will use a variety of Spanish and English, depending on their own background knowledge and experiences, and the teacher will make note of their language use.

The students are developing bilinguals and therefore will use all of their linguistic resources—in Spanish and in English—to participate in this and other academic activities. The teacher, however, will maintain use of academic Spanish throughout the unit, including when she is giving directions and disciplining students.

The first part of this unit provided students with key vocabulary in Spanish, and the teacher keeps these words prominently displayed in the classroom in a word bank.

As students share their observations, she directs them to use the previewed vocabulary. She provides any new Spanish vocabulary she observes that the students need and adds those words to the word bank.

The read aloud follows the same pattern as the picture walk. After previewing the concepts in the book first through the concrete activity and then again through the picture walk, the students are ready to comprehend. The teacher reads each page aloud and then stops and asks each student partnership to complete a sentence that begins with the prompt *Esta página trata de* ———. (This page is about ———.). These comments are not shared with the entire group, but the teacher observes and listens to the partnerships.

LANGUAGE EXPERIENCE APPROACH

The language experience approach (LEA) is a reading and writing strategy in which groups of students are involved in writing about a shared, comprehensible experience. The teacher records student dictation about the experience on chart paper or in some other highly visible manner. In some units LEA may appear in the reading comprehension part of the biliteracy unit framework, in others the writing part. What is key to the successful implementation of LEA is that it be based first on a highly comprehensible experience and that this experience is one that all the students have shared. In the sample units for 3rd grade, 4th grade, and high school, LEA is used in the writing portion of the unit. In the sample unit for 1st grade, LEA is used in the reading comprehension part of the unit. Students are asked to write a summary of the book the teacher read aloud to the students. The teacher uses the summaries to make formative assessments of the students' comprehension of the text and their language use.

Implementing the activities outlined in any unit that follows this framework can take many days or even weeks. With younger learners, who have short attention spans, just the LEA, for example, may take several days.

During the several days it takes to complete the LEA, the teacher can gain valuable information about student levels of comprehension as she listens to students talk with their partners. Each day, she focuses on a limited number of students, creating anecdotal records on those particular students or capturing student progress on a more formal device, such as one of the rubrics in Chapter 8.

FOCUSED READING

In focused reading, students read a variety of texts on the same topic at different readability levels.[1] This strategy exposes them to academic vocabulary from multiple sources. For example, in the 4th grade unit on regions of the United States, each student partnership is assigned to read several texts about one topic within the larger context of the local region: climate, topography, or natural resources. The social studies book provided by the district is one resource for reading about these topics. Students should also be encouraged to read, in Spanish, books from the library and articles from the Internet. Reading from multiple texts about a single topic helps students to clarify and refine their understanding of important concepts and to move to progressively more difficult texts on that same topic.

---

[1] Krashen (2004) describes a similar strategy called "narrow reading."

SAY SOMETHING

In the say something strategy, student partnerships or small groups read a portion of text and then stop and say one of four reactions, supported by a sentence prompt:

- Summary: *Esta página/parte del capítulo trata de* ———. (This page/part of the chapter is about ———.)
- Prediction: *Predigo que* ———. (I predict that ———.); *Creo que* ———. (I think that ———.)
- Question and answer: *¿Qué quiere decir* ———*?* (What does ——— mean?); *¿Qué es* ———*?* (What is ———?); *¿Por qué* ———*?* (Why ———?); *Yo creo que* ———. (I think that ———.)
- Personal or academic connection: *La parte del texto que describe* ——— *me recuerda* ———. (The part of the text that describes ——— reminds me of ———.)

The fishbowl strategy may be a useful way to model the language and behavior expected during paired reading. The teacher asks two student volunteers to model read a portion of their assigned section, stopping and saying something with the sentence prompts. As the students move into partnerships to begin the say something strategy, the teacher circulates, listening to the student–student interactions. These interactions provide the teacher with ample data for formative assessment.

The say something strategy may be adapted and used as say something/write something, which is identical except for the additional task of keeping a literature journal or note-making guide. After each oral interaction, each student is asked to record what he or she said. This strategy, which is used in the 4th grade and high school sample units, emphasizes the natural connection between reading and writing and allows the teacher to monitor the thinking and comprehension of all partnerships, something she or he cannot do if students are only speaking their responses.

Classroom Routines That Enhance Comprehension: Sustained Silent Reading and Readers' Interviews

The list of strategies described in this chapter for enhancing reading comprehension is not exhaustive, and we encourage teachers to investigate and develop their own teaching and learning strategies that emphasize comprehension. Two good resources are Allan (2004), and Harvey and Goudvis (2000).

Sustained silent reading (SSR) refers to a time dedicated to student reading. This practice is referred to by many terms, including drop everything and read (DEAR) and read and relax (R&R). During this time, students are free to choose anything they want to read, including magazines, newspapers, and books on any subject. When teachers can dedicate 15 to 30 minutes a day to SSR and couple this with readers' interviews (one-on-one meetings with individual students), they are providing students with an opportunity to practice comprehension in a low-stress environment that encourages reading for the sake of reading. The research on the benefits of SSR is extensive, as are information and suggestions about how to manage SSR in the classroom (see, e.g., Berglund and Johns, 1983; Garan and DeVoogd, 2008–2009; Hopkins, 1997; Routman, 1994). Readers' interviews allow teachers of biliteracy to model appropriate reading strategies, monitor what students are reading, and encourage students to read books in both languages.

The best way to meet the needs of bilingual learners during SSR in a biliteracy classroom is to offer a wide of range of attractive, interesting, and culturally relevant reading materials in Spanish and English. For the successful implementation of SSR, follow these suggestions:

- Establish a regular time for SSR three to five times a week.
- The first few times SSR is implemented, refer to it as reading for pleasure and explain the following:
  - How to choose a book
  - How to read quietly and without talking to anyone
  - How to ignore interruptions by others in the room
- For students with little experience reading silently for a sustained time, allow five minutes for a session of SSR, so they can be successful from the beginning.
- As students become more comfortable with the routine of SSR, increase the sessions to between 15 and 30 minutes a day, depending on the age of the students and the time available in the daily schedule.

Once SSR has become routine, begin the readers' interviews. Start by developing a system to monitor the books each student is reading, the language or languages the texts are in, and students' comprehension of the texts they are reading and their use of comprehension skills. Establish a schedule and routine for holding the interviews with students while the balance of the class engages in silent reading. Box 7.1 offers suggestions for questions teachers might ask during the student interviews.

While free book choice is a key element of SSR, teachers developing biliteracy in the United States should require the students to read books in Spanish and Eng-

BOX 7.1. **Questions for Readers' Interviews**	
Teacher asks open-ended interview questions	• What story/book/article are you reading? • What would you like to tell me about this story/book/article? • What is it about? • What made you choose this story/book/article? • Can you show me the place in the story/book/article where it talks about that? • Please read me a part of the story/book/article that you liked.
Teacher indicates a picture/word/sentence	• What does this picture/word/sentence refer to? • Tell me about what is happening in the story/book/article.
Teacher asks student to read a passage aloud, then asks questions about it	• What did you just read about? • What happens next in the story/book/article?

Note: Readers' interviews should be conducted in the language of the book.

lish during SSR to ensure that students do not read only English books. When we give students the option to read whatever they would like, in whatever language they like, many students will choose to read in English rather than in Spanish, in part because of the messages they receive from the school and society at large about the preference for reading in English. Some schools reinforce the minority status of Spanish through such practices as celebrating a student's choosing an English text as a sign of advancement in reading and judging students who choose to read in Spanish as struggling with reading. Some school libraries offer few books in Spanish and these may be in an inaccessible corner; others offer no books in Spanish.

Another very powerful contextual reason that U.S. students of biliteracy may choose to read in English is that they see the teacher choosing to read in English. Teacher modeling is extremely important in SSR. The teacher models how to choose a book and what it looks like to be actively engaged in reading for enjoyment. If the teacher is doing this modeling with an English text, she is sending the message that English is preferable to Spanish.

Students of biliteracy in the United States are also moved to choose books in English to read during SSR because often the newest, most colorful, and most interesting texts available to them are in English. Schools may on the surface support literacy development in Spanish by providing texts in Spanish, such as the incomprehensible text, *El pato pone la piña en el plato del papá*, described earlier, but these are not necessarily the books the students want to read when given a choice. These practices send the message that reading in English is the only reading that counts.

Because time constraints in most U.S. schools prohibit a teacher from implementing two sessions of SSR a day—one for English reading and one for Spanish reading—both languages are supported during a single daily SSR period. Teachers can reinforce the requirement that students read books in both languages during this single, bilingual SSR period by asking that students sign up for readers' interviews at least twice a month and requiring that one interview be about a book in Spanish and one about a book in English. (The English requirement can be waived for students, often newcomers, who have little proficiency in English until they have gained some proficiency in English.) This practice holds students accountable for reading in both languages and raises the status of Spanish reading to the level of English reading, while still allowing the student the freedom to choose texts in each language.

Reading Comprehension and the Three Premises

Modeling reading for pleasure in Spanish and including a structure in SSR for ensuring that students do not abandon reading in Spanish helps to raise the status of the language.

The strategies offered in this chapter encourage students to use all their linguistic resources and background experiences to interact with and make sense of text. They help students to understand that reading, in any language, means comprehending text. The use of universal strategies gives teachers and students a set of tools to help connect and take advantage of linguistic resources in two languages, especially during SSR and the readers' interviews, where teachers use the same interview structure, ask the same kinds of questions, and refer to and make connections with texts read in both languages. The focus on comprehension emphasizes what is common to Spanish and English literacy and helps students see the connection between their two languages.

ACTIVITIES FOR REFLECTION AND ACTION

1. This chapter emphasizes making sure students understand the text before they do word work or fluency activities with the key terms. How is this practice similar to or different from your current teaching practices?

2. Review the reading series, program, or materials you currently use for literacy instruction. How does the reading series or program suggest preparing students for reading a text? Which of the suggested active reading strategies could be used within your current literacy program?

3. "Say something" has been highlighted in this book as a strategy that integrates oral language and reading and that emphasizes comprehension. Review the description of the say something strategy in this chapter and then try the strategy in your classroom. Using the following questions, reflect on your use of the strategy:
   - What went well? Why?
   - What surprised you about your own teaching?
   - What surprised you about student learning?
   - What improvements or changes would you make in the future?

CHAPTER 8

Writing: A Multilingual Perspective

KEY POINTS

- Effective writing instruction and assessment use a multilingual perspective, recognizing and integrating the variety of cultural and linguistic norms that frame language use and influence written discourse patterns.

- Reading and writing instruction are naturally linked: comprehension and other reading skills can be taught through writing, and writing skills can be taught during reading instruction.

- Writing is a skill to be developed and a tool for enhancing other areas of learning.

Learning to Write in Spanish in the United States: An Integrated Approach

Students developing biliteracy in the United States will draw on all of their linguistic resources when they write. This premise is revealed in a writing sample by a 6th grade student who is responding to the prompt, "*Escribe acerca de tu deporte favorito*" ("Write about your favorite sport").[1]

> *Ayer fuimos a mi tía's casa y comimos carne asada que cocinó mi abuela. Mi abuela es de México y le gusta mucho cocinar y cocina muy rico. Y tomó mucho tiempo en cocinarse la carne so fuimos a hacer "skate boarding" en el "skate park" que queda muy cerca de la casa de mi tía. Fui con mis dos primos Alejandro y David que no saben muy bien andar en el "skate board" porque son muy pekeños y se caen mucho.*

> Yesterday we went to the house of my aunt and we ate barbecue. My grandmother is from Mexico and she likes to cook and she cooks very well. And it took a really long time to cook "entonces" we went skateboarding in the skate park which is close to my aunt's house. I went with my two cousins Alejandro and David who aren't very good at skateboarding because they are little and fall down a lot.

This writer uses English syntax for the possessive (*tía's*) and some English phonics (*pekeño*), and she integrates English words (skate boarding). But she also uses Span-

---

[1]The following paragraph is not an actual sample, though it is based on real classroom samples. It is offered for illustrative purposes only.

ish syntax (*la casa de mi tía*) and demonstrates an understanding of Spanish ortho-graphic accents (*cocinó*). In addition, her discourse pattern (how she organizes and focuses her writing) exemplifies an indirect, circular approach that is reflective of the Spanish norm. She sets the stage and explains that she was at her grandmother's house and gives some details about her grandmother before discussing her favorite sport. This mixture of elements from each of her linguistic resources is natural and expected and underscores the importance of taking a multilingual perspective in teaching writing to bilingual learners.

Effective writing instruction, as demonstrated in the biliteracy unit framework, recognizes the importance of writing throughout the day and throughout the curriculum. The language experience approach (LEA) activity in the sample unit for 3rd grade (in Chapter 4) and the say something/write something activity in the sample unit for 4th grade (on the Web site) are examples of how students can be involved in writing while they are reading. This chapter presents further strategies and routines that help establish writing as a tool used for learning content throughout the day and throughout the curriculum. It focuses on how to teach and assess writing effectively using a multilingual perspective and taking an integrated approach that draws on all the linguistic resources bilingual learners bring to their writing work and that links writing with other student work. Students whose teachers take an integrated approach to writing

- Write every day (or almost every day) in math, science, social studies, and language arts
- Write in a variety of genres, including fiction, personal narrative, expository writing across content areas, and reflection on various texts
- Read and write together
- Use writing as a tool to learn new concepts and as a product for the teacher
- Practice free writing
- Write every day (or almost every day) in both their languages
- Learn about the different discourse patterns in their languages

In this book, we refer to writing as the process of communicating through print to an outside audience, as in a poem or the answer to an essay question, or with oneself, as in math notes or a literature journal. And because the goal of all literacy instruction is the ability to read and write comprehensibly, writing is an integral part of the biliteracy unit framework and of biliteracy development. It is not simply an end product students produce for the teacher to demonstrate their ability to spell or to write complete sentences. Writing helps students to be better readers, and reading helps students to be better writers (Cloud, Genesee, and Hamayan, 2009; Freeman and Freeman, 1997).

From Oral Language to Print

At its earliest stages, writing is oral language in print. Young children begin to write in order to communicate the same things they communicate through oral language (Freeman and Freeman, 1997; Halliday, 1975; Hammink, n.d.). The earliest print produced by emergent writers is naturally reflective of their oral language. Young bilingual learners developing biliteracy in Spanish and English in the United States produce print that is reflective of all their linguistic resources, at both the word and at the discourse levels.

EMERGENT WRITING AT THE WORD LEVEL

Researchers studying how children write their first words or pseudo words—scribbles and drawings—refer to stages for both monolingual English and monolingual Spanish children. Ferreiro and Teberosky (1982) describe five stages of emergent writing in a monolingual Spanish environment; Gentry (2011) and others describe similar stages of emergent writing in a monolingual English context. The differences between the stages of the monolingual Spanish students and the monolingual English students are instructive.

Stages 1 and 2 are the same for both groups. At stage 1, the writing is scribbles and sometimes pictures that figuratively correspond to the items they represent. For example, Ferreiro and Teberosky found that adults' names had more scribbles than children's names because adults are bigger than children. At stage 2, students write identifiable but random letters and numbers that have no apparent relationship to the sounds in the words or syllables represented.

At stage 3, the first difference appears, reflecting the different internal structure of each language. Monolingual English students move from scribbles to individual letters—most often initial, and later final, consonant sounds—and only later add vowels as their writing develops. By this stage, monolingual Spanish students, in contrast, have developed the syllabic hypothesis and sounds-symbol understanding. They move from scribbles to vowels first, where each vowel represents a syllable, rather than an initial or final sound. They then move to stage 4, where they write consonant-vowel syllable combinations, often using unconventional spelling. At stage 4, monolingual English students also write letters for all the sounds and use unconventional spelling. By stage 5, both groups write easily identifiable words.

The characteristics of monolingual students from both language contexts appear in the earliest writing of emergent bilinguals. As students of biliteracy move from scribbles to random letters and then to matching letters with sounds, their writing reflects both the syllabic hypothesis found in Spanish literacy development and the partial alphabetical writing found in English literacy development (Geiser, Escamilla, Hopewell, and Ruiz, 2007). This natural multilingual development of writing has instructional implications for teaching word-level skills in both Spanish and English and also for teaching and assessing emergent writing across languages. Strategies and assessments must be in place that reflect and take advantage of all the linguistic resources of the students.

EMERGENT WRITING AND DISCOURSE PATTERN

The emergent writing of young bilingual learners reflects all of their linguistic resources at the discourse level as well as at the word level, including the cultural norms that govern the way language is used in different situations and contexts. How these norms are reflected in writing is described in the section that follows.

Cultural Norms of Language Use

Cultural norms of language use become apparent when we engage in contrastive analysis of Spanish and English. Montaño-Harmon (1991) points out differences between the writing of secondary students in Mexico and that of secondary students in the United States that reveal these cultural norms. The Spanish writing samples have

- Fewer sentences
- Longer sentences
- More run-on sentences
- More repetition and rephrasing of ideas or examples
- Little use of enumeration (first, then, next)
- More conscious deviations from the main theme or point of the text

In Chapter 1, we saw how oral language is used in two speech events about borrowing a suitcase, one among three Spanish speakers and the other between two English speakers. Montaño-Harmon's list is consistent with the speech patterns of the Spanish speaker, Ramona, who expresses her need to go to the store many times but without ever asking directly. From an English language perspective, she deviates from the main theme—her need to return to the store to exchange the defective suitcase—by setting the stage and describing the situation. In the English speech event, Emily, in contrast, goes directly to her main idea without repeating or rephrasing her needs.

Montaño-Harmon goes on to note that many of the students in the study who were raised in a bilingual environment (Arizona border towns) tended to exhibit more of the Spanish text features in their English writing. This tendency, she notes, leads many teachers to mark down their English texts as disorganized, informal, or too wordy. She writes, "the evaluation of class compositions and those written for the Advanced Placement Examinations in Spanish . . . were marked down if they did not follow the linear, deductive discourse pattern deemed logical and organized in American English." This criterion, she says, is artificial, pointing out that texts written in Spanish according to the cultural norms of English sound stilted, awkward, and juvenile to those evaluating the writings according to the cultural norms of monolingual Spanish. This mismatch—students writing in English being penalized for using a discourse pattern more reflective of Spanish cultural norms, and students writing in Spanish being expected to use a more typically English discourse pattern—presents a dilemma to teachers of biliteracy in the United States. Do we teach students to write in Spanish the way Spanish is written in Spanish-speaking countries? Or do we teach them to write in Spanish following the cultural norms of English because they are in the United States, where the more direct, linear discourse pattern is favored?

As challenging as this issue is, there is still more to consider. The question of discourse pattern is as important in reading as it is in writing. The novels of such Spanish-language writers as Gabriel García-Márquez, Isabelle Allende, and Carlos Ruíz Zafón, for example, include what monolingual English speakers may consider run-on sentences, repetitions, and deviation from the main theme. Comprehension of these novels and texts in other genres written in monolingual Spanish contexts is dependent on an understanding not only of the words but also of how to navigate these longer sentences, frequent repetitions, and deviations from the main topic. Students who have been taught to write using only the cultural norms of English and who have had access only to texts written in this way—such as course texts and literature translated from English into Spanish—will find Spanish-language texts written in a monolingual Spanish context challenging and difficult to comprehend.

Consider the following two definitions of chlorophyll. The first is from a Spanish academic text, the second from an English academic text.

La clorofila—que es una sustancia orgánica—capta la energía solar (luz), la luz provoca la ruptura de la molécula de agua, es decir se rompe el enlace químico que une el hidrógeno con el oxígeno.

Chlorophyll is the molecule that absorbs sunlight and uses its energy to synthesize carbohydrates from CO_2 and water.

The two passages have much in common, including purpose (to define), topic (chlorophyll), and audience (students). Where they differ is in the length and organization of the sentence. The Spanish sentence is longer, it has more repetition and rephrasing (signaled by the phrase *es decir*, "in other words"), and, by English-language standards, it is a run-on sentence. Similar comparisons can be made with other genres of writing. It is as important for students of Spanish and English biliteracy to receive explicit instruction in the different discourse patterns of Spanish and English texts of all genres as it is for all students of literacy, bilingual or monolingual, to be taught to read a variety of genres.

Students of Spanish and English biliteracy in the United States also benefit from explicit instruction in the assumed roles of the writer and the reader in the discourse pattern typical of some Spanish writing. The writer has these responsibilities:

- Offering the reader all the information needed to reach his or her own conclusion
- Leading the reader to a conclusion without explicitly telling the reader what that conclusion should be
- Providing many examples to lead the reader to the main focus
- Setting the stage for the central theme
- Rephrasing and rewording the information in order to provide the reader with several avenues to the central theme

The reader has these responsibilities:

- Reading and reviewing the many examples in order to deduce the author's central theme
- Reading between the lines and looking for clues to the main focus of the text
- Making connections among details in order to form a generalized understanding of the text

While many of these responsibilities are the same for readers and writers in English, in Spanish the reader is often required to do more inferring and reading between the lines, while in English the writer's role is to make the connections for the reader, often with as few words as possible. Each biliteracy program's goals determine how these elements are taught.

All students of Spanish literacy in the United States should understand that there are different discourse patterns in written text. Ensuring that students gain this understanding means making sure that they read many original Spanish texts, not just translations, throughout their education in Spanish and English biliteracy, beginning in pre-K and kindergarten. Many students of Spanish literacy in the United States are exposed only to texts translated from English to Spanish. While it is clear that these texts are more accessible and plentiful in the United States, especially for children in pre-K through 3rd grade—and may even be more comprehensible to our students than texts from Spanish-speaking countries because they deal with familiar themes and activities—students who read only translated texts are not exposed to Spanish discourse patterns. We strive to increase students' vocabulary in Spanish by explicitly bringing in words from their local communities and from other Spanish-speaking communities around the world. We must also strive to increase their literacy vocabularies by exposing them to and teaching them about a variety of written genres and discourse patterns in both Spanish and English.

Educators considering exposing students to this variety of genres and discourse patterns should keep in mind that teachers who are sequential bilinguals may have difficulty teaching students to write in the discourse patterns of their second language and that all teachers of biliteracy can benefit from professional development on how to recognize and teach these different forms of text.

The next section describes strategies to teach writing effectively and the differences in the discourse patterns across genres in the biliteracy classroom.

Writing Strategies That Respect and Reflect All the Language Resources of Two-Language Learners

At the word and sentence level, two-language learners will use phonics and syntax from English and Spanish. At the discourse level, they will use patterns that reflect the cultural norms of both languages. Effective instructional strategies take advantage of what students know and can do while increasing and developing their writing skills.

LANGUAGE EXPERIENCE APPROACH

LEA exemplifies the integration of reading and writing. As described in Chapters 4 and 7, it takes advantage of an initial highly comprehensible, shared experience that students then narrate to the teacher. For students at the earliest stages of literacy development, LEA is an effective way to model the move from oral language to print. For older students, it is a way to model the use of new vocabulary, new sentence structures in writing, and a variety of writing genres. LEA is used in the reading portion of the sample unit for 1st grade and the writing portion of the sample units for 3rd grade, 4th grade, and high school.

For students of all ages, LEA has three steps. The first step is sharing a concrete, comprehensible experience, which students do during the "Building oracy and background knowledge" part of the biliteracy unit framework. The second step is narrating the concrete experience while the teacher writes. As she writes what the students narrate, the teacher gives a writing mini-lesson, modeling a specific writing skill appropriate for the developmental stage of her students. The third step is reading or writing using the LEA document as a mentor text. Students can read the text in a choral reading or guided reading exercise or revise, edit, or use it to guide them in writing their own texts of the same genre (Table 8.1).

The movement from concrete experience to oral language to print makes LEA a highly effective strategy for writing instruction for two-language learners. When

TABLE 8.1.

Elements of the Language Experience Approach at Different Grade Levels

Grade Level	Sharing a Concrete Experience (Step 1)	Narrating While the Teacher Writes (Step 2)	Reading or Writing Activity Using Step 2 Transcription as Mentor Text (Step 3)
Primary (grades pre-K–2)	• Nature walk around the school to observe the characteristics of fall • TPR* about living and nonliving things • Concept attainment about three states of matter	• Left-to-right directionality of print • Writing on the line • Difference between letter, syllable, word, sentence • Syllabification • Capitals and periods • Complete sentences • Main idea and supporting details	• Matching letters and sounds (phonemic awareness) • Choral reading • Identifying vowels or syllables • Dictado†
Intermediate (grades 3–5)	• ART‡ about a fictional story • TPR about the rock cycle	• Writing dialogue • Paragraphing • Organizing an expository text; using connecting words	• Writing a personal narrative • Writing from a particular point of view • Writing expository text • Editing and revising text
Middle and high school (grades 6–12)	• Movie clip of *The Diary of Ann Frank* • YouTube video clip about unfair labor practices • TPR about different types of governments	• Complex sentences • Varied sentence structures and phrases for comparing and contrasting • Maintaining consistent verb tense	• Writing compare/contrast essays • Answering exam essay questions • Editing and revising text

*Total physical response: The teacher models academic oral language accompanied by pictures, realia, and movements.

†Dictado: The teacher dictates one or more sentences and the students write. This strategy is used to teach spelling and writing mechanics.

‡Adapted readers' theater: Teachers orally paraphrase a text that students will read, supplementing the oral storytelling by acting out key parts of the text and inviting students to join in as actions are repeated.

the concrete experience is complete, the teacher initiates the second step of LEA by asking students for a sentence and inviting them to collaborate with their partner to prepare it.

The teacher then calls on one student partnership and writes down its sentence. While students prepare their sentences with their partners, the teacher listens to their discussions to assess their understanding of the new concepts and the oral discourse patterns they use to discuss these new concepts. Then, as the students offer their sentences for placement within the LEA text, the teacher shapes each utterance to match the writing skill and genre she is teaching.

Through LEA, students learn how to move from oral language to print and how to shape their written work to reflect the skill, genre, style, or discourse pattern being taught. To shape student language, the teacher employs strategies from the three groups discussed in Chapter 6:

1. Model and redirect
2. Anchor charts comparing formal and informal language
3. Contrastive analysis of language

The teacher responds to student offerings and shapes the LEA text in Spanish to emulate a discourse pattern more reflective of Spanish or English, in keeping with the plan articulated by the school or district for teaching the different discourse patterns. For example, if the program goal is to teach the more linear, English discourse patterns—with shorter sentences and fewer words per sentence—teachers can rephrase student utterances to reflect more linear writing. This rephrasing gives the teacher the opportunity to talk explicitly about the difference in discourse patterns and why the change has been made.

In the sample unit for high school, the teacher uses LEA to teach the genre of compare/contrast in Spanish. She begins by model writing the first paragraph in a shared writing format, following the steps for LEA described in Table 8.1. As the teacher and her students write the first paragraph together, the teacher focuses on the structure of a compare/contrast essay in Spanish and the key words and phrases used in comparing and contrasting. She also does some metalinguistic analysis. For example, if she is modeling a Spanish discourse pattern for comparing and contrasting and a student offers a sentence that is more reflective of an English compare/contrast essay, she lines up the two sentences side by side and compares their structures.

Teachers of Spanish literacy in the United States must recognize, respect, and reflect in their teaching the following points:

- Spanish and English have a variety of discourse patterns.
- Students use these different discourse patterns in their oral language and in their writing.
- Students benefit from explicit instruction in the existence and characteristics of the different discourse patterns.

DIALOGUE JOURNALS

Dialogue journals are a free-writing exercise for students. Students choose the topic and the language, and the teacher determines the amount of time they spend writing. Teachers collect and respond to what the students write—hence the name "dialogue" journal—but do not mark the writing with a red pen or ask students to correct or revise what they have written. Dialogue journals can be used at any grade level, regardless of the writing abilities of the students. Once students have learned to write quietly for a set amount of time, journal time becomes an excellent transitional activity—from recess to class, from home to school, from school to home.

The teacher introduces dialogue journaling by modeling a free write on chart paper or with a projection device, emphasizing that all writing, on any topic, is acceptable. When the students see the teacher writing in Spanish, they are encouraged to use Spanish. With younger students, the teacher says the words as she writes them. For very young students, the teacher can model drawing pictures, labeling them or writing a few words on the lines below the picture. By explicitly not giving students a topic or list of topics, the teacher is modeling how to use writing to think about the world. Students learn that writing is not always a product directed by and produced for the teacher.

At first, only a few minutes a day is dedicated to this silent journaling. The point is to make students feel successful, and so it is important that students not be given so much time in the beginning that they run out of things to write. As students become more confident and feel free to write, the time can be increased. The daily time dedicated to journaling will depend on the age of the student and can range from 10 minutes to 25 minutes a day. For older students in middle and high school, journaling may become a homework activity, after initial modeling in class.

Teachers need to establish a schedule for responding to the student journals. Even though students write every day, in a class of 25 or 30 students in the lower grades or with a group of 100 to 150 students in junior high and high school, a teacher cannot possibly respond to each student every day. She might therefore decide to respond to five students a day or to each student once a month. Whatever the schedule, the responses should follow a standard form:

- Comment
- Connection
- Question

After reading all the entries since the previous teacher response, she responds in general to all the entries, in the language in which the student has written the journal. She begins with a comment that demonstrates to the student that she has read the journal entries. Rather than, "Nice job," she might write, "It is so interesting that you were able to see those puppies being born!" Next, she makes a connection, writing, for example, "I never had a dog when I was younger. You are so lucky to have one in your home!" This activity is what really makes the journal a dialogue. In a real conversation, individuals make connections to what others are saying. The teacher ends with a question, perhaps one that helps give the student something to write about next time if he or she is having trouble coming up with topics. For example, "Who takes care of the puppies at your house?" continues the dialogue. Once the dialogue journals become routine, students look forward to reading the teacher's responses, and the teacher has repeated opportunities to learn about her students' writing abilities and to get to know them as individuals rather than simply as students.

CONTENT-AREA JOURNALS

Content-area journals also help to integrate writing throughout the day. However, they are unlike dialogue journals, where the writing is for informal communication with the teacher and the students choose the topic and the language. Content-area journals provide a place for students to respond in writing to the content they are learning in math, science, social studies, or literature, using the discourse pattern and genre of the content area. The teacher assigns the topic and genre for student reflection through writing, and the writing is done in the language of instruction for the content area. The focus is on giving students practice with using writing to learn, while emphasizing that writing serves many purposes. Content-area journals are often used for recording the writing response part of say something/write something. Suggestions for other content-area writing assignments throughout the curriculum appear in Table 8.2.

TABLE 8.2.	
Assignments for Content-Area Journals	
Content Area	**Assignments**
Math	• Describe the steps followed to solve a math problem • Write original word problems • Explain how to play a math game or the best strategy for winning a math game
Science	• Describe daily or weekly observations of science experiments • Make, test, support, and refute an hypothesis using the scientific method • Summarize science experiments • Create science analogies, comparing complex scientific concepts to everyday things or experiences
Social studies	• Dialogue with characters in history and give them advice or ask them questions • Compare historical events or situations with contemporary ones • Describe the causes and effects of historical events
Literature	• "Talk" to the author or the characters in the book • Retell or summarize books or parts of books • Describe setting, characters, or other literary elements in the story

As in dialogue journals, teachers model what is expected of students in their content-area journals. And though they do not edit or revise the content-area journals, they do use the student writing for formative assessment. Reading content-area journals gives teachers insight into their students' thinking processes, their understanding of the concepts being studied, their ability to use different writing genres, and their proficiency with other writing skills, such as spelling and punctuation. With such insight, the teacher can address misunderstandings of concepts and underdeveloped writing skills in later writing mini-lessons or during the word-study portion of the biliteracy unit framework.

Teaching and Assessing Writing with a Multilingual Perspective

LEA, dialogue journals, and content-area journals offer many assessment opportunities. A sample of these opportunities appears in Box 8.1, including those areas of assessment common to all three strategies and areas of focus specific to each kind of journal.

The information that assessments yield can be used to guide further writing instruction. For example, if, through reading students' dialogue journals and content-area journals, the teacher discovers that many of her students still struggle with writing a complete sentence, she can focus on writing complete sentences during her writing mini-lesson in the second (narration transcription) part of an LEA. Teachers can use rubrics and anecdotal records to collect the kind of information they need to plan their writing mini-lessons.

BOX 8.1. Integrating Writing Instruction and Assessment: Language Experience Approach (LEA), Dialogue Journal, and Content-Area Journals

FOCUS OF ASSESSMENT COMMON TO ALL THREE JOURNALS

- Use of new vocabulary
- Code-switching
- Academic and social language use
- Understanding of new concept

FOCUS OF ASSESSMENT SPECIFIC TO LEA

- Oral language discourse pattern
- Oral language syntax

FOCUS OF ASSESSMENT SPECIFIC TO DIALOGUE JOURNALS

- Stage of emergent writing
- Written-language discourse pattern
- Use of writing mechanics
- Spelling
- Preference for English or Spanish

FOCUS OF ASSESSMENT SPECIFIC TO CONTENT-AREA JOURNALS

- Stage of emergent writing
- Understanding of content-area concept
- Written-language discourse pattern
- Use of writing mechanics
- Use of content-area genre
- Spelling

The most effective rubrics for assessing the Spanish writing of developing bilinguals reflect all their linguistic resources. Monolingual English writing rubrics, even if translated into Spanish, and writing rubrics developed in a monolingual Spanish setting cannot capture and communicate all that the bilingual learner can do. Educators have developed writing rubrics for the bilingual learner that teachers can use as a base to develop their own rubrics to match the needs of their students and the goals of their program (see, e.g., Geiser et al., 2007). For example, the Literacy Squared project has created rubrics that assess students' Spanish and English writing side by side (Escamilla, et al., 2010). The guiding questions in Table 8.3 can also be used to create writing assessment rubrics for two-language learners. Table 8.4 is a sample rubric based on these guiding questions that was specifically designed for assessing oral language generated during the second step, the narration, of an LEA and written language generated during the third step, writing activities based on the LEA mentor text. This rubric highlights and assesses the relationship between oral language and writing. Table 8.5 offers an example of a rubric designed for use in assessing the writing produced within an integrated unit of study. It assesses expository writing skills taught as part of the 4th grade sample unit. For each language, the teacher would document examples of the skills. For example, the teacher would note the use or lack of introductory sentence or paragraph. The bilingual strategies category allows the teacher to document where students are using phonology, morphology, syntax and grammar, and pragmatics appropriate to the language, and where they are using their knowledge from one language in the other.

TABLE 8.3

Guiding Questions for Developing Writing Assessment Rubrics for Two-Language Learners

Writing Element	Questions to Address	Example
Rhetorical or discourse structures	• How are discourse patterns reflected in the organization of text?	• Number of sentences • Length of sentences • Conscious deviations from central topic
Metalinguistics	• What evidence is there of conscious use of the other language?	• Quotation marks around English words in Spanish • Conscious attempts at cognates
Writing mechanics	• How is punctuation used, and which language rules are followed?	• Use of exclamation points at the beginning and end of sentences • Apostrophes for possessive
Language use	• Which language is used for which subjects? • How is social and academic language used? • What kind of code-switching, calques, borrowings, and extensions are used?	• Use of English for sports terms • Use of English syntax with Spanish words (*Mi favorito color es rojo.*)
Spelling	• Which orthographic patterns are followed?	• Qu or ck? • H or g/j? • F or ph?

This need for adaptation applies to writing programs as well as to writing rubrics and assessment tools. Many writing programs are designed either for the monolingual English speaker learning literacy in English only or for the English language learner learning writing with a focus on English literacy only. Writer's workshop programs, for example, often begin with an abstract or challenging activity, such as reading a mentor text or imagining and writing about a personal experience, rather than with the concrete and highly comprehensible activity recommended in the biliteracy unit framework. These programs are, in effect, asking a student like Antonio who is new to this country to imagine a time he played in the snow or asking a student like Paulo to listen to a read aloud of a mentor text full of vocabulary that is unfamiliar to him. Teaching writing in the biliteracy classroom necessitates adapting materials and processes to help the students understand the writing process and different genres.

The following questions can help guide the effort to adapt or implement a writing program for two-language learners:

- How does the program respect and take advantage of all of the linguistic resources of two-language learners?
- How does the program address the issue of different discourse patterns in Spanish and English?
- How does the program support participation and engagement for students with a range of linguistic abilities?
- How does the program encourage students to write across content areas using a variety of text types?

TABLE 8.4

Sample Oral and Written Language Rubric for Pre-K–2 (in Spanish)

Documentación del lenguaje expresivo de los estudiantes bilingües: Español

Años escolares Pre-K–2

Nombre del estudiante: _____

Fecha: _____

Componente	Circule las Descripciones Apropiadas	Comentarios y Evidencia
Redacción (organización de ideas)	La redacción tiene ejemplos de un discurso oral más circular y enfocado en las relaciones donde la narración se salta de una idea a otra pero donde todo está conectado. La redacción tiene ejemplos de un discurso más lineal y enfocado en los acontecimientos que incluye un orden cronológico que quizá integre el uso de palabras transicionales tales como primero, segundo, tercero, etc. El estudiante puede narrar una experiencia o un acontecimiento de manera completa y lógica que incluye detalles, causa y efecto y secuencia usando el discurso oral del español o del inglés o una combinación.	
Fluidez	El lenguaje expresivo fluye naturalmente sin pausas innecesarias No hay necesidad de parar para buscar palabras precisas.	
Lenguaje informal (vocabulario)	El lenguaje social representa el nivel de desarrollo y la edad del estudiante. (No sabo para niños de 3 a 5 años de edad, por ejemplo) El lenguaje social puede incluir expresiones no-convencionales del español (arcaísmos como "naiden" o "pos"; "ira" para "mira").	Anote ejemplos del uso del lenguaje social del estudiante.
Lenguaje formal (vocabulario)	El estudiante desarrolla lenguaje académico por medio del uso de banco de palabras, frases claves, etc. El estudiante usa el lenguaje académico que ha aprendido en diferentes contextos escolares.	Anote los apoyos y las estrategias que fomentan el aprendizaje del lenguaje académico.
Uso de los dos lenguajes	El lenguaje social representa el uso de la creatividad lingüística que representa el contexto sociocultural bilingüe del estudiante. Por ejemplo, puede usar: Cambio de código: Tengo el ball right here. Préstamo léxico: Socketines; wáchale Extensión semántica: Vamos a comprar las groserías. Calco: Vamos a mi tío Mario's casa.	Anote ejemplos de cómo el estudiante usa ambos recursos lingüísticos.
Conocimiento metalingüístico	El estudiante sabe distinguir entre el inglés y el español. Cuando se le pide al estudiante que hable en un lenguaje, puede hacerlo. El estudiante empieza a distinguir entre el uso del lenguaje social (la troca) y el uso del lenguaje académico (el camión de carga).	Anote ejemplos u otras observaciones.

TABLE 8.5		
Sample Expository Writing Rubric		
Spanish: Evidence and Notes	**Writing Element**	**English: Evidence and Notes**
	Includes elements of expository genre • Introduction to the topic and conclusion • Accurate factual details about topic (not opinion) • Follows logical organization	
	Writing mechanics • Complete sentences • Correct punctuation • Accurate spelling • Paragraphs	
	Bilingual strategies • Phonology • Morphology • Syntax and grammar • Pragmatics (language use)	

An Integrated Approach to Teaching Writing and the Three Premises

The integrated approach reflects the three premises of this book. As predicted by the first premise, which describes the minority status of Spanish in this country, much of what the students read in Spanish is translated from an English text. Teachers and programs explicitly need to include texts originally written in Spanish and explicitly teach the unique discourse patterns reflected in those texts.

Writing rubrics, other assessment tools, and writing programs used in the United States tend to favor elements of the more direct, linear discourse patterns reflective of English cultural norms. Teachers, schools, and districts need to adapt these programs and materials to reflect the abilities of two-language learners, who use all of their linguistic resources as they develop their literacy skills.

ACTIVITIES FOR REFLECTION AND ACTION

1. This chapter provides an overview of student linguistic creativity in their writing, and offers suggestions on how to build on and develop student writing skills throughout the curriculum. How did you first react to the writing sample early in the chapter from a 6th grade student who was responding to the prompt, *"Escribe acerca de tu deporte favorito"*? How, if at all, did your reaction change after reading this chapter? How, if at all, does the writing in the sample resemble your students' writing? Strategize ways of responding to this student's writing and your own students' writing that respect and build upon the languages in the students' linguistic repertoire.

2. This chapter provides a framework for developing writing rubrics and several sample rubrics. Using either a rubric from this chapter or one you create yourself, assess a

student's writing sample in Spanish. Then assess the same piece of writing using the rubric currently used by your school or district. Compare and contrast the information each rubric provides you. Finally, assess the same student's writing in English. Consider developing (or using) a bilingual rubric like the one in this chapter.

3. Review the texts that your students are assigned to read in school and those they choose to read on their own. In what language are the texts? Are they original to that language or translations? What genres and discourse patterns are reflected in these texts?

4. The language experience approach (LEA) has been highlighted in this book as a strategy that integrates oral language, reading, and writing. Review the description of LEA in this chapter and then try the strategy in your classroom. Using the following questions, reflect on your use of the strategy:
   - What went well? Why?
   - What surprised you about your own teaching?
   - What surprised you about student learning?
   - What improvements or changes would you make in the future?

CHAPTER 9

Word Study and Fluency: The Dictado and Other Authentic Methods

KEY POINTS

- Students learn discrete skills best by using words, sentences, and paragraphs they already understand.

- The explicit teaching of discrete word-study skills should come only after comprehension has been established.

- Student writing provides one of the best sources to determine what word-study skills to teach to two-language learners.

- The strategies used to teach word study and fluency should match how the language works. Fluency reflects comprehension.

A Constructivist Approach to Word Study

Much has been written and debated about how to ensure that students of Spanish literacy and students of English literacy learn discrete skills. We believe that students learn discrete skills (e.g., sounds, spelling, grammar, word order, punctuation, word meaning) best when they use words, sentences, and paragraphs they understand, in Spanish and English. Too often, students can sound out words and appear to read fluently but cannot explain what they have read. These students are then unable to take the discrete skills they are being taught and apply them to new situations. Therefore, we have placed word study and fluency after reading comprehension and writing in the biliteracy unit framework.

The following sentence and list of questions illustrate the importance of comprehension.

Luego de ponerse la chumpa, el patojo salió hacia el obelisco con su chucho para comerse una champurrada cuando se le atravesó un chompipe.

1. *¿Quién iba hacia el obelisco?*
2. *¿Qué se atravesó?*
3. *Dibuja al patojo, la chumpa, el obelisco, la champurrada y el chompipe.*

The following translation has maintained the key words from Spanish that illustrate the connection between meaning and learning to read.

After putting on a *chumpa*, the *patojo* left for the *obelisco* with his *chucho* to eat a *champurrada* when a *chompipe* crossed his path.

1. Who was headed to the *obelisco*?
2. What crossed his path?
3. Draw a *patojo*, a *chumpa*, the *obelisco*, the *champurrada* and the *chompipe*.

All the students featured in this book (Carmen, Paulo, Lucía, Hannah, and Antonio) could say and decode the key words in this example: *chumpa, chucho, champurrada, chompipe*. In a lesson that focuses on the *cha, che, chi, cho, chu* syllables, they would be successful in reading the words with *cha, cho*, and *chu*. Some readers might not understand the meanings of the words that begin with *cha, cho*, and *chu* and assume they are made up. However, they would most likely be able to decode them appropriately, and answer questions 1 and 2 by applying their knowledge of syntax to the text. This ability to answer questions about a text without comprehending it points to the need for teachers to use assessments that focus on meaning as well as on discrete skills. It also points to the importance of matching language users to the language they use. Decoding without understanding·is a difficult and useless exercise that only wastes time. Unfortunately, many students who learn to read and write go through this meaningless exercise in school almost every day.

All of the words in the sample sentence are real. But because some are from Guatemala, readers who are Spanish speaking but not from Guatemala are unlikely to know them. A *chumpa* is a *chamarra* or *chaqueta* (jacket) in Mexico; a *champurrada* is a delicious cookie made with sesame seeds in Guatemala; a *chompipe* (turkey) is a *pavo* in Spain and Mexico, where wild turkeys are *guajolotes*. Thus, though the text is comprehensible to Guatemalan students, it is not so for Carmen, Paulo, Lucía, Hannah, and Antonio. This example is a reminder that language varies by speaker and that teachers need to be careful about simply adopting materials from Spanish-speaking countries that require background knowledge for comprehension that does not match the background knowledge of most two-language learners in the United States.

The biliteracy unit framework takes a constructivist approach to reading and writing. Students practice and learn word-study skills with words they generate themselves and that are tied to a unit that integrates content and language arts. This approach maximizes their learning.

Matching Word Study to the Structure of the Language

A key element in developing biliteracy is the acknowledgment of the differences between English and Spanish. While many approaches to literacy instruction are similar in both languages, students also need instructional strategies that focus on the distinct rules of each language in the areas of phonology, morphology, syntax and grammar, and pragmatics.

One difference between Spanish and English is the set of *letras tramposas* (tricky letters) in Spanish that make the same sound and are difficult to learn. The most common *letras tramposas* are the following:

- "c," "s," "z" make the [s] sound
- "c," "q," "k" make the [k] sound
- "b," "v" make the [b] sound in word initial position

- "g," "j" make the [h] sound
- "y," "ll" make the [y] sound

Another difference is that English is made up of approximately 40 to 56 phonemes represented by 26 letters, while Spanish is made up of 24 phonemes represented by 27 letters, and every letter has one corresponding sound. This difference is one reason Spanish is often described as more regular and transparent than English. However, there are areas in Spanish that are complex, different than English, and that affect instruction. In English, "b" and "v" are two distinct phonemes, /b/ and /v/ (as in "berry" and "very"), and these phonetic differences are evident in their pronunciation and in their use in spelling (Calvert and Silverman, 1975). In Spanish, however, the pronunciation of the letters "b" and "v" is phonetically identical (Hualde, 2005), as in *bebé* and *Victor*. The spelling rules that indicate how to use "b" (known as *la b grande*) and "v" (*la v chica*) in Spanish are found in "How Spanish Works."

These examples underscore the need to teach spelling in Spanish differently than we do in English. Saying the letters out loud in Spanish is not enough to make a distinction that can help with spelling. To learn the rules for the use of *la b grande* and *la v chica*, for example, students need to see lists of words using these letters side by side on a word wall (Figure 9.1). Because of the complexity of this concept, students benefit from continuing to add examples to word walls starting in kindergarten or 1st grade and continuing through 5th grade and middle school (or higher) until the scaffolds are no longer needed.

The best approach to teaching spelling in Spanish, as for teaching all word-level skills, is to use comprehensible text. In a 1st grade bilingual unit on the theme "responsibility," for example, the teacher, Mrs. Johnson, works with the children to create a comprehensible text, which she later uses to teach spelling, focusing on several of the *letras tramposas*. Mrs. Johnson begins by using the concept attainment strategy to teach the students that when people meet individual and collective responsibilities, their families and communities are strengthened. The students view examples and describe in their own words children who are and who are not responsible. Mrs. Johnson then introduces the words *responsable* (responsible) and *irrespon-*

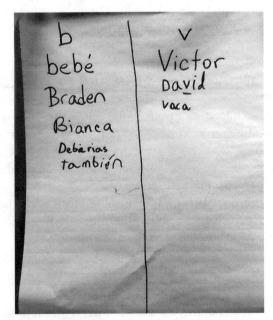

Figure 9.1. Word wall demonstrating the use of *la b grande* and *la v chica*.

sable (irresponsible) and engages the students in total physical response (TPR) using key words, such as *responsabilidad, colaborar, cumplir, organizar,* and *reciclar.* The TPR prepares them for a writing experience that follows the steps of the language experience approach (LEA). They read aloud a story about a boy named David who is not very responsible, and then, as a class, they write a letter to David to suggest ways he can be more responsible. When the shared writing is complete, Mrs. Johnson conducts a word-study mini-lesson on the *letras tramposas.*

Mrs. Johnson begins by guiding students in selecting words that contain the [k] sound, using what she calls the "*c de casa.*" Students identify the words *cumplir* (comply), *colaborar* (collaborate), and *reciclar* (recycle), circle them in the shared text, and place them on the word wall that contrasts the three letters that make the [k] sound in Spanish: "c, q, k." Learning to distinguish these letters is important for two-language learners, because the [k] sound in Spanish is represented most often by the letter "c," whereas the [k] sound in English is most often represented by the letter "k." The side-by-side lists of words on the word wall allow the students to visually contrast the three letters that make the [k] sound in Spanish.

Once Mrs. Johnson has led the students in identifying words that are spelled with the "*c de casa,*" she contrasts the [k] sound with the [s] sound by identifying words that contain what she calls the "*c de cine*" and she highlights the [s] sound in *reciclar.* She adds the word *reciclar* to that part of the word wall that contrasts the three letters in Spanish that make the [s] sound: "c, s, z." Her students quickly understand that the letter "c" in Spanish makes two different sounds (Figure 9.2). As they find examples, they start to learn the following spelling rules:

- The letter "c" is pronounced [s] when followed by the vowels "e" and "i" as in *cine* and *cerdo.*
- The letter "c" is pronounced [k] when followed by the vowels "a," "o," and "u" as in *casa, colaborar,* and *cuidar.*

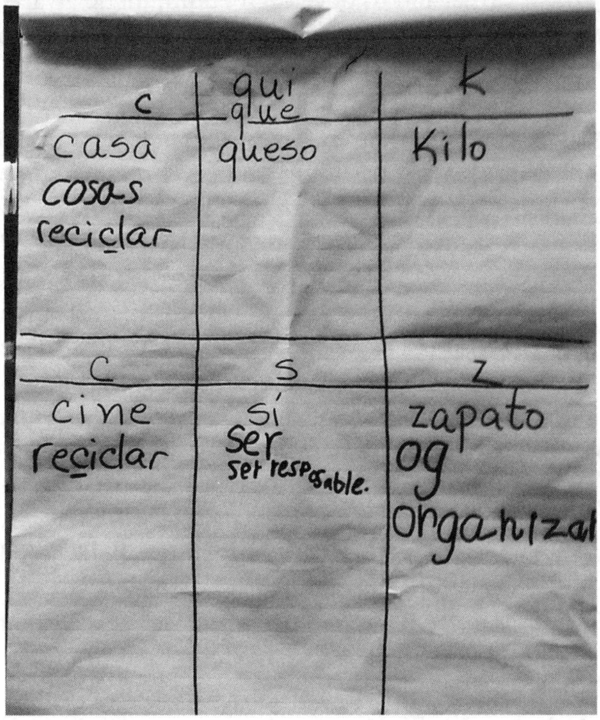

Figure 9.2. Word wall demonstrating the three letters that make the [k] sound in Spanish and the three letters that make the [s] sound.

- The letter "g" is pronounced [h] when followed by the vowels "e" and "i" as in *gigante* and *gente*.
- The letter "g" is pronounced [g] when followed by the vowels "a," "o," and "u," as in *gato*, *gordo*, and *gusano*.

Mrs. Johnson's 1st graders learn that these rules apply not just to words that begin with the letter "c" but also to words that have the letter "c" in the middle, such as *cocinar*. Key to this approach is that all the words the students select to add to the word wall are words they have used in other contexts, and they will be able to consult the word wall for their next writing exercise. Because the students have previously studied "b" and "v" and therefore have a *b grande / v chica* word wall, one student suggests adding *responsabilidad* to that word wall.

When the mini-lesson on spelling is over, Mrs. Johnson plans a dictado for the next day by reviewing student journals and consulting her instructional resources to identify the skills she wants to focus on. Finally, she selects the sentence from the student-generated text, the letter to David, that highlights these word-study skills and prepares the materials she will need.

Word Study and Initial Literacy Instruction in Spanish

Initial literacy instruction refers to the teaching of reading and writing when students first encounter print and are beginning to learn to match oral language with text. Typically, students receive initial literacy instruction in early childhood programs and in the primary grades. But some students who enter upper grades have not received formal schooling and need to develop initial literacy skills. Older students in Spanish-for-native-speakers classrooms may also benefit from focusing on these skills, not necessarily to learn to read, especially if they are proficient English readers and are transferring their skills from English to Spanish, but to understand how Spanish works and to develop metalinguistic awareness.

The initial literacy word-level skills students need to acquire to be able to read and write in Spanish match the way Spanish works. These skills, described in the following paragraphs, begin with syllable awareness.

Syllables. Syllable awareness emerges before phoneme awareness in Spanish and is a stronger predictor of reading success (Freeman and Freeman, 2006; Izquierdo, 2010; Vernon-Carter and Ferreiro, 1999). Understanding how to break words into syllables helps students learn to decode (Escamilla, 2000; Izquierdo, 2010; Mora, 2009). Spanish has strong syllable boundaries, and there are many more multisyllabic words in Spanish than in English. In Spanish literacy classes, it is important for teachers to emphasize syllabic awareness orally (marking each syllable) and then guide students in writing the syllables they hear. The role of syllabification in English is not as strong as in Spanish and it is emphasized later, in about 3rd grade.

Vowels and Consonants. Starting in kindergarten, students can learn the strong vowels (a-e-o) and the weak vowels (i-u). These are critical lessons because students will need to understand the distinction between strong and weak vowels in order to appropriately segment words into syllables. Syllables can be formed with the strong vowels (e.g., po-e-ta), but the weak vowels always accompany strong vowels (e.g., Ma-rio, E-duar-do), unless they are accented (e.g., Ma-rí-a). Vowels are the first building blocks of Spanish literacy, consonants the second. In contrast, the building blocks of English are the names and sounds of each letter.

Alphabet and Initial Sound. Learning letter names in Spanish is less important than matching vowels to consonants to form syllables. For some students, learning letter names in Spanish can be confusing because letter names do not directly match letter sounds; for example, "h" is *hache*, which some children call "*a*" or "*ch*"; "s" is "*ese*," which some children call "*e*" (Mora, 2009; Salgado, 2000). Names of letters in Spanish are learned formally only after students have learned the letter sounds and can form syllables. In English, however, knowing initial letter names and sounds is a predictor of reading success, and it is such an important skill that students are taught and tested regularly for mastery. The difference between the two languages shows up in the way word walls are organized. In English, word walls capture spelling patterns and are usually organized alphabetically, emphasizing initial letter sounds. In Spanish, they focus on aspects of the language that are irregular, such as the three letters "c," "s," and "z," which make the [s] sound, or words with the gender-specific article (*el problema, la mano*).

Sight Words and Spelling. All words in Spanish, though not necessarily comprehensible, are decodable, and spelling is transparent and regular. Thus, high-frequency word lists are not used in Spanish the way they are in English, where the spelling of words that cannot be decoded and do not follow regular rules must be memorized and spelling lists focus on different spelling patterns. In Spanish, spelling is taught through the dictado, a method that focuses on phonology, morphology, syntax and grammar, and pragmatics. Teachers can, however, create a list of frequently misspelled words, such as the conjunction *y* if students spell it as "*i*," or *voy* if students spell it as "*boi*." Student writing is the best source for identifying the words that can be included in this list.

Rhyming and Word Families. Because of the tight relationship between sound and symbol in Spanish, if you can say it, you can write it (though not necessarily understand it). Thus, in Spanish, phonological awareness continues to develop through writing. Word families in Spanish include words that share a common root and with ending changes, as in *flor–florería–florero*.

Word families in English, however, refer not to words with a common root meaning but to words that rhyme. In English, the words "bat," "cat," "sat," and "fat" are part of a word family because they all share the ending -at and they rhyme. During English literacy instruction, students are taught about word families through onset and rime activities, in which they take a common ending, like -at, and add different initial consonants, onset, to this common ending. Understanding and practicing onset and rime is fundamental to the ability in English to decode and understand the relationship between sound and symbol as it appears at the beginning of the words (c-at, f-at, s-at). This skill is learned and taught orally.

Accent and Accent Marks. The concept of the accent is very important in Spanish. An orthographic accent mark on a weak vowel, as in *Lucía*, indicates a syllable that is stressed; a diacritic accent mark differentiates between words that are spelled and pronounced the same but have different meanings (*se* vs. *sé*). The ability to use accents correctly in Spanish, like the ability to read with fluency, requires an understanding of how vowels and syllables are formed. In English, the accent is pronounced by placing oral emphasis on a sound but is not captured in writing. Thus, for example, the pronunciation of "present" is determined by its usage: prés-ent for the noun and pre-sént for the verb.

Spanish Word-Study Strategies

There are many highly effective and student-centered strategies that can be used to develop word-study skills for students in Spanish. All are based on words, sentences, and paragraphs that students understand and all are part of a comprehensible unit of study. Word-study activities based on these strategies can take place during a specially designated 10- to 20-minute word-study time or as part of a language arts block. They are based on two assumptions: (1) the words used to teach discrete skills are words the students know; and (2) the students are developmentally ready for the word-study skills and areas of focus.

The teacher makes this determination through, for example, formative assessment of writing samples and student responses in reader's workshop conferences. She models the skill; the students practice it as a whole group; and then she gradually turns responsibility over to students. She knows that the gradual release of control enhances understanding. The teacher also knows that metalinguistic awareness is a critical skill for two-language learners that prepares them for the contrastive analysis part of the Bridge. It helps students learn to "think about language" and to understand the explicit parts of language that together create the language system (Mora, 2009).

PHONOLOGICAL DEVELOPMENT IN THE PRIMARY GRADES

Nombres Cortos y Largos

This strategy is meant for students at the initial stages of literacy development, working together as a whole class or in small guided-reading groups. The words they use are words they know and comprehend. These can be drawn from a text, for example, about families that the students generated in an LEA exercise or they can be the students' first names. The teacher leads the students through the following series of activities that focus on, in this order: concept of word, syllable awareness, letter sounds, and strong and weak vowels (Escamilla, 2009).

1. As the group says all the students' names out loud, the teacher guides the students into classifying the names into short names (1 or 2 syllables) or long names (3 or more syllables). The teacher writes the names in two columns (Box 9.1).

2. Students write their own name on a piece of graph paper or the teacher gives it to them already written.

3. Students circle their whole name after watching the teacher do the same to her name.

4. Students say their name out loud, chunking it in syllables. They then circle each syllable in their name or highlight each syllable with a color. As names are divided, the teacher makes sure that the words are divided appropriately into syllables. For example, the name Eduardo is divided into E-duar-do because the vowel "u" is weak and remains so within the diphthong.

BOX 9.1. **Introducing the Idea of Syllables**	
Nombres Cortos (2 sílabas o menos)	**Nombres Largos (3 sílabas o más)**
Mario (Ma-rio)	María (Ma-rí-a)
Sara (Sa-ra)	Eduardo (E-duar-do)
Betty (Be-tty)	Elizabeth (E-li-za-beth)
Luis (Luis)	Guillermo (Gui-ller-mo)

5. The teacher reviews the vowels (a-e-i-o-u) and each student underlines or highlights the vowel in each syllable. This step can be done in different ways. Some students may look for vowels in general while others look for a specific vowel. Those who are ready for learning about the concept of strong and weak vowels can search for either the strong vowels (a-e-o) or the weak vowels (i-u). One way to introduce the concept of strong and weak vowels is by using concrete examples. If students notice that Mario does not have an accent on the "i" while the "í" in María is accented, the teacher can explain that María has three syllables (Ma-rí-a), because the weak "i" vowel became strong with the accent, while Mario has only two syllables because the "i" remains weak (Ma-rio).

This type of attention to the whole word, the syllables, the sounds, and the vowels can be repeated and practiced with other words that students understand.

Though kindergarten and 1st grade teachers most likely will not introduce the actual grammar rules, they should be sure that the rules are followed as they segment words into syllables with their students.

Sounds and Syllables

In the sample unit for 1st grade, the teacher uses the 15 minutes allotted daily to word study and fluency to focus on phonological development through a whole-group mini-lesson on an aspect of word study that might be a review for some students and an area of growth for others. For example, if students are still working on listening to syllables in words and then finding them in print, she can take a word or phrase from the student-authored text created during an LEA and find its syllables, play with different syllable combinations, or review syllable clusters. The text generated for a unit on the family naturally includes words that contain the syllable patterns conducive to teaching phonics to early readers.

The teacher follows these steps:

1. Review the vowels and their sounds. Introduce the consonant by showing students the letter and its sound (not its name). Show the students the consonant and the vowel together and say, *"La [m] y la [a] es igual a [ma]."*

2. Introduce the consonants based on those that are most used (high-frequency consonants). There is no set order, but most teachers follow the sequence: m, s p, l, t, d, n, r, ñ (within words), c/q, f, ch, b, g, j, z, v, ll, h, güe, güi, y, x, k, w.

3. Engage students in a TPR exercise (or other, similar exercise) by selecting five volunteers, who each stand and hold a card. Following the teacher's lead, the students chant *"[m] y [a] es igual a[ma],"* and repeat a gesture for every card that is used. This process is repeated various times. Then, the volunteers change and the vowel changes and the *"me"* syllable is created, then the *"mi,"* and so on, until all five syllables have been reviewed.

4. Following a graph that contains the same information, the students form syllables:

    m + a = ma
    m + e = me
    m + i = mi
    m + o = mo
    m + u = mu

5. Students generate words for each set of consonant first syllables anywhere in the word, not just in the initial position, as shown here:

ma	me	mi	mo	mu
mamá	dame	misa	mono	música
hermano	melón	camino	Guillermo	muleta
cama	México	millón	mole	mucho

The teacher acknowledges all approximations and places words that contain other syllables below and explains what the syllable combination is and that she will use the word at a later time.

6. The words generated for each syllable are then copied onto a *ma–me–mi–mo–mu* word wall that is placed where it can be seen for as long as the students use it.

The whole process is repeated as each new syllable family is studied.

WORD WALLS AND ANCHOR CHARTS IN SPANISH

Successful visual charts in Spanish match how Spanish works; they are student generated and correspond to students' developmental stages. Word walls focus on spelling patterns; anchor charts capture the characteristics of Spanish in the United States. Word walls in Spanish should highlight the parts of Spanish that are irregular, such as the *letras tramposas*. They should not look like word walls in English because each language works differently. A few suggestions for topics to use on grade-specific word walls are listed in Box 9.2. Notice that the word walls build on each other year after year, until students no longer need them.

The word walls and anchor charts presented in this chapter are created during the Spanish literacy portion of the day. Chapter 10 describes word walls that are introduced during the Bridge, such as cognate lists in both languages, word walls that allow for the comparison of the two languages, and word walls in English.

In going through the different types of word walls and anchor charts for Spanish, keep in mind the following practices:

- **Students generate the examples for word walls and anchor charts.** Teachers introduce blank word walls and anchor charts. Then, as the class engages in shared writing, dictation, and other literacy activities across the curriculum, the teacher points out words that are examples of certain spelling patterns and students write the examples on the word walls and anchor charts. As students become familiar with the pattern, they will begin to identify and suggest additional examples.
- **Words walls and anchor charts give explicit attention to word-study skills.** The more explicit the anchor charts, the more they act as scaffolding for developing metalinguistic awareness.
- **Multiple word walls and anchor charts are used in the classroom, reflecting different word-study skills and different student developmental stages.** For example, in Mrs. Johnson's classroom, some students still need word walls that capture syllables (words that have the "*ma*" syllable, as in *cama*), whereas other students are ready for the *letras tramposas* that make the [k] sound, the "*h muda*" (silent "h"), and the "b" and "v" comparison. Student writing provides excellent data on how to differentiate the areas of word study.

BOX 9.2. Creating Spanish-Specific Word Walls	
Primary Grades	*Intermediate, Middle, and High School*
KINDERGARTEN	**3RD GRADE (build on and use 2nd grade word walls)**
	Homophones: *ola/hola; a ver/haber; hacer/a ser*
How syllables join to make words: *pa + to = pato; ma + lo = malo*	Rules for "v"; rules for "b" Rules for "ll" and "y" Rules for accent marks Rules for "j" and "g"
Student-generated words that contain syllable patterns: *sa—sabana, saber, salir, saltar, mariposa, venenosa*	High-frequency words that are often misspelled
Words with articles: *la rana, el libro, el reloj*	Word families: *flor–florero–florería* *libro–librería–librero*
Words with *la b grande* compared with words with *la v chica: burro, vaca*; and words with the silent "h": *hermano, hormiga*	Notation devices: 3-2-03 = February 3, 2003 in Spanish, March 2, 2003 in English
1ST GRADE (build on and use kindergarten word walls)	English words that add a letter in Spanish but otherwise are the same: *problema*–problem; *justicia*–justice
High-frequency words that are often misspelled: (*boi = voy; llo = yo; bamos = vamos; sena = cena; i = y*)	Contrast English and Spanish days of week, months of year, and so forth
Words that have the same sound but different letters: • c (*cine*), s (*sonido*), z (*zapato*) • q (*queso*), c (*casa*)	Syntax (word order) My mother's green house–*La casa verde de mi mamá.*
Words that begin with the silent h	**4TH GRADE (build on and use 3rd grade word walls)**
Words with *la b grande* compared with words with *la v chica*	Compound words: *cumpleaños, rascacielos, quemacoco, tocadiscos, paracaídas*
Word families: *pan, panadero, panadería, pez, pescado, pescador*	Color-coded words that are spelled the same in Spanish and English but pronounced differently: *idea, natural*
High-frequency words that need accents/tildes/dieresis: *papá, mañana, piña, bilingüe*	

continued

BOX 9.2. **Creating Spanish-Specific Word Walls** *continued*	
	5TH GRADE AND UP (build on and use all the previous word walls as needed)
2ND GRADE (build on and use 1st grade word walls)	Cognates in technical vocabulary metamorphosis–*metamorfosis* revolution–*revolución*
Contractions: *a + el: al; de + el: del*	Study of morphology (e.g., prefixes, suffixes) de- : *devaluar*/devalue -ble : *admirable*/admirable
Common blends: *fr–frío; fl–flor; pl–plato*	Compare and contrast English and Spanish syntax and writing mechanics "You won't! Will you listen?" she demanded. —¡Seguro que no! ¿Me oyes?—preguntó.
How accents cause words to change meanings: *el Papa/el papá/la papa; hablo/habló*	
Frequently used words in writing: *favorito, familia, hermanos*	
Gender and number agreement: *los números son–el número es*	

Adapted from Escamilla, K. (1999). Teaching literacy in Spanish. In R. DeVillar & J. Tinajero (Eds.), *The power of two languages 2000* (pp. 126–141). New York: Macmillan/McGraw-Hill.

Students in the primary grades need to visualize how Spanish works. Word walls are most effective when they are introduced to students as early as kindergarten and maintained with the continual addition of new examples through high school. In the intermediate grades, the focus of the word walls shifts from phonology to word-study areas that address morphology, syntax, and semantics. Morphology, grammar, and language use tend to be the areas of focus for word walls in middle school and high school. The anchor chart shown in Figure 9.3 was created by a 6th grade dual-language class where students were studying ancient civilizations and focusing on the aspects of language that hold meaning, such as the suffix *-polis*.

Three types of anchor charts explore linguistic creativity: (1) informal and formal language (or home/community and school language), (2) archaic forms of Spanish, and (3) regional forms of Spanish. All are appropriate for all grade levels, though the titles and depth of analysis change as students move into the higher grades.

Figure 9.4 is an example of an anchor chart created by a 2nd grade transitional bilingual class comparing informal and formal Spanish. It takes the Spanish spoken in the community and explicitly shows students what parts of the utterances come from English and what parts come from Spanish. Students as young as kindergarten and 1st grade are ready to learn that *lonche* is a word that comes from English (lunch) and has been extended into Spanish. In the upper grades, this anchor chart could be titled *Préstamos Léxicos* (Linguistic Borrowings) (Potowski, 2005) rather than Informal and Formal Language. Older students benefit from studying just where their "Spanglish" comes from, and this anchor chart helps them do so. When students learn that linguistic borrowings sound like Spanish but are English words that have been borrowed, they are developing metalinguistic awareness.

Figure 9.5 is a sample anchor chart created by the authors that compares archaic forms of Spanish (*Arcaísmos españoles*) with contemporary Spanish. Many Spanish-speaking students come from families and communities that have retained archaic

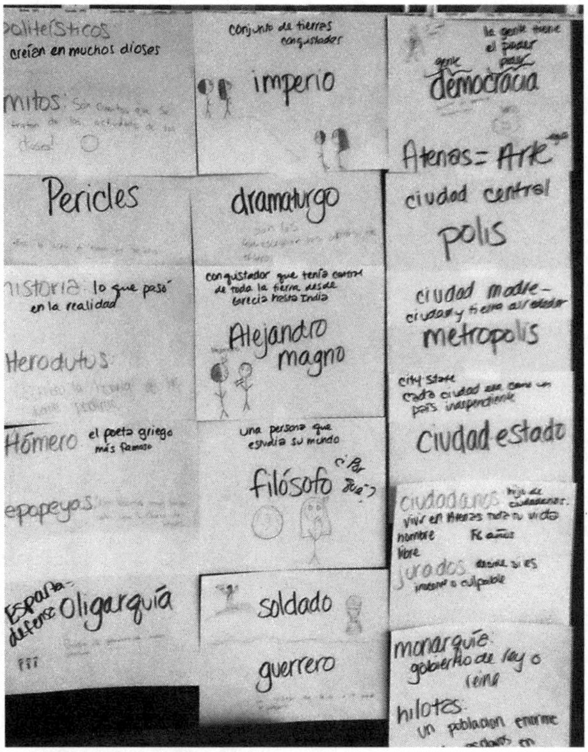

Figure 9.3. Word wall: Suffixes. (Courtesy of Meghan Potter's 6th grade dual-language class in Menasha, Wisconsin.)

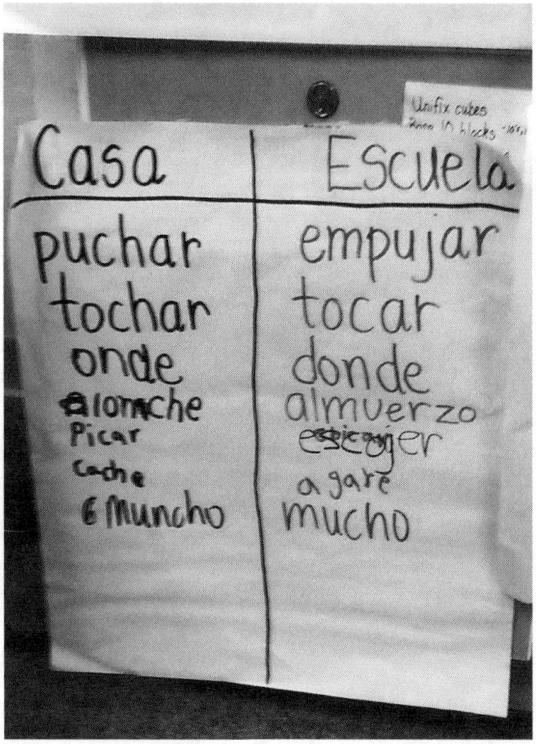

Figure 9.4. Anchor chart: Informal and formal Spanish. (Courtesy of Crystal Ramos' 2nd grade transitional bilingual class in Kennewick, Washington.)

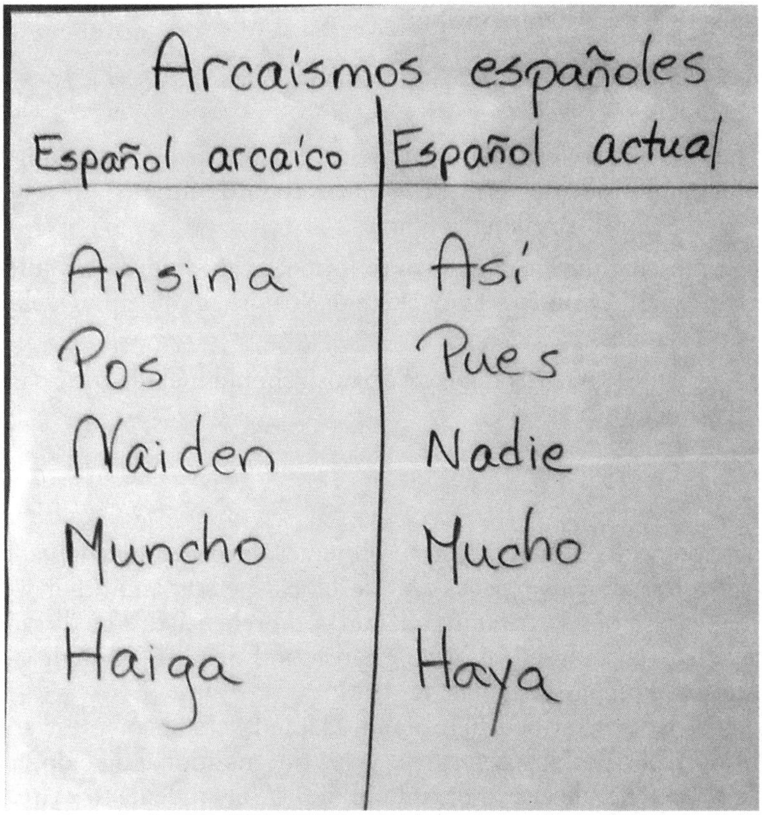

Figure 9.5. Anchor chart: *Los arcaísmos españoles*. (Examples drawn from Potowski, 2005; Valdés, 2011.)

Figure 9.6. Anchor chart: *Regionalismos*.

forms of Spanish. Their inability to recognize a word such as *así* if they use *ansina* may negatively affect their reading comprehension.

Finally, because Spanish in the United States is rich with many different regional varieties, it is important to have anchor charts that capture different ways of saying the same thing in different countries. Figure 9.6 is a sample anchor chart, also created by the authors, that compares regionalisms (*regionalismos*). Studying regionalisms reveals the following:

- Most regional ways of saying things in Spanish describe social or informal contexts.
- Despite differences in informal Spanish, all Spanish-speaking countries use the same academic terms. *Fotosíntesis* (photosynthesis), for example, is used in all Spanish-speaking countries.
- Comparing informal Spanish to formal Spanish increases student vocabulary, enriches student knowledge of Spanish, and helps develop metalinguistic awareness.
- A chart that records regional Spanish should include the Spanish spoken by the students.

THE DICTADO

The dictado, which, for teaching to biliteracy, has been updated and adapted from the traditional strategy, teaches and develops spelling and other word-study skills in a way that is holistic, meaningful, and comprehensive. The dictado is a universal strategy that can be used in both English and Spanish, though its origins are in Spanish- and French-speaking countries.

The dictado described here is an adapted version of the traditional dictado used in Spanish-speaking countries. With the traditional dictado, used about once a week, the teacher dictates a paragraph of text for students to write. Through their writing, they demonstrate their understanding and use of discrete skills, such as spelling (e.g., appropriate use of the *letras tramposas*), punctuation (e.g., appropriate placement of commas, exclamation marks, and hyphens to indicate dialogue), syntax, and semantics. The focus on the paragraph forces students to apply all the word-study skills they have learned, bringing together the different elements of Spanish to form a comprehensible text.

In Latin America the dictado is often used to convey messages to parents. The teacher dictates a message to parents and the children write it in their *cuaderno de comunicación* (communication notebook). These are authentic messages that require attention from parents, and therefore they should make sense and be written clearly. Students understand the message because it usually is related to a routine or event taking place at school. Teachers can use the exercise to introduce new academic language or conventions. A message might read, for example: *Señores Padres: El día de ayer de un total de 29 alumnos sólo 5 hicieron la tarea completa y 6 a la mitad. Gracias. Srta. Pochi. Matemática.* (Dear Parents: Yesterday, of a total of 29 students only 5 completed their homework and 6 did half of what was assigned for homework. Thank you, Srta. Pochi. Mathematics.)

The dictado as applied in teaching for biliteracy is used for both instruction and evaluation. The version presented here is influenced by the work of the Literacy Squared Project at the BUENO Center in Colorado (Escamilla and Hopewell, 2010). To prepare for the dictado, the teacher reviews samples of student writing, choosing one or more sentences that reflect a spelling pattern and element of writing mechanics that the students are ready to learn. The content of the dictado should come from content known and studied by the students. They must understand all of the words in the dictado. It would be most effective to use a text or part of a text generated by students during an LEA exercise. For example, 1st graders might create a passage in an LEA during the sample unit on families that looks like this:

> *La niña tiene una familia grande. Ella visita a sus* grandparents *los sábados y visita a sus abuelos los domingos.*[1]

The length of the dictado chosen by the teacher will reflect the developmental level of the students and, because students are often at different levels, may need to be differentiated. For example, while some 1st grade students are able to write several sentences, others may be ready only for a few key words or a single sentence.

The teacher uses the same dictado throughout the week. The dictado is used as an instructional opportunity on Monday through Thursday to focus on elements of spelling, mechanics, or fluency (Table 9.1). On Friday, the dictado moves from an instructional strategy to an assessment. The first day can include a mini-lesson on certain discrete skills. Different groups can work on different sets of skills. In the sample unit for 1st grade, the skills could include the following:

- Writing mechanics, such as the use of capitalization and periods
- Spelling of the word *niña*; accent on the word *sábados*

---

[1] The book used for the read aloud on which the text was based, *Me encantan los "Saturdays" y los domingos*, by Alma Flor Ada, is written in Spanish but contains some words in English. The main character visits her English-speaking grandparents on Saturdays and her Spanish-speaking grandparents on Sundays.

TABLE 9.1.				
Planning the Dictado				
Monday	**Tuesday**	**Wednesday**	**Thursday**	**Friday**
The teacher presents the dictado by reading it aloud several times. After the first reading, the students write as the teacher dictates. Then the teacher writes the dictado so the students may correct their own attempts. This first correction includes a mini-lesson on an element of writing mechanics or spelling.	The teacher presents a mini-lesson. This mini-lesson may be a review of Monday's mini-lesson, or may have a new focus, depending on the age and abilities of the students.	Students take turns dictating to each other; while one reads, the other writes. If the text has more than one sentence, the students can participate in a partner activity called "blind hand sequencing," in which each student has only a portion of the text, and, without looking at each other's text, the two work together to complete the text. The focus at this point is on reviewing the concepts introduced Monday and Tuesday, and on reading fluency.	Students add content to the dictado in small groups or individually. There is a continued focus on the spelling and writing mechanics introduced earlier in the week.	The teacher once again reads the dictado from Monday aloud and the students write as she dictates. The teacher then collects and evaluates the students' writing. It is at this point that the dictado moves from an instructional strategy to an assessment.

- Spelling of the word *visita* (*la v chica*)
- Rules for forming the plural (*el domingo y los domingos*)
- Masculine and feminine articles (*el domingo y la niña*)
- Suffix patterns such as *-ia* in Spanish (*familia*) that match -y in English (family) in preparation for the contrastive analysis during the Bridge, which can further develop this concept with examples, such as *historia*–history; *hereditaria*–hereditary; *obligatoria*–obligatory.

Figure 9.7 shows a dictado that was taken from a student-dictated text generated during an LEA exercise in a 2nd grade classroom. Note that the teacher uses graph paper for the dictado. The graph paper helps students see whole words and their syllables. It also provides an added level of support for students working on fine motor skills. Graph paper can be used for dictados through 5th grade.

Assessing Word-Study Growth

The word-study strategies described in this chapter offer opportunities to document student progress. Classroom-based assessment that is anchored in good instructional practices generates the type of data and information that is most helpful

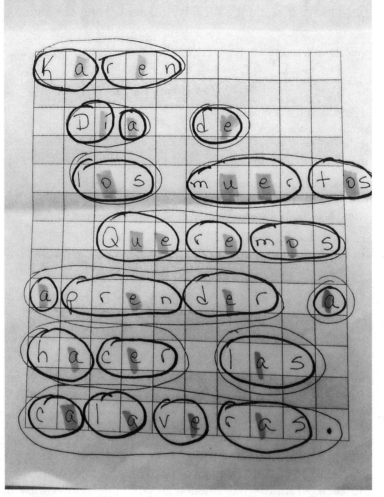

Figure 9.7. Using graph paper to practice syllable segmentation.

to teachers in planning lessons and in differentiating instruction according to student need. The following structures can accompany these word-study strategies and can be used routinely:

- **Personalized word-study collection:** When the word wall is full and more space is needed, students collect their favorite words from each word wall as part of a "word graduation ceremony." During a mini-lesson, the teacher models how students can use their collections as a checklist to refer to when reviewing their work. The word-study collections can follow students through the grade levels.

- **Word-study checklist:** The teacher can develop a checklist to evaluate student application of word-study skills throughout the week and in their weekly dictado. Table 9.2 presents a sample checklist.

- **Anecdotal records:** Teacher data are collected and recorded using student writing produced through dialogue journals, content-area journals, and the writer's workshop.

TABLE 9.2
Documenting Student Skill Development Using the Dictado

Weekly skill: _____

Skills	Comments and Observations
The student has demonstrated understanding of the use of the word-study skill throughout the week.	
The student has used the weekly word-study skill appropriately in the dictado.	
The student has applied the weekly word-study skill in other writing.	
Other	

Fluency

Fluency reflects comprehension (Damico, 2010). Practicing fluency with incomprehensible text is as meaningless as decoding with incomprehensible text. We take a constructivist approach to fluency, and therefore we do not want students practicing fluency by reading incomprehensible words and texts. When working on fluency, it is important to focus on meaningful uses of language and to ensure that meaning is emphasized as much as skill. Poetry, plays, songs, and tongue twisters related to a unit theme and big idea can be used effectively to practice fluency and are fun for students to recite.

- *Declamación de poesía* (**poetry recitation**): Memorizing and reciting poetry on special occasions is a cultural tradition in many Spanish-speaking countries. This tradition can be incorporated into a classroom routine at any age and used to practice vocabulary, syntax, and other word-level skills along with fluency. The popular poem *Abuelita*[2] works well in the 1st grade sample unit on the family.

  > *Abuelita*
  > *La mamá de mi mamá*
  > *Es mi abuelita querida,*
  > *La viejita consentida.*
  > *Que sus caricias me da.*

---

[2] http://www.pacomova.es/poesias/familia/abuelita.htm

El papá de mi papá
Es mi abuelito querido,
El viejito consentido
Que sus consejos me da.

- **Reader's theater:** Students can practice fluency by reading a published play or one they write themselves. Taping the reading provides constructive feedback.
- ***Trabalenguas:*** Memorizing and reciting tongue twisters, chants, and songs all support fluency and phonics development. The following two emphasize basic syllable patterns and can be used in the 1st grade sample unit on the family.

Compró Paco pocas copas y,
Como pocas copas compró,
Pocas copas Paco pagó.

Mírame sin mirar, Miriam
Mírame mientras me muero
No me mires, Miriam mía,
No me mires que me muero.

Word Study and Fluency and the Three Premises

The word-study strategies described in this chapter address the three premises directly. By focusing on how Spanish works, they help raise the status of Spanish. The anchor charts that recognize and analyze how Spanish and English are in contact in the United States acknowledge that students use all their languages in learning to read and write in Spanish. Work on the charts builds on what students already know and can do, helping to develop their metalinguistic awareness in Spanish and prepare them for the Bridge into English. And, finally, the word-study strategies, which avoid texts translated from English, match how Spanish works.

ACTIVITIES FOR REFLECTION AND ACTION

1. In the biliteracy unit framework described in this book, word study and fluency practice come after oral academic language, comprehension, and writing activities. At what point in a unit of instruction are you currently teaching word study and fluency? What are the benefits of teaching word study and fluency after oral academic language, comprehension, and writing activities? What are the challenges?

2. Compare the word walls currently in use in your classroom with those suggested in this book for your grade level. Try implementing one new word wall—one you do not currently use—and note how students react to and use this new resource.

3. Try a dictado with your students. Begin by using words or sentences that reflect something the students are familiar with, like a comment about the school or a description of the classroom. Using the following questions, reflect on your use of the strategy:

- What went well? Why?
- What surprised you about your own teaching?
- What surprised you about student learning?
- What improvements or changes would you make in the future?

CHAPTER 10

The Bridge: Strengthening Connections between Languages

KEY POINTS

- Two-language learners who understand how their languages are similar and different achieve higher levels of academic achievement.

- Though some two-language learners make connections between their languages on their own, many need explicit instruction in the transfer of language and concepts. This instruction comes during the Bridge.

- Students who experience the Bridge as part of biliteracy development will begin bridging on their own and will continue to do so as they learn more about how their languages are similar and different.

- The Bridge is preplanned and matches the language and content allocation plan of the program. Specific elements of the Bridge vary according to program models.

Bridging Rather Than Transitioning: Moving from a One-Way Street to a Two-Way Bridge

The ability to transfer knowledge and skills between languages is the theoretical underpinning of bilingual education. As described elsewhere in the book, many traditional bilingual programs assume that cross-linguistic transfer, also called transition, happens only once and is one-way and permanent (Escamilla, 2009). When the transition occurs, students are considered to be English proficient and to have no further need of Spanish. From then on, they are educated as monolingual English speakers. Before the transition, while developing oral English, these students have been taught almost exclusively in Spanish. In many school districts, students make the transition from Spanish literacy and content instruction to English at the end of 2nd or 3rd grade. In other districts, students make the transition from Spanish to English when they attain a specific score on an English proficiency test. Some dual-language programs also follow this pattern of transitioning students from literacy in one language to literacy in two languages at a predetermined time. In some of these programs, English speakers develop initial literacy in English while English language learners develop initial literacy in Spanish. Other programs teach all students initial literacy in Spanish and content areas (math, social studies, and science) in English, thereby delaying formal biliteracy instruction. This programmatic interpretation of cross-linguistic transfer does not reflect what we know about students and how they use their two languages. Waiting to teach literacy in the students' other language fails to build on what bilingual students know and can do, and it delays their biliteracy development. Moreover, programs that take an English-only approach to cross-linguistic transfer send the message to students that once they have transitioned into English instruction they no longer need to use Spanish and that using Spanish represents regression. This kind of transitioning is likely to produce students who write "choclit" in English even if they can write "*chocolate*" in Spanish, who cannot see "*sumar*" in "sum," and who find nothing familiar in the words "tranquil," "carnivore," and "lunar."

The biliteracy unit framework and the three premises address the needs of students who are developing biliteracy by interpreting cross-linguistic transfer as the bridging that occurs continuously in the learner's mind. The strategic use of two languages through planned literacy instruction in Spanish and English every day, for example, supports bridging and is possible even in programs that include more time spent in Spanish in the primary grades, such as in an 80% Spanish and 20% English dual-language program. Programs that look at cross-linguistic transfer as bridging—as occurring throughout a student's education, as bidirectional between Spanish and English, and as continuing even after formal support of Spanish has stopped rather than as a one-time, irreversible transition—enrich students' linguistic resources and encourage higher-level thinking. Bridging occurs as early as preschool and continues to be used as long as students use both languages for learning. The earlier we start tapping into our students' two linguistic resources and the longer they maintain them, the better they will do in school. Building on recent research in the area of transfer (Dressler, Carlo, Snow, August, and White, 2011), this chapter guides teachers in planning ways to tap into those resources and ensure cross-linguistic transfer in developing biliteracy.

Bridging and the Strategic Use of Two Languages

The purpose of the Bridge, as discussed in previous chapters, is two-fold: to help students transfer academic language learned in one language to the other language and to engage in contrastive analysis by focusing on how Spanish and English are similar and different. It requires the active engagement of the students. In the biliteracy unit framework, Spanish and English are used strategically. The unit begins with literacy instruction in one language through an integrated language arts and content unit. During the next stage, the Bridge, Spanish and English are placed side by side as teachers and students generate the labels in the other language for what has already been learned, and then teachers help students analyze how Spanish and English are similar and different in phonology, morphology, syntax and grammar, and pragmatics. The unit ends with extension and application activities in the language to which the students bridged. Teachers undertake formative assessment in both languages throughout the unit.

In earlier discussions of the biliteracy unit framework, and in the examples that follow in this chapter, literacy instruction begins in Spanish with a Bridge to English. The biliteracy unit framework, however, is versatile, and depending on the program model and the goals of the program, the languages can be switched. Literacy and content can be developed in English with a Bridge to Spanish and reinforced through extension activities in Spanish.

Key Characteristics of the Bridge

The biliteracy unit framework is anchored in a theme, its related big idea, and in the integration of literacy with content to provide meaningful context for literacy activities. Discrete skills are emphasized once comprehensibility has been established, and students use all four language domains in Spanish: listening, speaking, reading, and writing. The order in which the literacy elements are placed is intentional. The teaching of literacy skills that develop comprehension, writing, word study, and fluency come after the establishment of a comprehensible context in which a concrete activity is used to make the unit's big idea understandable to all students, who by then are ready for the Bridge.

FOCUS ON LANGUAGE THROUGH THE USE OF A CONCRETE ACTIVITY

The practice of introducing key language and concepts at the beginning of a unit with dynamic, student-centered, and concrete activities ensures that students build background knowledge and vocabulary before engaging in literacy activities. This proactive approach, as presented in the biliteracy unit framework, avoids the assumption that all students have the language they need to engage in the unit's literacy tasks. As reiterated throughout this book, it is expected that two-language learners will use all of their linguistic and cultural resources as they learn, but that the teacher will carefully plan her language use in order to reach deep levels of academic Spanish. To support student acquisition of key formal Spanish, she uses specific strategies to introduce the theme and the big idea and to get students to use this language orally. She then guides the students' transfer of concepts and key terms from Spanish to English during the Bridge by using the same concrete activity, or one similar to it, that she used to initiate the unit in Spanish.

Language instruction, not concept instruction, is the focus of the Bridge. Bridges that occur once students have learned the new concepts and skills demonstrate to the students that what they learned in Spanish can be used and applied in English, or vice versa; that is, they can express their understanding of the key concepts in two languages. Bridges also provide the teacher with rich assessment opportunities. Consider the example in Figure 10.1. This is a photograph of a Bridge anchor chart produced in a 1st grade bilingual classroom, where students learned about the solar system in Spanish. They generated the Spanish list on the left side of the chart when their teacher asked them to choose the most important words they had learned about the solar system. The teacher had introduced many of these words at the beginning of the unit using total physical response (TPR) movements (for "*sol*," a big circle with both hands; for "*rotación*," spinning in place; for "*gas*," fingers shaking as they go up in the air). After all the reading and writing activities her students had done in Spanish, the teacher knew they understood the meaning of the words well and that they understood the components of the solar system. To bridge, the teacher put on her magic scarf, indicating she was moving into English, and instructed her students to stand and do the same movements she was doing as she said the key words in English. Then drawing on what they had just learned, the students provided the English equivalent for the words learned in Spanish, and the teacher added the English words to the column on the right side of the chart. Doing TPR in English gives students like Paulo, Lucía, and Hannah whose English is well developed a reference for words they might already know in English. But because even they might not know the words for the elements of the solar system,

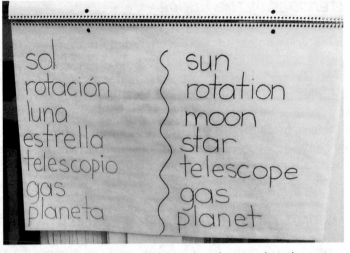

Figure 10.1. Side-by-side Bridge anchor chart on the solar system. (Courtesy of Karina Chavez's 1st grade transitional bilingual classroom in Villa Park, Illinois.)

a Bridge activity like this is as important for them as it is for all other bilingual learners. Combining the TPR gestures and corresponding words in English helps students like Carmen and Antonio learn English science terms. They have not yet developed enough English to be able to generate the English equivalent, informally or formally, of what they learned in Spanish. The key for all students is that they are attaching new words in English to concepts they already learned in Spanish.

Many strategies can be used to bridge meaning and attach English words to concepts learned in Spanish. Among these are the following, which are described in Chapters 4 and 6, as they might be used for teaching academic content and language in Spanish:

- TPR or adapted reader's theater (ART): The teacher narrates the story in English as students act it out.
- Concept attainment: Visual examples of two different concepts are provided while the teacher gives students the names of the concepts in English.
- Fishbowl: Two or more students model for the rest of the class how to generate words in English for what they have learned in Spanish using pictures and other supports.
- Field trip, experiment, movie: As the class watches the movie or talks about the field trip, the teacher provides the English words for what was learned in Spanish. Photos, notes, graphs, or artifacts from the experience are used to connect the English words to those learned in Spanish.
- Word sort with sentence prompts: Using the same pictures and realia used in Spanish, the teacher introduces the English equivalent with sentence prompts and other supports.

ACTIVE STUDENT ENGAGEMENT

During the Bridge, students generate a list of words for the concepts they have just learned, first in Spanish and then in English, and they do so while engaged in activities that focus on meaning. They might, for example, produce an anchor chart like the one pictured in Figure 10.1 about the solar system. On the surface, this chart looks like a simple translation of words from Spanish to English that the teacher supplied. But it is not, because the Bridge is not a translation and the words are not supplied by the teacher. To produce this chart, students had an active role in making meaning and generating language. They took the concepts they learned in Spanish and, building on the knowledge they have in both languages, bridged them to English. In any classroom, bilingual students who are becoming biliterate have different levels of language development ability in Spanish and English. Teachers must therefore plan and implement bridging activities that are based on their knowledge of what their students know and can do in both their languages. The following sections describe strategies to use with students of different proficiency levels in English to help them bridge. Two specific goals of the Bridge for all students, regardless of their language proficiency levels, are to learn the English equivalent of the vocabulary and language they have in Spanish and to explicitly connect the background knowledge and vocabulary they developed in Spanish to English activities. A third goal of the Bridge is for students to have the opportunity to develop their English-language skills based on their language proficiency levels. One Bridge can meet the needs of students at different proficiency levels, but the language activities of the Bridge will need to be differentiated.

Bridging with Students at the Beginning Stages of Language Development

At the end of the Spanish literacy portion of a unit, students like Carmen and Antonio will understand the key concepts and language that have been taught. In addition to planning for students to meet the first two goals mentioned earlier, teachers will want to plan for students like Carmen and Antonio to develop their English listening skills first and then add speaking skills and reading and writing during the extension activities in English.

Before moving into English, students express what they have learned in Spanish, and they or their teacher captures this learning visually using drawings and illustrations or a list like the one in the left column of the anchor chart in Figure 10.1. After generating that list of words about the solar system, the students were ready to learn the English words for what they learned in Spanish. Since they were at the beginning stages of language development, the teacher provided the English words. She could have used any one of many possible concrete activities. In this instance she chose TPR, which she had also used to teach the concepts in Spanish at the beginning of the unit. For example, as she made a big circle with both hands, she said, "sun," and the students followed her and made a big circle. Then she spun in place and said, "rotation," and again the students followed her and spun in place. The students understood the meaning of the words they were using in English because they had done the same movements during the literacy activities in Spanish. The teacher assessed her students' understanding of the words in English by observing them do the gestures to the words in English.

Most students at these early stages of language development demonstrate their understanding of the words in English only by engaging in the movements and not speaking because they are focusing on comprehension of the words. These students will need to practice the movements and the new words several times. As their knowledge of English develops, they will begin to use listening and speaking together to express their learning.

Bridging with Students at the Intermediate Stages of Language Development

Students whose language development is at the intermediate stages will participate differently in the Bridge, and the expectations of their language use will differ from those for students at the beginning stages of language development. They may speak English, but their vocabulary may be somewhat limited and their ability to use language functions, such as comparing or sequencing, may still be developing. While the focus for students at the beginning stages of language development might be listening and speaking, teachers can plan for students at the intermediate stage to broaden their vocabulary and language in English through the use of language supports.

Students who have intermediate levels of language development can be more active participants in generating language during the Bridge than students at earlier stages of language development. Once they have expressed in Spanish what they have learned, the teacher can ask them to provide the labels in English, inviting them first in small groups to come up with various ways of expressing the new concepts in English. For example, once students have worked in groups, the teacher can read *"rotación"* from the anchor chart and say, "Who knows how to say that in English?" Students may respond with "turn around," demonstrating what they know in English. After acknowledging and accepting "turn around" as one way of expressing the meaning of *rotación* in English, the teacher can introduce the word "rotation" and point out that it is a cognate and that the two words are almost the same in both languages. "Rotation" may be a new word for some students, and others may realize they knew this word but had not remembered it. Like the students in the early stages of language development, they will continue to develop their vocabulary and language through the use of sensory language supports (visuals, concrete objects, TPR), interactive language supports (sentence prompts, word banks, small-group work), and graphic language supports (graphic organizers, tables, charts). Bridging in this way and using these language supports meet the needs of a wide range of students and ensure that students at different levels of language development are successful.

Bridging with Students Who Are English Proficient

Students from bilingual families and students like Hannah who come from English-speaking families and are proficient in English can play a very active role in generating the English equivalent to what was learned in Spanish. The teacher may still have to teach them the precise formal language she is looking for by first accepting and acknowledging what they say and then introducing formal language related to the topic. Language goals for the Bridge with English-proficient students would be to learn formal language in English that builds on concepts they have generated in Spanish and to use this formal English in the extension activities.

Linguistically Appropriate Bridging Strategies

Guiding students to create an anchor chart with side-by-side lists of words in Spanish and English like the one pictured in Figure 10.1 is an excellent bridging strategy for different grade levels and language-development levels. Younger students, however, might benefit from the use of a more graphic anchor chart like the one pictured in Figure 10.2. The kindergarten students who generated this chart were

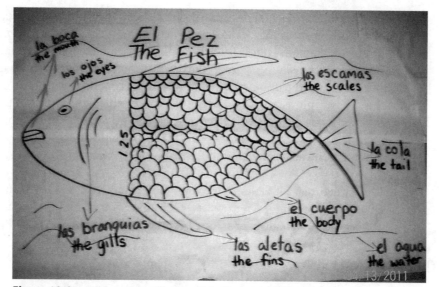

Figure 10.2. Bridge anchor chart on fish. (Courtesy of Kim Hansen and Marco Gomez's dual-language kindergarten classroom in Woodstock, Illinois.)

studying fish, and they used the visual of the fish to summarize their learning in Spanish and then bridge into English.

Bridging strategies for older students can include a more complex use and analysis of language and text. One such strategy is así se dice, which comes from the work of the Literacy Squared Project developed at the University of Colorado's BUENO Center. It is similar to the "side-by-side" strategy but is appropriate for students who have higher language development levels in both languages. Así se dice involves the following steps (adapted from Escamilla, Geiser, Hopewell, Sparrow, and Butilofsky, 2009):

1. Students create or select a statement, paragraph, poem, or other linguistic expression in Spanish (or English in a unit that begins in English and bridges to Spanish).

2. The teacher leads students through a process of paraphrasing the text to the other language by first modeling and then inviting students to continue to paraphrase either in cooperative groups or as a whole group.

3. In the process of translating the text, teachers and students engage in contrastive analysis, identifying the phonological, morphological, syntactic, grammatical, and pragmatic similarities and differences that exist in these two texts.

4. The class chooses a paraphrased version that best captures the meaning of the original text in Spanish and discusses why it is the best version.

The final step of the strategy is flexible: students can compare different English versions and analyze them or students can compare their own version against the mentor text from step 2. Teachers using this strategy should focus on the process because it is what teaches students about how the two languages are similar and different. For example, students may produce a summary of how they determined when a text is a fable that looks like this:

Aprendimos que todas las fábulas tienen varias características en común, empezando con el uso de animals u objetos como personajes principales. Se emplea el uso de la personificación al describir a los animales u objetos de la fábula.

To translate a text (self-authored or otherwise) for así se dice, students must comprehend its meaning. Translating a text requires understanding and applying the linguistic elements phonology, morphology, syntax and grammar, and pragmatics. Successful translations also require an understanding of language use and cultural norms, which can be analyzed and taught to students as part of the así se dice process. In paraphrasing the description of the fable, students and their teacher will most likely focus on passive and active voice and syntax, among other things, and they will learn that translating word for word is not effective. A paraphrased así se dice about what makes a text a fable could look like this:

> We learned that all fables share common characteristics. The main characters in all fables are either animals or objects. Personification is used to describe the animals or objects who are the main characters in the fable.

CONTRASTIVE ANALYSIS

Once the teacher and students have placed Spanish and English side by side, using a strategy such as Spanish–English side by side or así se dice, they are ready to engage in contrastive analysis, studying how the two languages are similar and different. Teachers who use the Bridge report that they find it easier to start with the similarities between the two languages and then go to the differences.

Phonology and Morphology

During the contrastive analysis, attention to the sound system and structure of language should be developmentally appropriate and meaningful to students. For example, students who understand the silent "h," one of the *letras tramposas*, which is found at the beginning of many words in Spanish, can understand that the "h" in the English word "chrysalis" is silent. Students at all levels may find it easier to understand cognates, words in the two languages that have common origins. For Spanish and English, the common origin is Latin, the root language of many academic English words. Scholars estimate that there are between 10,000 and 15,000 Spanish–English cognates (Dressler et al., 2011), and that up to 70% of the words on the Academic Word List are Spanish–English cognates (Coxhead, 2000). Many of these cognates are words frequently used in Spanish that correlate to academic words less frequently used in English.

Because cognates are the most obvious similarity that bilingual students notice between Spanish and English, we suggest that they be a big part of the contrastive analysis of the Bridge at all levels, starting as early as kindergarten. Teachers also must be very explicit in teaching about cognates because research has shown that simply being bilingual does not ensure that students will identify cognates on their own (Dressler et al., 2011). Students should be taught to look for cognates, and cognates should be widely displayed on Bridge anchor charts in their classrooms. For example, teachers could use an anchor chart like the one in Figure 10.3 to teach about cognates, beginning by saying the cognates out loud in both languages so students can "hear" the similarities. Then, pointing out that cognates need to have similar prefixes or suffixes, the teacher carries out the following three steps:

1. Invites a student or group of students to "search" for cognates and cognate patterns
2. Asks students to circle the cognates on the visual used for the Bridge

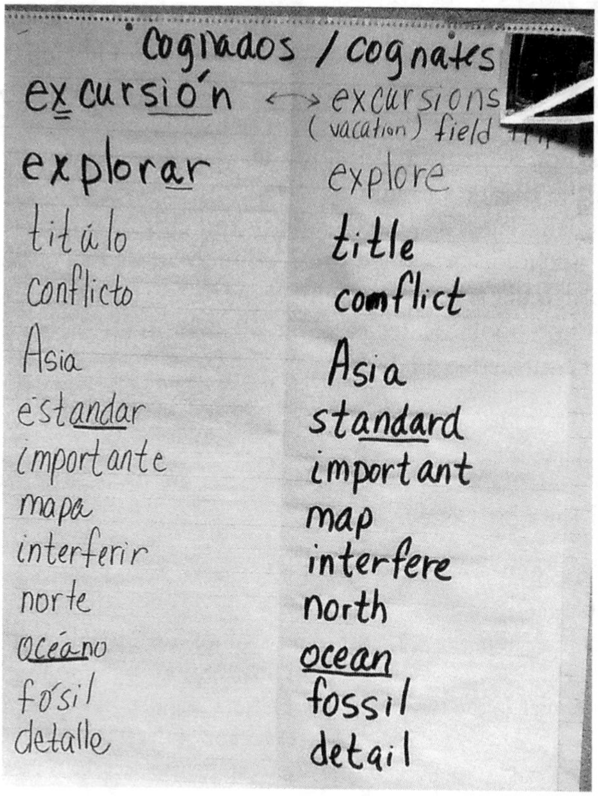

Figure 10.3. Side-by-side Bridge anchor chart in social studies: Cognates. (Courtesy of Blanca Harvey's 6th grade dual-language classroom in Kennewick, Washington.)

3. Invites one or more students to add the cognates from the Bridge visual to the Bridge anchor chart (or cognate list) in the room

When cognate lists become so long they are unwieldy, the teacher can guide students in classifying them or invite students to select several favorite cognates to add to their Bridge notebook. Students can use this notebook to capture examples and explanations about how Spanish and English are similar and different. They can take it with them throughout the grades as they continue to develop their biliteracy skills.

The cognates the students will most likely identify in Figure 10.1 on the solar system are *rotación*–rotation; *telescopio*–telescope; *gas*–gas; and *planeta*–planet. The *-ción/*-tion pattern can be a focus of a mini-lesson if the teacher thinks the students are ready for it. Drawing their attention to the pattern and then asking them to come up with additional examples to exhibit on an anchor chart helps students see, and therefore understand, the patterns and similarities in their two languages. The photograph in Figure 10.3 was taken in a 6th grade classroom. Notice the morphological patterns found in the prefixes and suffixes of these social studies words. (For more examples and explanations of cognates and other Spanish rules, see "How Spanish Works.")

Syntax and Grammar and Pragmatics

Teachers preparing a bridging lesson on syntax and grammar and pragmatics, or language use, should plan areas of focus by identifying predictable patterns inherent in the unit theme and by analyzing student writing. Attention to syntax and grammar and pragmatics, as for phonology and morphology, should be developmentally appropriate and meaningful to students.

For younger grades, simply noticing patterns and rules suffices. Naming the rules and patterns is not as necessary or even appropriate. For older students, the Bridge is the ideal context for gathering data for spontaneous or future mini-lessons that focus on aspects such as grammar and punctuation as reflected in the two languages. For students at all grade levels, the patterns and rules that are discovered during the Bridge should be moved into Bridge anchor charts. It is important that the two languages be side by side in the classroom so that students can refer to the Bridge anchor charts once the Bridge analysis has ended. As with cognates, when the word walls take up too much space, specific patterns can be "graduated" into student notebooks. Refer to Table 10.1 for descriptions and examples of each of the areas of contrastive analysis.

TABLE 10.1.

Areas of Focus for Contrastive Analysis

Element and Area of Focus	Examples
Phonology (sound system) • Sounds that are different in the two languages • Sounds that are similar in the two languages	• Sound-symbol correspondence (e.g., the [k] sound: "qu" or "c" in Spanish; "c" or "k" in English) • Silent letters (e.g., "h" and "u" in Spanish; many in English) • The existence of the [th] sound in English but not in Spanish; therefore, students select the closest Spanish phoneme, which is /d/
Morphology (word formation): prefixes and suffixes shared between the two languages (cognates)	*in*formal–**in**formal *in*for*mar*–**in**form *social*ismo–social**ism** *desastroso*–disastr**ous** *pre*parar–**pre**pare *profe*sión–profe**ssion** *educa*ción–educa**tion**
Syntax and grammar (sentence structure) • Rules for punctuation, grammar, word order, and so forth, unique to each language • Areas that are similar and areas that are different	• Spanish uses the initial inverted exclamation point; English does not (e.g., *¡Me encanta!*–I love it!) • Articles have gender in Spanish but not in English (e.g., *el título*–the title; *la revolución*–the revolution) • In Spanish, accents change the meaning of words (e.g., *el papa vive en Roma; la papa es deliciosa; mi papá es muy trabajador*) • Spanish has many reflexive verbs; English has few (e.g., *Se me cayó*) • Conjugation of verbs in Spanish reduces the need for the pronoun (e.g., *¡Voy!*) • An adjective follows a noun in Spanish and precedes it in English (e.g., *centímetros cuadrados*–square centimeters) • English contains possessive nouns; Spanish does not (e.g., my grandmother's house–*la casa de mi abuela*)
Pragmatics (language use) • Cultural norms or contexts that are reflected in language use • Use of overlapping cultural norms in a bilingual context	• Questions about age avoid the world "old" in Spanish because it has negative connotations (*¿Cuántos años tienes?*) • Figurative language from English is translated directly into Spanish: *Estoy encerrado afuera* (I am locked out!) rather than *Me quedé afuera*. • Spanish constructs are used during English (*Mis padres ganan mucho dinero*—my fathers win lots of money).

Important Elements of the Bridge

The specifics of the Bridge, including who does the bridging, when and how often bridging is done, and what is bridged, depend on student needs, program goals, and program language and allocation plans.

THE FOCUS OF THE BRIDGE

Once students have learned the unit concepts in one language, they are ready to bridge to the other language. Not everything, however, has to be bridged. Doing so would defeat the purpose of bilingual education. We bridge to maximize our students' bilingualism by developing metalinguistic awareness, and we bridge sentence structures, discourse patterns, and terms students need in order to be successful in the other language. For example, many students in dual-language programs in the United States learn math in English and science in Spanish in grades K–5. They would therefore bridge from English to Spanish in math and from Spanish to English in science. In this instance, the Bridge in science is essential to ensure that students do well on standardized science tests administered in English. They are learning science exclusively in Spanish but taking a test in English. If the Bridge is used as part of every science unit, students are prepared to demonstrate their science knowledge in English when they take the test. Even though federal accountability measures do not require students to take standardized tests in Spanish, bridging into Spanish as part of every math unit would ensure that students have the language in Spanish for what they have learned in English. This approach meets the dual-language program goal of bilingualism and biliteracy across the content areas and reinforces to students that they can transfer and access knowledge learned in one language in the other language.

The Bridge addresses the anxiety that many educators feel about teaching subjects in Spanish on which students must be tested in English. As long as educators have a plan that clearly outlines which subjects will be taught in which language at which grade levels and they are systematic about bridging, students can learn content in Spanish, engage in bridging, and be able to demonstrate their learning in English.

FREQUENCY OF THE BRIDGE

Knowing how often Bridges should occur depends on the language program being followed and the language development of the students. All two-language learners benefit from bridging. Our experience indicates that the simpler the plan, the easier it is to carry out. Thus, teachers in both bilingual and dual-language programs may find it easier to think of bridging once concepts have been learned in one language. But the Bridge can be used at other points, according to the program model. For example, in SNS classes or Spanish as a foreign language classes, bridging from English to Spanish at the beginning of a unit may make a big difference in the acquisition of Spanish.

The following questions should be considered in determining when to incorporate bridging into the program:

- Who are the students and what is their language development like?
- What are the program's vision and goals?
- How can bridging help students academically and linguistically?

An important consideration in scheduling the Bridge is the impact it will have on the allocation of minutes in Spanish and English. Because many programs seek to elevate the status of Spanish and to protect Spanish time, teachers in these programs may tend to schedule the Bridge during English time. In a program that includes monolingual and bilingual teachers, monolingual English teachers can conduct the Bridge as long as they meet with their Spanish teaching colleagues and are prepared to lead the students through the bilingual Bridge analysis.

EXTENSION ACTIVITIES

Students need an opportunity to extend their learning from one language to the other. At a minimum, extension activities should include all four language domains (listening, speaking, reading, and writing) and authentic literacy tasks. The extension activities in the discussion that follows are based on a biliteracy unit that begins with the development of literacy knowledge and skills in Spanish with a Bridge to English. They focus on language rather than content and include work in all four language domains. Instruction during these extension activities is differentiated so that language is scaffolded through the use of English-language development standards and goals for English language learners. (Spanish-language development standards and goals for Spanish language learners are used in a program that bridges from English to Spanish.)

The photographs in Figure 10.4 show a side-by-side chart created as part of a Bridge and two extension activities, one in science and one in math, from a kindergarten dual-language program. According to the content allocation plan for this program, language arts, social studies, and science are taught in Spanish by one teacher and math and language arts are taught in English by another teacher. The students generated the Bridge after finishing a science unit on worms. Worms lived in their classroom for several weeks, and students read and wrote in Spanish about the worms. They generated the list on the left side of the chart with their Spanish teacher and then they walked into their English teacher's classroom with the list. Their English teacher used TPR to teach them the English equivalent of each Spanish word, and they and their teacher completed the right side together.

For the first extension activity, the English teacher used the language experience approach (LEA), and the students dictated to her in English what they had learned about worms (see Figure 10.4B). The students in this classroom, who comprised English language learners and native English speakers, included a mix of English language development levels. To build on the background knowledge and vocabulary the students had built in Spanish, the teacher then used the topic of worms to develop story problems with her students as part of her math lesson in English (see Figure 10.4C). The extension activities allowed the students to practice the English words they had learned for content delivered in Spanish. They were not used to teach the content in English. Doing so would have been a misinterpretation of the Bridge.

KNOWLEDGE OF SPANISH THAT STUDENTS MAY USE IN ENGLISH

Extension activities provide bilingual teachers with rich information about how students use their knowledge in two languages to read and write. They can use this information to plan English literacy activities and areas of focus for mini-lessons. They can expect students, for example, to write "the" as "da," and "like" as "leik." Because the [th] sound does not exist in Spanish, students use the closest Spanish

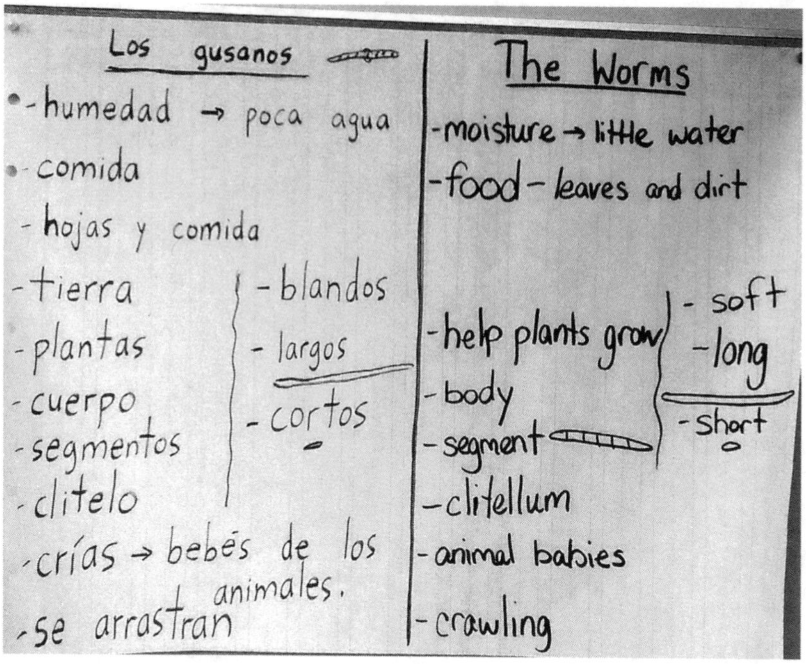

Los gusanos / The Worms anchor chart:

Los gusanos	The Worms
- humedad → poca agua	- moisture → little water
- comida	- food - leaves and dirt
- hojas y comida	
- tierra } - blandos	
- plantas } - largos	- help plants grow } - soft
- cuerpo } - cortos	- body } - long
- segmentos	- segment } - short
- clitelo	- clitellum
- crías → bebés de los animales.	- animal babies
- se arrastran	- crawling

A

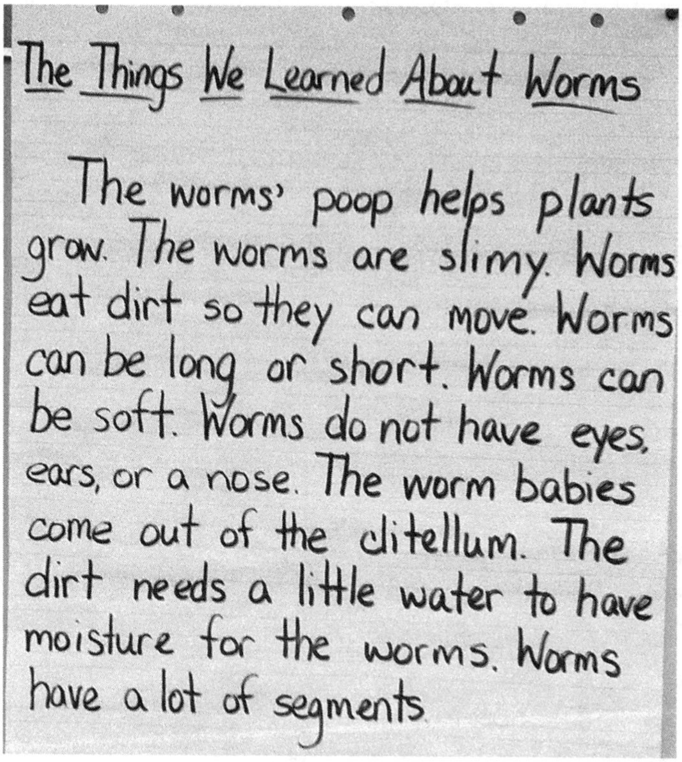

The Things We Learned About Worms

The worms' poop helps plants grow. The worms are slimy. Worms eat dirt so they can move. Worms can be long or short. Worms can be soft. Worms do not have eyes, ears, or a nose. The worm babies come out of the clitellum. The dirt needs a little water to have moisture for the worms. Worms have a lot of segments

B

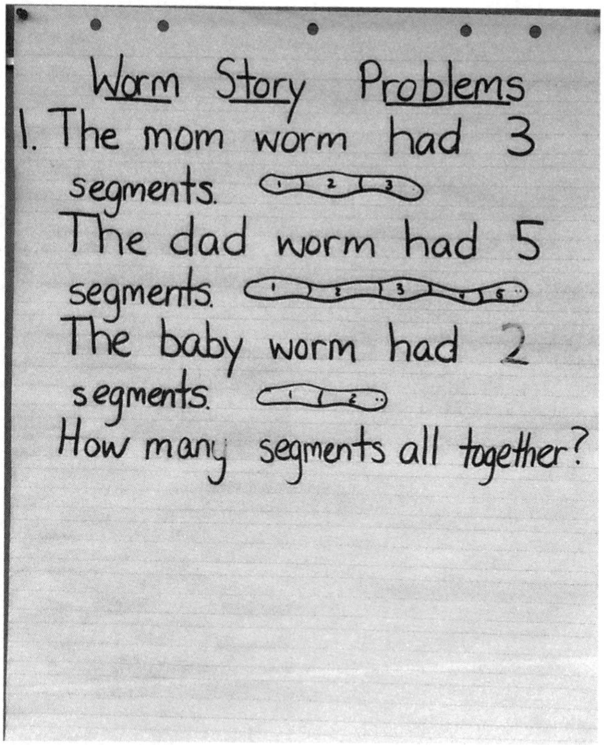

Worm Story Problems
1. The mom worm had 3 segments.
The dad worm had 5 segments.
The baby worm had 2 segments.
How many segments all together?

C

Figure 10.4.   **A,** Side-by-side Bridge anchor chart on worms. **B,** LEA extension activity. **C,** Math extension activity. (Courtesy of Kim Hansen and Marco Gomez's dual-language kindergarten classroom in Woodstock, Illinois.)

sound, which is [d]. Table 10.2 summarizes some of the predictable uses of Spanish phonology during English literacy.

Consider the English writing in Figure 10.5. The author of this text is the 1st grader Armando, who engaged in Spanish literacy activities using the book *¡No, David!* by David Shannon. As described in Chapter 9, these activities included TPR

TABLE 10.2.

Spanish Phonology in English Writing

Spanish-to-English Transfer	Approximation Based on Spanish Word Knowledge	Standard English Equivalent
Phonology	ey	a
	laiket	like it
	jor	her
	fit	feet
Spelling	cald	called
	juer	where
	litel	little
	mek	make
Phonemes	brader	brother
	der	there
	initig	anything

Adapted from Escamilla, K., & Hopewell, S. (2007, April 9–13). *The role of code-switching in the written expression of early-elementary, simultaneous bilinguals.* Paper presented at the Annual Conference of the American Education Research Association, Chicago.; and Mora, J. K. (2009). From the ballot box to the classroom. *Education Leadership, 66*(7), 14–19.

Figure 10.5. Writing extension activity. (Courtesy of Rosalva Portillo's 1st grade transitional bilingual classroom in Moline, Illinois.)

movements that identified the rules David should follow in school. As part of the extension activities after the Bridge, the students wrote in English about David and what his behavior in school should be like. During the Spanish literacy unit, Armando had written, "*David debería sentarse bonito.*" In English, he wrote, "David should set un hes sit. David cud (end up) en yellow." ("David should sit in his seat. David could [end up] in yellow.") Yellow refers to the behavior system David's teacher uses. She moves their name tags to the yellow light when they have been given a warning about their behavior. An analysis of Armando's writing in English indicates that he is using sounds he knows from Spanish in English and making many approximations using his Spanish knowledge. For example, Armando uses "e" for "i" ("set" instead of "sit" and "hes" instead of "his") and the Spanish sound of the vowel "i" for "ea" in English ("sit" instead of "seat").

Students need opportunities to engage in writing like this so that they can use what they know in all of their languages. This piece of writing provides the teacher with rich information about how Armando understands English sounds and spellings, and it helps her plan further literacy activities in English. Armando would benefit from a list of English sight words, a dictado, and an LEA exercise that would allow him to use his oral language to dictate to his teacher. High-frequency words such as "the" and "his" could come out of the LEA.

Considerations for Successful Uses of the Bridge

Knowing when, why, and how to bridge requires a complex and sophisticated understanding of teaching for biliteracy. Because the field of bilingualism has for so long kept the two languages separate, at first glance bridging may feel uncomfortable and look like simple translation. The three biggest areas to consider to ensure successful uses of the Bridge are time and frequency, purpose, and process.

TIME AND FREQUENCY

Fundamental to successful bridging is embracing the concept and research of cross-linguistic transfer: students can learn new concepts in one language and then bridge their learning to the other. Thus, bridging is effective only in a language program that clearly defines when each language is used, by what teacher, and for what content. The Bridge needs to be integrated within a carefully crafted language and content allocation plan that minimally includes language arts in both languages every day (not necessarily the same percentage of time) and that has identified in which language math, science, and social studies will be taught in each grade.

Bridging is not done randomly or whenever students code-switch. Because it comes after students learn concepts, bridging cannot be required to be part of the teacher's daily schedule, though it should be part of the overall instructional plan.

WHERE THE BRIDGE FITS INTO THE OVERALL INSTRUCTIONAL PLAN

To review, the biliteracy unit framework has three parts: (1) learning new concepts and literacy skills in one language, (2) the Bridge, during which both languages are side by side, and (3) extension activities in the other language. Students developing biliteracy need to engage in reading and writing in both languages daily. The Bridge, however, does not necessarily occur daily since it occurs only after students have learned concepts in one language. The extension activities may go on for several days or even weeks and become, in effect, the English literacy portion of the day.

PROCESS: STUDENTS ANCHOR THE BRIDGE

The teacher organizes and guides students in producing the language on Bridge anchor charts, using many of the strategies presented in this book, but the teacher does not generate the language of the Bridge. Unsuccessful Bridges usually are so because students did not generate the words and therefore do not understand them and are not able to engage in comparing the two languages or extending their learning into the other language. It is crucial to ensure that the Bridge is student centered and to guide students in expressing their learning through dynamic instructional strategies. The following section provides examples from the sample units for 1st grade and high school. You can find the complete sample 1st grade and high school units on the Web site.

Sample Extension Activities for 1st Grade and High School

In the 1st grade unit, all the activities before the Bridge are conducted in Spanish and focus on the family and the big idea, "We all have families, but each family is unique." The Bridge provides students with the English equivalent for the key words they learned in Spanish, and using the Bridge visual, students focus on the similarities and differences that exist in the two languages. They will then apply the concepts learned in Spanish by engaging in extension activities in English.

Before using the concrete activity to bridge, the students generate a list of key words they learned in Spanish about the family by reviewing the LEA they wrote and selecting key words about family. At this grade level, the language development of many English language learners is between the beginning and intermediate stages. Therefore, the teacher plans to bridge by using the following:

- The same concrete activity used at the beginning of the lesson to provide students with the English words (the photo of her family using sentence prompts and a word bank, and the photo of her students' families)
- The side-by-side bridging activity for the Bridge focus, with students adding the English words to the right-hand column
- Contrastive analysis focused on morphology: cognates (*la familia*–the family; *especial*–special); and syntax and grammar: gender-specific articles in Spanish (*la mamá*–the mom, *el papá*–the dad). (Students will add the cognates to their cognate wall and start a new anchor chart in Spanish that includes examples of feminine and masculine nouns and their corresponding articles.)

Students may notice other aspects of language, and the teacher will accept them. For example, students may notice that both languages have patterns to indicate the relationship in stepfamilies. All family names of step-relatives include the word "step" in English, whereas Spanish uses "*-astra* or *-astro*" (*madrastra, padrastro, hijastra, hijastro*).

Extension activities in English can include reading and writing books about families, such as a classroom big book that describes the similarities and differences among student families.

Students in the high school class explore in Spanish how folk tales reflect the values and beliefs of a culture. At the beginning of the unit, they learn the key words related to folk tales through a word sort, read and compare several versions of the *Llorona* legend, and write a compare/contrast essay about these versions. To bridge, students select a section of the essay and then highlight the words that represent key folk tale elements. Using the así se dice strategy, students paraphrase the statement into English. If students are at the beginning or intermediate stages of English development, it may be important to first create a side-by-side Bridge visual of key words related to folk tale elements in both languages. The Bridge focus includes an analysis of how English word order is different than Spanish, a study of the organization of ideas and how cultural norms are manifested in the two languages, and a look at the morphological patterns and meaning of words that ends in the creation of a list of cognates and false cognates.

After the Bridge, for an extension activity students read folk tales in English, identify the key elements, and write a comparative essay in English about two of the folk tales, using the folk tale elements they studied in Spanish.

Bridging and the Three Premises

The Bridge is the part of the biliteracy unit framework that most directly addresses each of the three premises. The Bridge elevates the status of Spanish by highlighting its unique aspects. Students realize that Spanish is valuable and what they learn in Spanish helps them in English, just as what they learn in English helps them in Spanish. The Bridge builds on the linguistic resources of bilingual learners and helps them develop an understanding of the third premise: that Spanish and English are governed by distinct linguistic and cultural rules.

ACTIVITIES FOR REFLECTION AND ACTION

1. This chapter outlines the benefits of students understanding the similarities and differences between their languages through contrastive analysis. Analyze your schedule and program using the following questions:

   • When are students using both languages side by side in a planned and structured manner?

   • How is contrastive analysis explicitly taught and supported throughout the day and throughout the curriculum?

   • How can your current bridging practices be supported or enhanced?

2. On the one hand, this book has described the benefits of the strategic use of two languages as opposed to the random use of two languages, or flip-flopping. On the other hand, this book supports bringing the two languages together in order to engage students in contrastive analysis. Create a presentation to explain this "third space," in which English and Spanish are brought together in a strategic and planned way, to the key stakeholders in your school community. Use artifacts, videos, photos, student

evidence, and the research and resources provided in this book to explain bridging to stakeholders.

3. A number of bridging strategies were introduced in this chapter, including the side-by-side strategy and the así se dice strategy. Analyze the language development levels of your students in both languages, and plan a Bridge and an extension activity using several of the strategies in the chapter. Using the following questions, reflect on your use of the strategy:

   • What went well? Why?

   • What surprised you about your own teaching?

   • What surprised you about student learning?

   • What improvements or changes would you make in the future?

4. This chapter describes and illustrates a number of Bridge anchor charts. As part of a Bridge strategy, implement one of the Bridge anchor charts and reflect upon the following:

   • How does this anchor chart add to the contrastive analysis of your Bridge?

   • What did you learn about your students' metalinguistic knowledge?

   • What additional Bridge anchor charts will you use in the future as result of this experience, and why?

GLOSSARY

academic language: The oral and written language used in academic texts and settings, also referred to as "formal language" or "school language." This is the language students need to perform tasks in the content areas at grade level. It is the language students may not know but must acquire to be successful in school-based activities.

active reading strategies: Activities, such as **say something/write something**, that emphasize text-level activities rather than word-level tasks.

adapted readers' theater (ART): Instructional strategy used to introduce a text students will read. The teacher orally paraphrases the text while acting out key parts and inviting students to join in as she repeats the actions.

additive bilingualism: Outcome of programs that support, build on, and continue to grow all the linguistic resources of **sequential bilingual learners** and **simultaneous bilingual learners.** Contrasts with **subtractive bilingualism.**

anchor chart: Visual support that organizes information for students. In this book, the term refers to information related to Spanish in the United States (such as comparing informal language and formal language). See also **Bridge anchor chart.**

arcaísmos españoles (archaic forms of Spanish): Spanish terms that can be traced back 500 years and that continue to be used today in certain areas of the Spanish-speaking world. Formerly a prestigious form of Spanish that has become less prestigious and is often associated with Spanish-speaking students from rural areas.

así se dice: **Bridge** strategy for students at about 3rd grade or higher. Students generate a statement or **big idea** in one language about what they have learned and then paraphrase it in the other language. This strategy allows the **contrastive analysis** between Spanish and English to include word choice, punctuation, **syntax** and grammar, and cultural norms.

big idea: Statement, also referred to as an essential or enduring understanding, grounded in learning standards and a theme.

bilingual learner: Student whose knowledge is shared across two languages. In this book, used synonymously with **two-language learner.**

biliteracy: The ability to read, write, and speak in two languages for a range of communication purposes.

Bridge, the: The instructional moment in teaching for biliteracy when teachers bring the two languages together, guiding students to actively engage in **contrastive analysis** of the two languages by visually placing them side by side and to transfer the academic content they have learned in one language to the other language.

Bridge anchor chart: Visual support that demonstrates similarities and differences between Spanish and English.

bridging: Making cross-linguistic connections.

calco (calque): Phrase copied from one language and used in the other, retaining the original meaning; similar to **linguistic borrowing.**

circular discourse pattern: Communication style often associated with Spanish that involves the use of multiple words and details to get to the point indirectly. Contrasts with **linear discourse pattern.**

code-switching: Use by a bilingual person of both languages in conversation, usually in a social context where the mixing of languages is appropriate (e.g., "*Llegaste tarde* again). Phrases that include code-switching follow grammar and phonological rules.

cognates: Words that emanate from the same root and have similar meanings, spellings, and pronunciations. Spanish and English share between 10,000 and 15,000 cognates in the area of **academic language** (e.g., photosynthesis–*fotosíntesis*; energy–*energía*; electricity–*electricidad*).

concept attainment: Instructional strategy in which students are provided with a series of appropriate and inappropriate examples of a new concept. Students analyze these appropriate and inappropriate examples to formulate a definition of the concept (Bruner, Goodnow, and Austin, 1956).

content allocation: Language in which each academic subject will be taught, by grade level, in a bilingual or **dual-language program**.

content-area journal: Place for students to respond in writing to the content they are learning. The focus is on using writing to learn.

contrastive analysis: Practice in which bilinguals compare and contrast specific areas of their languages. Areas for contrastive analysis include **phonology**, **morphology**, **syntax** and grammar, and **pragmatics**.

cross-linguistic transfer: Application of a skill or concept learned in one language to a second language.

***declamación de poesía* (poetry recitation):** Tradition in Spanish-speaking countries that involves accurate intonation and emotion; also an instructional strategy used to develop fluency.

dialogue journal: Place for free writing. Students choose the topic and language and the teacher responds to the content, not the mechanics, often using a standard formula: comment, connection, question.

dictado/dictation: Instructional strategy in which the teacher dictates words, sentences, or paragraphs that are familiar to the students, and the students write what the teacher is saying. The dictado is holistic; it teaches and develops spelling, punctuation, and **syntax** and grammar (and other word-study skills) in a way that is meaningful and comprehensive.

discourse: Patterns of language use (both oral and written) common to specific contexts in which a language is used. For example, the discourse pattern in a conversation among scientists differs from the discourse pattern in a negotiation for the purchase of a used car.

dual-language program: Additive bilingual program using two languages for literacy and content instruction that aims for true biliteracy, bilingualism, and biculturalism for all students in the program. Students may include **language-minority students** (English language learners and two-language learners) and **language-majority students**, or language-minority students only.

emergent bilingual: Student who speaks a language other than English at home and has been identified as becoming English proficient. In some contexts, this term is used in preference to **English language learner.**

English language learner (ELL): Student who speaks a language other than English at home and has been identified as becoming English proficient. In some contexts, this term is being replaced by **emergent bilingual.**

fishbowl: Instructional strategy that involves two or more students modeling the language and behavior the rest of the class is to use as they work in pairs or small groups.

focused reading: Instructional strategy in which students read a variety of texts at different readability levels on the same topic.

formal language. See **academic language.**

formative assessment: Assessment that occurs throughout a lesson or unit to provide feedback that is used to modify instruction.

funds of knowledge: Cultural resources and knowledge held by bilingual students and their families.

genre: A categorization of writing or speaking, such as humorous or persuasive. Examples of writing or speaking may reflect several genres.

guided reading: A method of literacy instruction currently popular in U.S. schools. Small groups of students with similar levels of literacy development are provided targeted instruction in areas of need with appropriately leveled texts.

***Habla con tu compañero(a) o pareja* (Talk to your partner):** Cooperative learning strategy in which two or more students talk with each other about a particular topic, usually using **sentence prompts**. The purpose is to give students the opportunity to actively use the language being taught in a low-anxiety situation.

heritage language speaker: Student brought up in a home where Spanish or other minority language is spoken and who has some proficiency in the language.

informal language. See **social language.**

initial literacy instruction: The teaching of reading and writing when students first encounter print and are beginning to learn to match oral language with text.

internal structure of a language: The natural way a language is organized. Literacy instruction that matches the internal structure of the language is characterized by the use of strategies that support literacy development in that language, such as studying vowels first in Spanish and consonants first in English.

language allocation: Percentage of the instructional day spent in each language in a bilingual or **dual-language program**.

language experience approach (LEA): A method of writing instruction in which the teacher puts students' oral language into print, enabling students to create a comprehensible text in their own words directly related to a shared experience.

language-majority student: Speaker of the language used by the majority of the people in the country (e.g., English speaker in the United States).

language-minority student: Speaker of a language other than the one used by the majority of the people in the country (e.g., Spanish speaker in the United States); also referred to as an English language learner or a two-language learner.

letras tramposas **(tricky letters):** Letters in Spanish that produce the same sound (e.g., b/v; c/s/z; c/qu/; j/g; ll/y). They are described as "tricky" because the **phonology** of Spanish is otherwise regular and transparent. They are often the focus of a **word wall** in Spanish.

linear discourse pattern: A communication style often associated with English that involves the use of a minimal number of words to get to the point directly. Contrasts with **circular discourse pattern**.

linguistic borrowing: A characteristic of Spanish in the United States; the use of English words that retain the English meaning (e.g., *"lonche"*–lunch; *"bills"*–bills; *"puchar"*–push).

linguistic creativity: Term used in this book to describe the ways students use Spanish and English together.

literacy: The ability to use listening, speaking, reading, and writing in a variety of contexts and for a variety of purposes to interact with and understand the world.

metalinguistic awareness: The understanding of how language works and how it changes and adapts in different circumstances. The teaching of metalinguistic awareness means helping students learn to "think about language" and understand the explicit parts of language that together create the language system. In bilingual learners of Spanish and English, it is the understanding of how the two languages are similar and different.

morphology: The study of the meaningful parts of words, such as prefixes and suffixes.

newcomer: Student new to the United States, usually a sequential bilingual who has developed one language and is learning a second language.

nombres cortos y largos: Strategy for teaching initial literacy skills in Spanish (concept of word, syllable awareness, letter sounds, and strong and weak vowels) based on meaningful text: the students' names.

oracy: The ability to use, understand, and produce a variety of oral language (listening and speaking) **genres**.

oral discourse pattern: Speech pattern of a particular group of people, reflecting the social expectations of the cultural context in which their language is developed.

phonological awareness: Understanding of how words sound, apart from what words mean. For example, understanding that the word "kitchen" has two spoken parts (syllables), that the word "bed" rhymes with "bread," and that the words "cat" and "king" begin with the same sound (Burns, Griffin, and Snow, 1999).

phonology: The study of the sound system of a language.

picture walk: Active reading strategy in which students look at pictures from a book and turn and talk about them with a partner, using **sentence prompts** and a word bank.

pragmatics: The study of how language is used and the larger context in which it is used.

reader's interview: A part of **SSR** in which the teacher meets with a student to discuss what he or she is reading. The interview is an opportunity for **formative assessment** of individual student comprehension skills and reading preferences and should be conducted in the language of the book.

realia: Real, concrete objects used in classroom instruction.

rubric: Documentation of student learning using specific criteria that match learning goals.

say something; say something/write something: Instructional strategy in which student partnerships or small groups read a portion of text and then stop and say and, sometimes, write a reaction, supported by a **sentence prompt** for summary, prediction, question and answer, or personal or academic connection.

semantic extension: A characteristic of Spanish in the United States; the expansion of the original meaning of Spanish words to include the meaning of a similar English word (e.g., "*groserías*"–groceries; "*carpeta*"–carpet).

semantics: Study of the meanings of words, especially the differences in word meanings based on context.

sentence prompt (*frase clave*): A few words provided by the teacher to give students the structure of the language so they can use language appropriately as they participate in a learning activity.

sequential bilingual learner: Student who has developed one language and is learning a second language.

simultaneous bilingual learner: Student who has been exposed to two languages since before age 3.

single-dominance perspective: A way of looking at **two-language learners** that assumes their abilities in both languages are not equal and identifies a dominant language, often resulting in the determination that the **simultaneous bilingual learner** is "low" in both languages.

social language: The relatively informal conversational language anchored in context, usually reflective of the language used in students' homes and communities; also referred to as "informal language," "home language," or "community Spanish."

Spanglish: Mixture of Spanish and English that follows a set of grammar and linguistic rules; often used in social settings where it is considered appropriate.

Spanish for native speakers: A form of Spanish-as-a-foreign-language program that has been adapted to meet the needs of Spanish speakers.

Spanish literacy: The broad range of teaching and learning activities undertaken through the medium of the Spanish language, focusing on the integrated development of oracy, reading, and writing throughout the curriculum.

subtractive bilingualism: The outcome of programs that focus on developing English skills, and in which students lose their native language as they learn English. In subtractive bilingual programs, any native language support is provided only until students achieve English proficiency. Contrasts with **additive bilingualism.**

summative assessment: Assessment that occurs at the end of lessons or units to evaluate what students have learned.

sustained silent reading (SSR): A time dedicated to individual student reading. During this time, students are free to choose anything they want to read, including magazines, newspapers, and books on any subject and in either Spanish or English.

syntax: Refers to word order within phrases and sentences (how phrases and sentences are constructed), and the rules that govern word order. Often paired with "grammar" to encompass the whole system of rules that describe a language.

total physical response (TPR): Instructional strategy used to introduce academic concepts in a concrete and comprehensible manner. The teacher models academic oral language accompanied by pictures, realia, and movements.

transitional bilingual program: Program that uses Spanish for a limited number of years while students learn English. Once students are considered to be English proficient, they are educated as monolingual English speakers and are assumed to have no further need of Spanish. This is a subtractive program that aims for English proficiency. It is often early exit, lasting for 3 years or less.

two-language learner: Student whose knowledge is shared across two languages. In this book, used synonymously with **bilingual learner**.

two-way-immersion (TWI): A **dual-language program** that supports **additive bilingualism**, in which **language-majority students** and **language-minority students** learn together to become bilingual, biliterate, and bicultural.

word sort: Instructional strategy in which pairs of students are asked to categorize words, pictures, or **realia** into predetermined categories (a closed word sort) or into categories of their own choosing (an open word sort).

word wall: A collection of words posted in the classroom to teach spelling or vocabulary and to which words are continually added, for example, side-by-side lists of words that capture examples of the *letras tramposas* in Spanish.

HOW SPANISH WORKS

Here we highlight aspects of the internal structure of Spanish that have a direct impact on the teaching of literacy in Spanish and the development of metalinguistic awareness, a key element of biliteracy. Understanding these aspects of Spanish and their counterparts in English helps teachers select the methods, strategies, and materials that ensure that they take an authentic approach to teaching literacy in Spanish and help them plan for the contrastive analysis part of the Bridge.

Vowels and Syllables

Spanish is a highly regular, consistent language that has a one-to-one correspondence between letter and sound and clearly defined boundaries between syllables. Twenty-seven letters produce 24 phonemes, and 5 vowels produce 5 sounds (Mora, 2009). Three vowels (a-e-o) are strong, or open, and two (i-u) are weak, or closed.

Syllables are made up of letters that are pronounced all at once. They are formed with one or more vowels or one or more vowels in combination with a consonant. The consonant can come before or after the vowel. The following rules for dividing words into syllables (adapted from Morris and Rosado, 2009) are applied in Spanish without exception.

1. When one consonant appears between two vowels, the consonant joins the second vowel to create a second syllable: *tu-bo; ma-no*. These are *sílabas directas* or *sencillas*.

2. When two consonants appear between two vowels, the two consonants are separated to create two syllables: *rit-mo; cer-ca*. These are *sílabas compuestas* or *cerradas*.

3. The digraphs CH, LL, RR are never divided (*e-llos*). The following consonant combinations are also never divided: BL, BR (*bra-zo, blu-sa*); CL, CR (*cre-cer, cli-ma*); DR (*dra-ma*); FL, FR (*flo-re-ro, fra-ter-ni-zar*); GL (*glo-sa-rio*); PR, PL (pri-mo, plu-ma); and TR *(tra-ba-jo)*.

4. A diphthong is a combination of two vowels pronounced as one sound (Thonis, 1983), as in *iglesia, ruido, ciudad,* and *puerta*. Diphthongs are made up of two weak vowels, as in *ciudad,* or one weak and one strong vowel, as in *puerta*. Diphthongs are not divided unless the weak vowel is accented. If the weak vowel is accented, the diphthong is broken and separated into two syllables. For example, the past tense of the verb *rociar* (to spray), *roció*, as in *El roció las flores* (He sprayed the flowers), is divided into two syllables, *ro-ció*, because the weak vowel, "i," is not accented and therefore the two vowels form a diphthong. In the present tense, however, *rocío*, as in *Yo rocío las flores* (I spray the flowers), the word is divided into three syllables, *ro-cí-o*, because, upon receiving the orthographic accent, the weak vowel becomes strong, thereby breaking the diphthong. Other examples include *bebía (be-bí-a); tío (tí-o); reír (re-ír); maíz (ma-íz), María (Ma-rí-a)*.

5. Triphthongs, which appear less frequently in Spanish than diphthongs, are made up of three vowels that are pronounced all at once. The traditional pattern is one strong vowel (a-e-o) between two weak vowels (i-u), as in *guau; miau; con-fiéis*. The four vowel combinations that form triphthongs in Spanish are
   - *iai* (as in estudi**ái**s)
   - *iei* (as in estudi**éi**s)
   - *uai* (as in continu**ái**s or *uay* as in *Uru**guay***)
   - *uei* (as in continu**éi**s or *uey* as in ***buey***)

6. Two strong vowels together, called a hiatus (*hiatos*), always form a separate syllable, as in *poeta (po-e-ta); caer (ca-er); museo (mu-se-o); oeste (o-es-te)*.

Phonology and Irregular Orthography: *The letras tramposas*

"B," "V"

In Spanish, the [b] sound can be written as either "b" or "v"; the difference between "b" (*"b" de burro o "b" larga*) and "v" (*"v" de vaca o "v" corta*) is orthographic because these two sounds are allophones, or variations of the same phoneme. Saying the words *"burro"* and *"vaca"* illustrates their similarity. The distinction between "b" and "v" is made clear only through their use in spelling. In English, the difference between "b" and "v" is phonemic. Saying the words "berry" (as in "I love to eat berries") and "very" (as in "I am very happy") illustrates their difference. The distinct sounds these letters have in English helps to identify them.

"C," "Q," "K"

"C," "q," and "k" all produce the sound [k]. "C is pronounced [k] when followed by the vowels a-o-u or when followed by a consonant, for example, *casa, coche, cuando, clases*. "Q" makes the [k] sound when followed by a mute "u" and only in the two combinations *que* as in *querer* and *qui* as in *quitar* or *quiosco*. "K" is used in a few foreign words that have been adopted into Spanish, such as "*kilo-gramo*" and "*kiwi*."

"C," "S," "Z"

"C," "s," and "z" all produce the sound [s] on the American continent. "C" is pronounced [s] when written before "e" or "i," as in *cerro* or *cimiento*. "S" is pronounced [s] as in *silla*. "Z" is pronounced [s] as in *zapato*.

In Spain, "c" (before "e" and "i") and "z" are pronounced as a fricative, similar to the [th] sound in English. This is called the *seseo* in Spanish.

LAS LETRAS MUDAS ("H," "U")

"H" is always mute in Spanish. It is used mainly in words of Greek or Latin origin, such as *hierba, hacer,* and *huevo*. Words that begin with -*ie* and -*ue* are preceded by the silent "h."

"U" is mute when it appears after "g" and "q" and before the vowels "e" and "i," as in *Querétaro, quizá, guerra,* and *guitarra*. "U" after "g" and before the vowel "a," however, is not mute and is pronounced, as in *Guatemala* and *guayaba*.

LA DIERESIS Ü

"Ü" is pronounced [u] when it contains the dieresis "ü," as in *bilingüe* and *pingüino*.

"G," "J," "X"

"G" is pronounced [h] when used before "i" and "e" (*girasol, gente*); "j" is pronounced [h] in all positions (*jícama, jocote, Junípero*), and "x" is pronounced [h] in *México*.

The *letras tramposas*

Letter	Examples
"B" is used in • Verbs that end in *aber, buir, bir* • Verbs that end in *aba, abas, ábamos* • Consonant blends (*br, bl, bs*) • Compound syllables (*bla, ble, bli, blo, blu*) • Words in which "b" is followed by "u" (*bu, bus, bur*), except *vuestros* in all its forms	*haber, distribuir, concebir* *jugaba, llevabas, caminábamos* *brisa, blusa, absoluto* *blanco, cable, biblioteca, blindado, hablo, diablura* *burro, buque, burbuja, burlar, buscar*
"V" is used in • Verbs that end in *servar* • Adjectives that end in *ava, ave, avo, eva, ivo, iva, evo* • Verbs *ir, estar, andar,* and *tener* when conjugated in the preterite • Words that begin with *ven*	*reservar, observar, conservar* *brava, suave, esclavo, nueva, superlativo, primitiva, agresiva, nuevo* *estuve, anduve, tuve, ve, va, van* *venenoso, ventajoso, venidero, venta, venganza, ventaja*
"C" is pronounced • [s] when followed by "e" or "i" • [k] when followed by "a," "o," or "u"	*cerro, cimiento, cocina* *casa, comer, cuando, cocina*
"H" is used in • Words that begin with *um* + vowel • Words that begin with *ue, ui, ia, ie,* and their derivations • Words that begin with *iper, ipo, idr, igr, emi, osp* • Words that begin with *hecto, hepta, hexa, hetero, homo, helio* • Words that begin with *erm, orm, ist, olg* • All forms of verbs in which it appears in the infinitive	*humano, humo, húmedo, humilde, humor* *hueco, huir, hiato, hielo* *hipérbole, hipopótamo, hidroavión, higrómetro, hemiciclo, hospedaje* *hectómetro, heptaedro, hexágono, heterogéneo, homófono, helio* *hermano, hormiga, historia* (exceptions: *ermita, ola*) *he, has, ha, habré, haciendo, hecho, haré, hablé, hablaré*
"U" is • Mute in words where it comes after "g" and "q" and before "e" and "i" • Pronounced when followed by the vowel "a" • Pronounced when there is a *dieresis*	*guerra, guitarra, querer, quitar* *Guatemala, Guadalajara* *bilingüe, pingüino*
"G" is pronounced [h] when used before "i" and "e."	*general, gigante*
"J" is pronounced [h] in all positions.	*jamás, Jaime*

Adapted from Escamilla, K. (1999). Teaching literacy in Spanish. In R. DeVillar & J. Tinajero (Eds.), *The power of two languages 2000* (pp. 126–141). New York: Macmillan/McGraw-Hill; and Morris, L., & Rosado, L. (2009). *Desarrollo del español para maestros en programas de educación bilingüe.* Arlington, TX: LM Educational Consultant.

Word Families

zapato	*zapato, zapatero, zapatería*
sol	*solana, solazo, solearse*
criar	*criado, crianza, criatura*
nube	*nuboso, nublado, nubecillo*
vestir	*vestidura, vestimenta, vestido*
poner	*deponer, disponer, entreponer, exponer, imponer, posponer, proponer, reponer, sobreponer, superponer*

Adapted from Thonis, E. (1983). *The English-Spanish connection.* Miami: Santillana USA.

Latin Roots

Spanish and English contain words that have Latin and Greek suffixes and prefixes. Words in both languages that share these common origins are called cognates.

Latin Root	Spanish Example	English Example
ambi (both)	**ambi**guo **amb**os	**ambi**guous
bene (good)	**bene**volente	**bene**volent
circun(m) (around)	**circun**stancia	**circum**stance
dict (to say)	**dict**ado	**dict**ation
mit (to send)	trans**mitir**	trans**mit**

Greek Roots

Greek Root	Spanish Example	English Example
auto (self)	**auto**biográfico	**auto**biographic
dis (bad; hard; unlucky)	**dis**funcional	**dys**functional
logía (study of)	psico**logía**	psycho**logy**
micro (small)	**micro**scopio	**micro**scope
fobia (fear)	claustro**fobia**	claustro**phobia**

Prefixes

Prefix	Examples
de- (opposite)	*devaluar* (devalue)
in-, *im-* (in)	*ingreso* (income) *inmigración* (immigration)
in-, *im-*, *il-*, *ir-* (not)	*indirecto* (indirect) *impaciente* (impatient) *ilegal* (illegal) *irregular* (irregular)
re- (again)	*repasar* (review)
sub- (under)	*subordinado* (subordinate)

Suffixes

Suffix	Examples
-al, *-ial* (having characteristics of)	*universal* (universal) *facial* (facial)
-er, *-or* (one who; person connected with)	*doctor* (doctor) *profesor* (professor)
-al (noun; person, place, or thing)	*animal* (animal) *manual* (manual)
-al (adjective; descriptor)	*brutal* (brutal) *criminal* (criminal)
-ble (adjective; descriptor)	*admirable* (admirable) *favorable* (favorable)

Cognate Patterns

	Suffix Pattern	Spanish	English
Nouns	-ista → -ist	*artista*	artist
		lista	list
	-ismo → -ism	*socialismo*	socialism
		mecanismo	mechanism
	-ncia → -nce	*arrogancia*	arrogance
		paciencia	patience
	-dad → -ty	*actividad*	activity
		electricidad	electricity
	-ción → -tion	*combinación*	combination
		institución	institution
	-ía, ia, io → -y	*agencia*	agency
		batería	battery
		salario	salary
Adjectives	-ivo → -ive	*decisivo*	decisive
		efectivo	effective
	-oso → -ous	*gracioso*	gracious
		delicioso	delicious
	-ico → -ic	*fantástico*	fantastic
		artístico	artistic
	-nte → -nt	*conveniente*	convenient
		importante	important
	-ido → -id	*espléndido*	splendid
		sólido	solid
	-il → -ile	*frágil*	fragile
		automóvil	automobile
	-ario → -ary	*arbitrario*	arbitrary
		imaginario	imaginary
Infinitive	-ar → -ate	*acentuar*	accentuate
		estimar	estimate
		terminar	terminate
	-ar → vowel + consonant + "e" (drop)	*acusar*	accuse
		comparar	compare
		analizar	analyze
Verbs	-tar or -tir → vowel + consonant + "t"	*consultar*	consult
		representar	represent
		convertir	convert
Verbs	-ificar → -ify	*simplificar*	simplify
		justificar	justify
Adverbs	-mente → -ly	*automaticamente*	automatically
		normalmente	normally

Apócope and Contractions

Words in Spanish can be shortened or lengthened by the use of diminutives, *chiquitita* (very little), and augmentatives, *grandotota* (very big). *Apócope*, words that are shortened, and contractions are other ways that words are reduced in Spanish.

Rule	Examples
Words such as **uno**, **bueno**, **malo**, **grande**, **alguno**, and **ninguno** may be shortened if they precede the noun.	**Algún** *día vendrá.* **Un** *galán me ama.* **Ningún** *hombre es igual al mío.* *La* **gran** *dama es mi mamá.*
Cualquiera and **cualesquiera** may be shortened by dropping the final "a" before either singular or plural forms.	*Dame* **cualquier** *cosa.* **Cualesquier** *de los dos está bien.*
Ciento drops its **to** before *mil* and before plural nouns of either gender. **Santo** (sacred, holy) is shortened before a saint's name unless the name begins with *Do* or *To*. **Santa** is never shortened.	**Cien** *mil hojas* **San** *Pablo* **Santa** *Clara*
de + el = del **a + el = al**	*Me gusta el olor* **del** *perfume.* **Al** *señor le gusta comer papitas.*

Placement of Accent Marks within Words

Words in Spanish have prosodic syllables (syllables that are the strongest when pronounced). Depending on where the prosodic syllabic is located, it either does or does not become a syllable that is accented. There are four possible places for each syllable, beginning with the last and moving to the left: the ultimate, or last (*aguda*), the penultimate, or second to last (*llana o grave*), the antepenultimate, or third from last (*esdrújula*), and the fourth from last (*sobreesdrújula*). Two examples, which are consistent with the Basic Accent Rules, show how a change in the placement of the orthographic accent changes the meaning of a word.

Example 1: *Paulo se terminó toda la leche.* (Paulo finished all the milk.)

The ultimate syllable is prosodic and the word ends in a vowel; therefore, the syllable is accented:

Antepenultimate *(esdrújula)*	Penultimate *(llana o grave)*	Ultimate *(aguda)*
ter	mi	nó

Example 2: *Me gusta la carne cocinada al término medio.* (I like meat cooked medium well.)

The antepenultimate syllable is prosodic; therefore, it is accented:

Antepenultimate *(esdrújula)*	Penultimate *(llana o grave)*	Ultimate *(aguda)*
tér	mi	no

BASIC ACCENT RULES

- *Palabras agudas*: Words whose last syllable is strongest and DO end in the consonants "n" or "s" or a vowel (a-e-i-o-u) require an orthographic accent: *terminó, acción; detrás, cantó, bambú, mamá.*
- *Palabras llanas o graves:* Words whose penultimate syllable is strongest require an orthographic accent if they DO NOT end in "n," "s," or a vowel: *lápiz, árbol, fácil.*
- *Palabras esdrújulas*: Words whose antepenultimate syllable is strongest ALWAYS require an orthographic accent: *vámonos, pájaro, poético, depósito, sílaba.*
- *Palabras sobreesdrújulas*: Words whose fourth from last syllable is strongest ALWAYS require an orthographic accent: *devuélvemelo.*
- When used in a question, the following words are always accented: *¿Qué? ¿Cómo? ¿Cuándo? ¿Dónde? ¿Quién? ¿Por qué?* (Note that when used in a question the word *porque* is divided into two words.)
- Most monosyllabic words (*sol, gas, sin*) are not accented.

Accent Rules That Determine the Meaning of Words

Most monosyllabic words in Spanish do not have a written accent mark. The following words, however, are exceptions: homonyms whose meaning is determined by the presence or absence of an accent mark.

Unaccented Word	Function and Example	Accented Word	Function and Example
aun	even (conjunction) ***Aun** sin conocerte, te amaba.*	*aún*	yet (adverb) *Tú **aún** no me quieres.*
de	of (preposition) *Yo soy **de** México.*	*dé (dar)*	to give ***Dé** todo lo que tiene.*
el	the (article) ***El** periódico no es mío.*	*él*	he (pronoun) ***Él** es mi hijo.*
mas	but (conjunction) *Yo lo amo, **mas** él a mí no.*	*más*	more (adverb) *Quisiera **más** postre.*
mi	my (possessive pronoun) ***Mi** casa es amplia.*	*mí*	me (direct object) *Ése regalo es para **mí**.*
se	reflexive pronoun ***Se** me olvidó tu cumpleaños.*	*sé*	I know (verb, *saber*) ***Sé** que vendrás.*
si	if (conjunction) ***Si** quieres, te recojo a las 6 p.m.*	*sí*	yes (interjection) ***Sí**, gracias por venir por mí.*
te	you (pronoun) ***Te** tienes que bañar.*	*té*	tea (noun) *Me encanta el **té** de hierbabuena.*
tu	your (possessive pronoun) ***Tu** carro nuevo está precioso.*	*tú*	you (personal pronoun) ***Tú** eres mi mejor amiga.*

Adapted from Mora, J. K. (2009). From the ballot box to the classroom. *Education Leadership, 66*(7), 14–19; Morris, L., & Rosado, L. (2009). *Desarrollo del español para maestros en programas de educación bilingüe.* Arlington, TX: LM Educational Consultant; and Thonis, E. (1983). *The English-Spanish connection.* Miami: Santillana USA.

Punctuation Elements in Spanish

Punctuation in Spanish operates very similarly to punctuation in English, with several exceptions.

- Exclamation and interrogation marks are used at the beginning and end of sentences: *Amas a tu novio, ¿se van a casar?; ¡No me digas!*

- A hyphen (*guión*), rather than quotation marks, is used to indicate the beginning of a dialogue between characters in a text or to indicate a change in interlocutor.

    -¿Qué estás diciendo?

    -No pensé que estuvieras tan molesto.

- There are three types of quotation marks in Spanish:

    1. *Las comillas españolas* («/») are used to highlight one word in a text: *Luego la mamá dijo: «Sí».*

    2. *Las comillas inglesas* ("/") are used to quote something: *Simón Bolivar dijo: "Nada es tan peligroso como dejar permancer largo tiempo en un mismo ciudadano el poder."*

    3. *Las comillas simples* ('/') are used to quote a short phrase: *Al ver el cuadro nuevo, Juan dijo: 'que basura' se ha comprado Raúl.*

- Words in the following categories are not capitalized:

    1. Days of the week: *lunes, martes*

    2. Months of the year: *enero, febrero*

    3. Nationalities: *mexicano, estadounidense*

    4. Religions and their followers: *el catolicismo y los católicos*

    5. Names of people and tribes: *los incas y los mapuches*

    6. Languages: *el inglés y el español*

- Names of disciplines are capitalized (unlike in English, where disciplines are not capitalized, except when referring to a specific course):

    *A mi me gusta estudiar **Q**uímica y **M**atemáticas* (I like studying chemistry and math.)

- Titles of books, stories, poems, articles, movies, songs, and plays have only an initial capital letter: *Las aventuras de Don Quijote* (The Adventures of Don Quixote); *De amor y de sombra* (Of Love and Shadows)

Punctuation Mark	Name in Spanish	Name in English
:	*dos puntos*	colon
;	*punto y coma*	semicolon
-	*guión*	hyphen
–	*raya*	dash
« »	*comillas españolas*	quotation marks (Spanish style)
' '	*comillas simples*	single quotation marks
" "	*comillas inglesas*	quotation marks (English style)
¿ ?	*signos de interrogación*	question marks
¡ !	*signos de exclamación*	exclamation marks
( )	*paréntesis*	parenthesis
[ ]	*corchetes, paréntesis cuadrados*	brackets
{ }	*corchetes*	braces, curly brackets
*	*asterisco*	asterisk
...	*puntos suspensivos*	ellipses

Gender

Nouns in Spanish are either feminine or masculine. Most feminine nouns end in -*a* (*hembra, muchacha y chica*), and most masculine nouns end in -*o* (*macho, muchacho y chico*).

Variations of the Rule	Feminine	Masculine
Some nouns that end in -*a* or -*o* match the opposite gender.	*la mano, la foto, la radio*	*el día, el mapa, el problema*
Nouns ending in -*i* or -*u* are mainly masculine.		*el colibrí, el espíritu*
Nouns ending in -*l*, -*n*, -*r*, or -*s* are mainly masculine.		*el árbol, el mes, el pan* *el color*
Nouns suffixed by -*miento*, -*dor* (denoting an agent), or -*al* are masculine.		*el sufrimiento, el obrador* *el manantial*
Nouns suffixed by -*on*, -*ión*, -*d*, -*tad*, or -*tud* are feminine.	*la razón, la nutrición, la voluntad, la pared, la actitud*	**Exceptions** *el avión, el camión, el bastión, el césped, el huésped*
Nouns ending in -*z* are feminine.	*la luz, la paz* *la voz*	**Exceptions** *el arroz, el pez, el lápiz*
Nouns of Spanish origin suffixed by -*ma* and -*ta* are feminine. Nouns of Greek origin suffixed by -*ma* and -*ta* are masculine.	*la llama, la dama, la rata*	*el idioma, el clima, el poeta* *el profeta*
Nouns suffixed by -*sis* are feminine.	*la síntesis, la hipótesis*	
Nouns of common gender can be used with both -*ista* and others.	*la artista, la deportista* *la cónyuge, la estudiante*	*el artista, el deportista* *el cónyuge, el estudiante*
The gender of certain nouns changes according to the meaning.	*la capital* (city) *la cura* (cure) *la frente* (forehead) *la mañana* (the morning) *la orden* (command) *la pendiente* (slope)	*el capital* (money) *el cura* (priest) *el frente* (front) *el mañana* (tomorrow) *el orden* (system of rules) *el pendiente* (earring)

REFERENCES

Allan, J. (2004). *Tools for teaching content literacy.* Portland, ME: Stenhouse.

Asher, J. J. (2000). *Learning another language through actions* (6th ed.). Los Gatos, CA: Sky Oaks Productions.

August, D., & Hakuta, K. (1997). *Improving schooling for language-minority children: A research agenda.* National Research Council Institute of Medicine. Washington, D.C.: National Academy Press.

Baker, C., & Prys Jones, S. (2006). The Development of Bilingualism in Children. In K. Brown (Ed.), *Encyclopedia for Language and Linguistics ELL2* (pp. 36–38). St. Louis: Elsevier.

Berglund, R. L., & Johns, J. L. (1983). A primer on uninterrupted sustained silent reading. *The Reading Teacher, 36,* 534–539.

Bloomfield, L. (1933). *Language.* New York: Henry Holt.

Brisk, M. E., & Harrington, M. (2007). *Literacy and bilingualism: A handbook for all teachers.* Mahwah, NJ: Lawrence Erlbaum.

Bruner, J. R., Goodnow, J. J., & Austin, G. A. (1956). *A study of thinking.* New York: Wiley.

Burns, M. S., Griffin, P., & Snow, C. E. (1999). *Starting off right: A guide to promoting children's reading success.* Washington, DC: National Academy Press.

Calvert, D., & Silverman, S. (1975). *Speech and deafness.* Washington, DC: Alexander Graham Bell Association for the Deaf.

Campbell, R., & Kreeft Peyton, J. (1998). Heritage language students: A valuable language resource. *ERIC Review, 6*(1).

Capps, R., Fix, M. E., Murray, J., Ost, J., Passel, J. S., & Hernandez, S. H. (2005). *The new demography of America's schools: Immigration and the No Child Left Behind Act.* Washington, DC: Urban Institute.

Center for Applied Linguistics. (2010). *Foreign language.* Retrieved July 6, 2012, from http://www.cal.org/topics/fl/immersion.html

Center for Applied Linguistics. (2011). *Directory of two-way bilingual immersion programs in the U.S.* Retrieved July 6, 2012, from http://www/cal.org/twi/directory

Cloud, N., Genesee, F., & Hamayan, E. (2000). *Dual language instruction: A handbook for enriched education.* Boston: Heinle & Heinle.

Cloud, N., Genesee, F., & Hamayan, E. (2009). *Literacy instruction for English language learners.* Portsmouth, NH: Heinemann.

Coxhead, A. (2000). A new academic word list. *TESOL Quarterly, 34,* 213–238.

Crawford, J. (1999). *Bilingual education: History, politics, theory, and practice.* Los Angeles: Bilingual Education Services.

Cummins, J. (1980). The entry and exit fallacy in bilingual education. *NABE Journal, 4*(3), 25–29.

Cummins, J. (1981). The role of primary language development in promoting education success for language minority students. In C. F. Leyba (Ed.), *Schooling and Language Minor-*

ity Students: A Theoretical Framework (pp. 1–50). Los Angeles: Evaluation, Dissemination, and Assessment Center.

Cummins, J. (1996). *Negotiating identities: Education for empowerment in a diverse society.* Los Angeles: California Association for Bilingual Education.

Damico, J. (2010, December). *The false promise of phonemic awareness in English language learners.* Paper presented at the annual statewide conference for teachers serving linguistically and culturally diverse students, Oak Brook, IL.

de Jong, E. J. (2011). *Foundations for multilingualism in education: From principles to practice.* Philadelphia: Caslon.

Dressler, C., Carlo, M. S., Snow, C. E., August, D., & White, C. E. (2011). Spanish-speaking students' use of cognate knowledge to infer meaning of English words. *Bilingualism: Language and Cognition, 14*(2), 243–255.

Duke, N. K. (2007, June 7). *Comprehension in early education.* Paper presented at Promoting student literacy through comprehension: Enhancing teacher preparation and professional development, Albany, NY. Retrieved January 15, 2011, from http://nycomprehensivecenter.org/docs/Duke-June07.ppt

Duke, N. K., & Pearson, P. D. (2002). Comprehension instruction in the primary grades. In C. C. Block & M. Pressley (Eds.), *Comprehension instruction: Research-based best practices* (pp. 247–258). New York: Guilford.

Echevarria, J., Vogt, M., & Short, D. (2003). *Making content comprehensible for English language learners: The SIOP model.* Boston: Allyn and Bacon.

Escamilla, K. (1994). The sociolinguistic environment of a bilingual school: A case study introduction. *Bilingual Research Journal, 18,* 1&2. Retrieved June 6, 2008, from http://www.ncela.gwu.edu/pubs/symposia/reading/article8/escamilla94.pdf

Escamilla, K. (1999). Teaching literacy in Spanish. In R. DeVillar & J. Tinajero (Eds.), *The power of two languages 2000* (pp. 126–141). New York: Macmillan/McGraw-Hill.

Escamilla, K. (2000). Bilingual means two: Assessment issues, early literacy, and Spanish-speaking children. In *A research symposium on high standards in reading for students from diverse language groups: Research, practice, and policy proceedings.* Washington, DC: Office of Bilingual Education and Minority Language Affairs (OBEMLA).

Escamilla, K. (2009, July). *Literacy in Spanish: What's the same/what's different?* Paper presented at Two-Way CABE Conference, San Diego, CA.

Escamilla, K., Butvilofsky, S., Escamilla, M., Geisler, D., Hopewell, S., Ruiz, O., and Sparrow, W. (2010). *Transitions to biliteracy: Literacy squared.* Final Technical Report of Phase I of the Literacy Squared Research Report.

Escamilla, K., & Coady, M. (2001). Assessing the writing of Spanish-speaking students: Issues and suggestions. In J. Tinajero & S. Hurley (Eds.), *Handbook for literacy assessment for bilingual learners* (pp. 43–63). Boston: Allyn & Bacon.

Escamilla, K., Geiser, D., Hopewell, S., Sparrow, W., & Butilofsky, S. (2009). Using writing to make cross-language connections. In C. Rodriguez-Eagle (Ed.), *Achieving literacy success with English language learners: Insights, assessment, instruction*. Worthington, OH: Reading Recovery Council of North America.

Escamilla, K., & Hopewell, S. (2010). Transitions to biliteracy: Positive academic trajectories for emerging bilinguals in the United States. In J. Petrovic (Ed.), *International perspectives on bilingual education*. Charlotte, NC: Information Age.

Espinosa, L. (2007). Second language acquisition in early childhood. In R. S. New & M. Cochran (Eds.), *Early childhood education*. Westport, CT: Greenwood.

Fairbairn, S., & Jones-Vo., S. (2010). *Differentiating instruction and assessment for English language learners: A guide for K–12 teachers*. Philadelphia: Caslon.

Ferreiro, E., & Teberosky, A. (1982). *Literacy before schooling*. (K. Goodman Castro, Trans.). Exeter, NH: Heinemann.

Freeman, R. (2004). *Building on community bilingualism*. Philadelphia: Caslon.

Freeman, Y., & Freeman, D. (1997). *La enseñanza de la lectura y la escritura en español en el aula bilingüe*. Portsmouth, NH: Heinemann.

Freeman, Y., & Freeman, D. (2006). *Teaching reading and writing in Spanish and English in bilingual and dual language classrooms* (2nd ed.). Portsmouth, NH: Heinemann.

Garan, E. M., & DeVoogd, G. (2008–2009). The benefits of sustained silent reading: Scientific research and common sense converge. *Reading Teacher, 62*(4), 336–344.

García, O. (2009). *Bilingual education in the 21st century: A global perspective*. Malden, MA: Wiley-Blackwell.

Geiser, D., Escamilla, K., Hopewell, S., & Ruiz, O. A. (2007, April). *Transitions to biliteracy: Focus on writing of Spanish/English emerging bilinguals*. Paper presented at the annual meeting of the American Education Research Association, Chicago.

Genesee, F. (1987). *Learning through two languages*. New York: Newbury House.

Genesee, F. (2008). Early dual language learning. *Zero to Three Bulletin, 29*(1), 17–23.

Genesee, F. (2010). Dual language development in preschool children. In E. García & E. Frede (Eds.), *Young English Language Learners: Current Research and Emerging Directions for Practice and Policy* (pp. 59–79). New York: Teachers College Press.

Gentry, J. R. (2011). *Twenty-first century practices for teaching beginning reading and writing: Preschool–grade 2*. Retrieved August 5, 2011, from http://jrichardgentry.com/text/begin_reading_k-2_1-16.pdf

González, N., & Moll, L. (2002). *Cruzando el puente*: Building bridges to funds of knowledge. *Educational Policy, 16*(4), 623–641.

Goodman, D. (2007). Performance phenomena in simultaneous and sequential bilingual: A case study of two Chilean bilingual children. *Literatura y Lingüistica, 18*, 219–232.

Gottlieb, M. (2006). *Assessing English language learners: Bridges from language proficiency to academic achievement*. Thousand Oaks, CA: Corwin Press.

Gough, P. B., & Tumner, W. E. (1986). Decoding, reading, and reading disability. *Remedial and Special Education, 7*, 6–10.

Grosjean, F. (1982). *Life with two languages*. Cambridge, MA: Harvard University Press.

Grosjean, F. (1989). Neurolinguists, beware! The bilingual is not two monolinguals in one person. *Brain and Language, 36*, 3–15.

Guerrero, M. (1997). Spanish academic language proficiency: The case of bilingual education teachers in the U.S. *Bilingual Research Journal, 21*(1), 25–43.

Halliday, M. (1975). *Learning how to mean: Explorations in the development of language*. London: Edward Arnold.

Hammink, J. (n.d.). *Emergent writing in the primary grades*. Retrieved July 12, 2011, from http://hamminkj.tripod.com/hamminkEW.pdf

Harvey, S., & Goudvis, A. (2000). *Strategies that work: Teaching comprehension to enhance understanding*. Portland, ME: Stenhouse.

Hopkins, G. (1997). "Sustained silent reading" helps develop independent readers and writers. *Education World*. Retrieved October 29, 2011, from http://www.educationworld.com?1_curr/curr038.shtml

Hord, S., & Rutherford, W. (1998). Creating a professional learning community. *Cottonwood Creek School: Issues about Change, 6*(2), 1–8.

Hualde, J. I. (2005). *The sounds of Spanish*. Cambridge: Cambridge University Press.

Hymes, D. (1972). Models of interaction of language and social life. In J. Gumperz & D. Hymes (Eds.), *Directions in sociolinguistics: The ethnography of communication* (pp. 35–71). New York: Holt, Rinehart, Winston.

Irujo, S. (2004, September/October). Differentiated instruction: We can no longer just aim down the middle. *ELL Outlook*. Retrieved September 6, 2009, from http://www.coursecrafters.com/ELL-Outlook/2004/sept_oct/ELLOutlookITIArticle2.htm

Irujo, S. (2006, March/April). Flexible grouping: Nobody ever said teaching was easy. *ELL Outlook, 2006*. Retrieved September 6, 2009, from http://www.coursecrafters.com/ELL-Outlook/2006/mar_apr/ELLOutlookITIArticle3.htm

Izquierdo, E. (2010, November). *Biliteracy: What is it?* Paper presented at La Cosecha Conference, Santa Fe, NM.

Jimenez, R. T., García, G. E., & Pearson, P. H. (1996). The reading strategies of bilingual Latino/a students who are successful English readers: Opportunities and obstacles. *Reading Research Quarterly, 31*(1), 90–112.

Koda, K., & Zehler, A. M. (Eds.). (2008). *Learning to read across languages: Cross-linguistic relationships in first and second language literacy development*. New York: Routledge.

Krashen, S. D. (2004). The case for narrow reading. *Language Magazine, 3*(5), 17–19. Retrieved September 20, 2010, from http://www.sdkrashen.com/articles/narrow/all.html

Montaño-Harmon, M. R. (1991). Discourse features of written Mexican Spanish: Current research in contrastive rhetoric and its implications. *Hispania, 74*, 417–425.

Mora, J. K. (2009). From the ballot box to the classroom. *Education Leadership, 66*(7), 14–19.

Morris, L., & Rosado, L. (2009). *Desarrollo del español para maestros en programas de educación bilingüe*. Arlington, TX: LM Educational Consultant.

Office of Civil Rights. (2006). *Questions and answers on the rights of limited-English proficient students*. Retrieved January 15,

2009, from http://www.ed.gov/about/offices/list/ocr/qa-ell.html

Ovando, C., Combs, M. C., & Collier, V. (2006). *Bilingual and ESL classrooms: Teaching in multicultural contexts* (4th ed.). Boston: McGraw-Hill.

Paradis, J., & Genesee, F. (1996). Syntactic acquisition in bilingual children: Autonomous or interdependent? *Studies in Second Language Acquisition, 18*, 1–25.

Pardo, L. S. (2004). What every teacher needs to know about comprehension. *Reading Teacher, 88*(1), 272–280.

Pease-Alvarez, L., & Hakuta, K. (1992). Enriching our views of bilingualism and bilingual. *Educational Researcher, 21*, 419.

Poplack, S. (1980). Sometimes I'll start a sentence in Spanish *y termino en espanol:* Toward a typology of code-switching. *Linguistics, 18*(7/8), 581–618.

Potowski, K. (2005). *Fundamentos de la enseñanza del español a hispanohablantes en los EE.UU.* Madrid: Arco Libros.

Potowski, K. (2007). *Language and identity in a dual immersion school.* Clevedon, U.K.: Multilingual Matters.

Potowski, K. (2010). Language diversity in the USA: Dispelling common myths and appreciating advantages. In K. Potowski (Ed.), *Language diversity in the United States* (1–24). New York: Cambridge University Press.

Ramirez, J. D., Yuen, S. D., Ramey, D. R., & Pasta, D. J. (1991). *Final report: National longitudinal study of structured-English immersion strategy, early-exit, and late-exit transitional bilingual education programs for language-minority children* (2 vols.). San Mateo, CA: Aguirre International.

RAND Reading Study Group. (2002). *Reading for understanding: Toward a research and development program in reading comprehension.* Santa Monica, CA: Office of Education Research and Improvement.

Romaine, S. (2000). *Language in society.* New York: Oxford University Press.

Routman, R. (1994). *Invitations: Changing as teachers and learners K–12.* Portsmouth, NH: Heinemann.

Salgado, H. (2000). *Cómo se enseña a leer y escribir.* Buenos Aires: Magisterio del Río de la Plata.

Swanson, C. B. (2009). *Perspectives on a population: English language learners in American schools.* Bethesda, MD: Editorial Projects in Education. Retrieved February 1, 2009, from http://www.edweek.org/go/copies

Tabors, P. (1997). *One child, two languages: A guide for preschool educators of children learning English as a second language.* Baltimore: Paul H. Brookes.

Tabors, P., & Snow, C. (1994). English as a second language in preschools. In F. Genesee (Ed.), *Educating second language children: The whole child, the whole curriculum, the whole community* (pp. 103–125). New York: Cambridge University Press.

Thomas, W. P., & Collier, V. P. (1997). *School effectiveness for language minority students.* Washington, DC: National Clearinghouse for Bilingual Education.

Thomas, W. P., & Collier, V. P. (2002). *A national study of school effectiveness for language minority students' long-term academic achievement.* Retrieved March 15, 2009, from http://repositories.cdlib.org/crede/finalrpts/1_1_final/

Thonis, E. (1983). *The English-Spanish connection.* Miami: Santillana USA.

Tomlinson, C. A. (1999). *The differentiated classroom: Responding to the needs of all learners.* Alexandria, VA: ASCD.

Tomlinson, C. A. (2001). *How to differentiate instruction in mixed-ability classrooms* (2nd ed.). Alexandria, VA: ASCD.

UNESCO. (2005). *Literacy for Life: The Quality Imperative.* Global Monitoring Report. Retrieved July 6, 2012, from http://unesdoc.unesco.org/images/0014/001497/149780e.pdf

U.S. Census Bureau. (2001). *Profile of the foreign-born population in the United States: 2000.* Current Population Report P23–206. Washington, DC: U.S. Census Bureau. Retrieved July 6, 2012, from http://www.census.gov/prod/2002pubs/p23-206.pdf

U.S. Census Bureau. (2005). *School enrollment: Social and economic characteristics of students: October 2003.* Current Population Report P20–554. Washington, DC: U.S. Census Bureau.

Valdés, G. (2011, November 17). *Spanish/English bilingualism: Developing personal, academic, and professional resources.* Paper presented at La Cosecha Conference, Santa Fe, NM.

Vernon-Carter, S., & Ferreiro, E. (1999). Writing development: A neglected variable in the consideration of phonological awareness. *Harvard Education Review, 69*(4), 395–415.

Wagner, S. (2001). *Crossing classroom borders: Pathways to the mainstream via teacher collaboration.* Unpublished doctoral dissertation, University of Illinois at Chicago.

Wiley, T. G., & Valdés, G. (2000). *Heritage language instruction in the United States: A time for renewal. Bilingual Research Journal, 24* (4), i–v. Retrieved January 20, 2009, from http://brj.asu.edu/v244/articles/art1/html

Wong-Fillmore, L. (1991). Second-language learning in children: A model of language learning in social context. In E. Bialystok (Ed.), *Language processing in bilingual children* (pp. 49–69). New York: Cambridge University Press.

Page numbers followed by b, f, or t refer to boxes, figures, or tables, respectively.